Rights of Passage
Struggles for Lesbian and Gay Legal Equality
DIDI HERMAN

Proponents of social reform have always sought change through law reform. But what forces produce these new legal constructions, and how open is the law to reform? Didi Herman provides a critical analysis of lesbian and gay struggles for legal equality in Canada. She begins by exploring the historical development of 'sexual orientation' protection in human rights law and considers the strategies employed by lesbian and gay movements, by politicians, and by judges. Herman continues by placing recent campaigns within a broader theoretical framework which identifies legal arenas as sites of struggle between opposing social movements. An important focus of the book, therefore, is the New Christian Right – the key force opposing the extension of lesbian and gay rights. This section draws on original interviews with leading Christian activists.

Herman contends that we can neither uncritically extol nor derisively dismiss the strategies used by lesbians and gay men fighting for their rights. She argues that within these legal battles dominance has been achieved by a liberal 'minority rights paradigm.' This model itself becomes a mode of regulation, constructing sexuality in ways that may not be fully liberating. Yet traditional moralities have also been under siege and, to some extent, significant shifts in social understanding have occurred.

Although *Rights of Passage* is specifically about lesbian and gay rights, its analysis provides insights into the relationship between social movements and the legal process more generally. This book makes an important contribution to current debates in sociology, legal studies, and political theory.

DIDI HERMAN is a lecturer in the Department of Law, University of Keele, United Kingdom.

DIDI HERMAN

Rights of Passage: Struggles for Lesbian and Gay Legal Equality

UNIVERSITY OF TORONTO PRESS
Toronto Buffalo London

© University of Toronto Press Incorporated 1994
Toronto Buffalo London
Printed in Canada

ISBN 0-8020-0441-5 (cloth)
ISBN 0-8020-7231-3 (paper)

Printed on acid-free paper

Canadian Cataloguing in Publication Data

Herman, Didi
  Rights of passage : struggles for lesbian and
  gay legal equality

  Includes bibliographical references and index.
  ISBN 0-8020-0441-5 (bound) ISBN 0-8020-7231-3 (pbk.)

  1. Gay liberation movement – Canada.   2. Gay
  liberation movement.   3. Homosexuality – Law and
  legislation – Canada.   4. Homosexuality – Law and
  legislation.   I. Title.

  HQ76.8.C3H4 1994   305.9'0664'0971   C94-930393-3

University of Toronto Press acknowledges the financial assistance to its
publishing program of the Canada Council and the Ontario Arts Council.

Contents

vi   Contents

Acknowledgments

Many people made the writing of this book much easier.

I could not have undertaken the initial research without the financial assistance of both the Laidlaw Foundation of Canada and the Social Science and Humanities Research Council of Canada.

I would like to thank those who gave their time for interviews: Judy Anderson, Karen Andrews, Chris Bearchell, Ian Binnie, Gwen Brodsky, Margrit Eichler, Don Hutchinson, Brian Mossop, Ken Popert, and Jim Sclater. Thanks also to the volunteers at the Gay Archives of Canada. Special thanks to Gwen Brodsky for keeping me in touch with the *Mossop* case, and for the ongoing discussions.

Several people provided helpful comments and encouragement when I first started thinking about some of these issues. Thanks to Brenda Cossman, Judy Fudge, Shelley Gavigan, Toni Williams, and Lisa Wyndels.

A number of people helped me along the way. They know how, and I would like to express my thanks to Joel Bakan, Susan Boyd, Kitty Cooper, Charles Cooper, Martin Durham, Lorna Erwin, Lisa Herman, Nina Klowden Herman, Nikki Lacey, Leanne Macmillan, Annecka Marshall, Peter McVey, Bruce Ryder, Carl Stychin, and Jeffrey Weeks.

Thanks to Virgil Duff at University of Toronto Press for his initial interest in and subsequent encouragement of this project and to Beverley Beetham Endersby for copy-editing.

Many thanks to Jim Beckford, who co-supervised the doctorate upon which this book is based, for providing essential feedback and general support.

Many thanks to Carol Smart – for her initial interest in my doctoral research, critical supervision, patience, and support.

Marlee Kline actively supported my writing in many ways: sending me stuff; encouraging me to continue; helping my work get around in Canada; and just being there.

Finally, Davina Cooper is responsible for more than just my being in Britain. She has provided me with an atmosphere of intellectual provocation, caring, love, good food, and good humour.

Note Regarding Previously Published Material

Earlier versions of parts (ranging from a few paragraphs to several pages) of the following chapters were published as indicated.

Chapter 3, 'The Politics of Law Reform: Rights Struggles into the 90s.' In J. Bristow and A. Wilson. eds., *Activating Theory* (London: Lawrence and Wishart 1993)

Chapter 4, 'Beyond the Rights Debate.' *Social and Legal Studies* 2 (1993), 25–43

Chapter 7, '"Sociologically Speaking": Law, Sexuality, and Social Change.' *Journal of Human Justice* 10 (1991), 57–76

Abbreviations

AG	Attorney General
CFV	Coalition for Family Values
CGRO	Coalition for Gay Rights in Ontario
CHRA	Canadian Human Rights Act
CLS	Critical Legal Studies
EEOC	Equal Employment Opportunity Commission
EGALE	Equality for Gays and Lesbians Everywhere
FFA	Focus on the Family Association
GATE	Gay Alliance Towards Equality
LEAF	Women's Legal Education and Action Fund
LP	Liberal party
NCC	National Citizens' Coalition
NCR	New Christian Right
NDP	New Democratic Party
NOW	National Organization of Women
MPP	Member of Provincial Parliament
PAW	People for the American Way
RTPC	Right to Privacy Committee
RW	REAL Women of Canada
SCC	Supreme Court of Canada

RIGHTS OF PASSAGE: STRUGGLES FOR LESBIAN AND GAY LEGAL EQUALITY

1

Introduction

In the later decades of the twentieth century, lesbian and gay movements, particularly those located within Western democracies, diversified and deepened their political struggles. The rise of lesbian feminism, internal divisions partly emerging from a politics based on 'identity,' AIDS and Queer Nation activism, and openly gay conservatives contributed to the complex and often contradictory social analyses and strategies that exemplify modern lesbian and gay politics. It is thus far more accurate to speak of lesbian and gay movements, than to assume any monolithic, homogeneous entity.[1]

Lesbian and gay movements have always contained, amid a range of activities, individuals and organizations committed to achieving change through law reform. In many countries, this pursuit of change began with demands, mainly by gay men, for the decriminalization of 'homosexual' (male) offences, and expanded to include other coercive practices of the state – police harassment, obscenity laws, and similar issues. In many jurisdictions, criminal law reforms still remain near the top of the agenda – for example, the age of consent in Britain, and sodomy statutes in many American states.

Somewhat later, criminal-law reform organizations were joined by a law-oriented movement of a different sort – the modern lesbian and gay rights movement.[2] Reflecting a shift in politics from demands to 'keep the state off our backs' (through decriminalizing same-sex sexual activity, ending prosecutions of gay publications and bookshops under obscenity laws, and so on), the rights movement demanded legal *protection*, primarily through inclusion within antidiscriminatory statutes and the extension of social benefits to lesbian and gay couples. Recently, lesbian and gay law-reform politics has come full circle with demands to criminalize homophobic abuse as 'hate crimes' (see Petersen 1991).

During this period, there have been many different kinds of lesbian and gay rights law-reform initiatives entailing a variety of strategies and attendant mobilizations. Among them have been political campaigns to amend existing antidiscriminatory legislation to include a 'sexual orientation' ground, and individual lawsuits launched under these statutes and others either to protect jobs or housing, or to demand various social benefits currently restricted to heterosexual couples or families.

The anticipated achievements through law reform are, on one level, obvious. A gay couple litigating against a state refusal to register their marriage seeks the legal recognition of their relationship as a marriage, with all the benefits (and burdens) that attend such an acknowledgment. A lesbian and gay organization lobbying for statutory reform to legislative definitions of 'spouse' hopes for the official recognition of lesbian and gay identity within state welfare, taxation, and other similar schemes.

But the goals of law-reform initiatives, in most cases, also go farther. Lesbian and gay rights movements, from their inception, have engaged in legal struggle partly on the basis of what changes in legal provision *signify* more generally. Aside from the tangible benefits that are sought, organizations and individuals have proceeded on the law front with the belief that law reflects societal fears and prejudices. In keeping with the demands of other marginalized groups, lesbians and gay men have argued that *progressive* law reform signals to bigots, and to those who would discriminate, that such attitudes and behaviours are no longer acceptable. In so doing, legal liberalization marginalizes those who were formerly the moral majority, and at the same time encourages lesbians and gay men to 'come out' with at least the official promise that their security and safety will be maintained.

Yet the acquisition of rights reforms does more than encourage gays and lesbians to 'come out'; perhaps as significantly, the positive legal recognition of lesbian and gay sexuality (as opposed to negative criminal-law constructions) promotes feelings of self-worth, citizenship, and community identity. Furthermore, the very struggle for these goals, whether or not they are achieved, is a politicizing process facilitating mobilization, identification, heightened public awareness, and the development of a lesbian and gay consciousness, practice, and theory.

For lesbians, gay men, and their supporters, the efforts of rights campaigners have been the subject of both unqualified praise and critical comment. There are those who advocate rights for lesbians and gay men without hesitation,[3] and those who, in contrast, question the goals and accompanying strategies of rights acquisition.[4] Many who fall into the latter group articulate a politics, drawn from socialist and feminist traditions, which problematizes the possibility of achieving substantial shifts in social relations through the reform of dominant legal ideologies[5] and institutions.

Consequently, I chart a course somewhat different from that of those who uncritically advocate and argue for the extension of legal equality to lesbians and gay men; yet I do not prophesy doom as a result of such developments. My intention is to present lesbian and gay rights as a 'problematic' – a location from which questions arise (Smith 1987, 89–91). I take as my problematic that rights movement with which I am most familiar, as participant and observer – the movement for lesbian and gay rights in Canada.[6]

This book focuses on three central questions: 1 / How are lesbian and gay subjects and subjectivities constituted through human rights law and what forces produce these legal constructions? 2 / How open is law to receiving new constructions of homosexuality? 3 / What is the relationship between the lesbian and gay rights movement and its principal opponents, the New Christian Right and 'the state,' and how do the struggles of social movements for interpretive authority shape the law-making process (and vice versa)?

Key Arguments and Themes

The Dominance of a Liberal Sexual Politics

My first argument is that, in lesbian and gay law-reform battles in Canada, liberal and conservative sexual politics dominate public debate. Since the mid-1980s, a liberal minority rights paradigm has been ascendant while radical sexual politics, *of both the left and the right*, are not as visible within public discourse on rights and sexuality. The dominance of the liberal equality paradigm has contributed to the public presentation and perception of lesbians and gay men as a discrete minority community, whose innate 'difference' should not result in prejudice and discrimination.

Many gay activists have found the idea that sexuality is neither a personal nor a political choice appealing; the 'sexuality is immutable' argument has provided a way out of medicalization, experimentation, and behaviour modification. Nevertheless, I argue that this idea may have outlived its usefulness, at least in the present political climate of Western, capitalist democracies. I further show how the liberal equality paradigm and the concept of immutability, are fundamentally at odds with those theories of sexuality which deconstruct the naturalness of heterosexuality and gender identities.[7] I argue that much lesbian and gay legal struggle obfuscates, rather than illuminates, such analyses. A feminist sexual politics is largely marginalized by mainstream lesbian and gay rights discourse and this, I suggest, is unfortunate.

Having said that, however, I also explore the extent to which dominant legal ideologies themselves shift and are reconstituted through social struggle. I examine human rights laws as disciplinary regimes of regulation,[8] considering their somewhat different contribution to the construction of sexual subjects from that produced by previous criminal law. Dominant frameworks of meaning cannot be harnessed by social movements without those frameworks in turn shaping and reconstituting actors and communities.

I address three subsidiary questions within this first argument. Why is the minority rights paradigm so hegemonic? When and why do liberal perspectives predominate over conservative ones? What happens when radical sexual politics enter public arenas, particularly law-related ones?

In responding to the first of these questions, I argue that the extension of formal equality rights to lesbians and gay men in capitalist democracies is not necessarily in conflict with a modern application of traditional Western liberal values. I go on to suggest that social-policy decision makers, including politicians, media chiefs, and judges, are drawn predominantly from groups exemplifying dominant political ideologies, as is reflected in their discourse and decisions on gay rights issues. I also show how law, as a regime of truth and knowledge, admits some external discourses but excludes others.[9] Finally, I argue that social-movement activists, in deciding to enter any public sexuality debate, whether legal or otherwise, engage in a process of self-censorship whereby the movement's internal politics are deliberately transformed and rendered compatible with the perceived prevailing social climate.

In exploring when and why liberalism predominates over conservative sexual politics (and vice versa), I trace several distinct but related dimensions of the law-reform struggle. For example, in discussing one gay rights case (*Mossop*) I show that litigation results were partially dependent upon the luck of the draw – which decision makers were selected to hear the case at its various stages. Yet, the progress of gay rights is not determined by individual whim. The decisions of adjudicators and politicians are historically and culturally contingent. Among other things, decision makers are severely constrained by their perceptions of the prevailing social climate – what (or whose) construction of homosexuality is ascendant in the public sphere at that historical moment. Liberalism's hegemony, for example, is clearly shown in several examples, such as the (slow and uneven) development of lesbian custody case law, the increasing success of gay rights legislative amendments, and the transition from the criminal pathologization of homosexuality to the provision of lesbian and gay equal opportunity policies in the armed services and police.

This prevailing social climate is in part shaped by shifts in medical-moral discourse, and the outcome of gay rights law-reform initiatives tends to follow the winds of change in psychiatric and other professional constructions of homosexuality. Thus, the role of experts in the law's construction of sexuality is something I closely consider. At the same time, however, powerful professional discourses, while significant constituters of social meaning, are not determinative of sexuality; the struggles of social movements, and the interjection of other knowledges, are also important in shaping social understandings. Legal discourse is not completely immune from such invasions.

Thus, another factor influencing the liberal or conservative fate of lesbian and gay rights reform is the role played by social-movement activists. Individuals and groups can infiltrate and influence political parties *despite and against* the prevailing social climate (and, in the process, hope to create a new one). In Canada, the Conservative party has its 'pro-family' wing, and the left-of-centre New Democratic Party its 'lesbian and gay caucus.' In Britain, for example, Martin Durham (1991) has argued that section 28 was an initiative of the 'moral right' in the Conservative government and did not have the active support of the party mainstream. So, the temporary success of political factions can often lead to the unexpected extension or withdrawal of rights.

Finally, I argue that attitudes and existing policies towards homosexuality both reflect and produce the balance of power between opposing social movements. The process of law making is, in this conceptualization, a terrain of struggle where diverse interests vie for popular support in what one conservative Christian text calls the 'war of words' (Dobson and Bauer 1990).

In addressing the third subsidiary question I posed above – what happens when radical perspectives on sexuality, of both right and left, *do* enter public arenas? – I consider various interventions in gay rights campaigns and litigation by both supporters and their New Christian Right opponents. I show that such perspectives are sometimes ridiculed, or, more often, simply ignored. At the same time, however, definitions of 'radical' are not static and unchanging. As John D'Emilio (1983, 244) has noted, early pioneers in lesbian and gay rights reforms were radical in their time; and, of course, Christian prohibitions on homosexuality, now deemed quaint and unscientific, were once the law of the land. Furthermore, the impact of radical interventions must be evaluated in the long term, and not simply by calculating specific wins or losses. As Gusfield (1981) has argued, social movements effect shifts in meaning over time, even though individual battles may be lost.

Liberalism and Social Change

Given that liberalism has, to some extent, been able to provide a certain measure of lesbian and gay rights, what are its limits? My second principal argument is that while liberalism (with respect to sexuality) is hegemonic, it is not impervious to change, and, perhaps, not inherently facilitative of the status quo (see Mouffe 1988, 1982). Liberal paradigms may allow for the recognition of new identities as represented by new social movements such as those of lesbians and gay men. These movements have been somewhat successful in shifting the boundaries of legal liberal constructions of homosexuality – from the 'deviant and dangerous offender,' to the 'minority' subject of human rights protection, to the 'spousal' recipient of social benefits previously available only to heterosexual couples.

In the process, the articulation of principles such as 'equality' together with 'lesbian and gay' has, to some extent, caused cracks in the firmament of 'universal' heterosexuality. Lesbian and gay law-reform struggles have prompted the concomitant defence of heterosexuality and traditional gender identities, a task unthinkable in a previous era of homosexual pathologization. In this way, lesbian and gay rights campaigns, even those which appear ostensibly less radical in demands and rhetoric, can be seen to be, perhaps, as in Judith Butler's analysis (1990), 'subversive' of gender and hence 'troubling.' I thus contend, for example, that while legal liberalism has, arguably, succeeded only in entrenching and obscuring class divisions (see Fudge and Glasbeek 1992 and Mandel 1989), the same is not the case for sexuality where concrete shifts in social meanings and practices *have* taken place.

I also discuss the role of rights, as demands and rhetoric, within lesbian and gay legal equality campaigns. In avoiding the polarities of the 'rights debate' in social theory, I argue that rights are neither good nor bad. Instead, rights claims and rhetoric play unpredictable and contradictory roles in social struggle; and their effects are complex and changing. In many ways, I advocate a 'decentring' of rights, not so much within social struggle (where I see rights demands as largely inevitable), but within academic analyses of such struggles.

Finally, however, I argue that the connection between rights acquisition for lesbians and gay men and the transformation of social relations which produce lesbian, gay, and other identities is not necessarily obvious or inevitable. Such a bridge must be built, not awaited. Furthermore, the inclusion of lesbian and gay identity within human rights law has, as I argued above, contradictory effects, including the entrenchment of a minority identity and politics.

Law and the State

I also use the example of lesbian and gay rights struggles in Canada to complicate analyses of law and the state which see the two as one, and that one as monolithic in character – whether as a tool or instrument of the capitalist class (Mandel 1989), or patriarchy (Mackinnon 1983, 1987), or as reflecting 'a' dominant ideology (Collins 1982; Gabel and Feimman 1982). I also question post-structuralist analyses of law, which tend to reject notions of the state and, in my view, reify the capabilities of legal discourse to produce subjects.

Instead, this book proceeds from a conceptualization of law-making processes *in the field of sexuality* as sites of struggle (see Hunt 1985). In my view, there is no one 'state' with 'a' position on or 'interest' in lesbian and gay law reform. The perspectives are variable: those of the federal Justice Department, the federal Minister for Women's Issues, the Secretary of State's funding administrators, the judges at the courts of appeal, the adjudicators administering human rights laws, individual employer-managers in the public service, and members of Parliament from all political parties – all these and more – are linked through their location in state structures but cannot be said to share much beyond that. In the arena of lesbian and gay rights, *confusion* and *contradiction* are far more prevalent than any common intention or strategy.

Emerging within this book, therefore, is a view of legislation and policy in the area of lesbian and gay rights that sees such developments as both reflecting and contributing to the constitution of the balance of power between social movements. In some ways, my understanding of the relation between social movements and the state is an instrumentalist one in that my analysis suggests that state bureaucracies and processes can be won (temporarily) by those seeking to shape the regulation of sexuality.[10]

Outline of Chapters

This first chapter concludes with a discussion of some of the ethical issues involved in doing the research upon which this book is based. The second chapter provides a brief and selective history of the Canadian lesbian and gay movement's engagement with human rights law reform, from the 1970s to the present. Besides offering an explanation for *why* some lesbians and gay men chose to advocate such reforms, I explain the structure of human rights regimes, and provide an overview of sexual orientation legislation and case law in Canada. I also consider several different paradigms of sexuality expressed by lesbians and gay men in their campaigns and litigation.

The third chapter launches into the substance of the book. Taking the struggle for a sexual orientation amendment to Ontario's Human Rights Code (popularly known as Bill 7) as a case-study, I explore the processes leading up to the enactment of the amendment in 1986, its effects and implications, and the politics of the debate between opposing social movements. I argue that this struggle had diverse implications. On the one hand, the lesbian and gay subject publicly emerging from the conflict was one informed by liberal legalism, not one that challenged such constructions. Further, the campaigns tended to strengthen and legitimate existing legal frameworks, thus undermining attempts to reform and replace them. At the same time, however, the struggle succeeded in rendering visible lesbian and gay sexuality and occasioning public debate – albeit within a liberal paradigm of tolerance.

Chapter 4 uses Bill 7 and other examples to consider debates about the politics of rights. I focus upon the role of rights as rhetoric, examining conflicting theories of rights efficacy in social-movement struggle. I suggest an analysis which, with respect to the Bill 7 contestation, moves beyond discussing the role of rights in the abstract to exploring the meanings of rights within particular contestations. I argue that the lesbian and gay rights movement can be seen as a modern movement for inclusion in frameworks of social citizenship and that the deployment of rights rhetoric must be assessed within this context. While I agree with some of the positions of the 'rights critics,' I none the less put forward a view of rights which considers such struggles in perspective, and in their specificity.

The fifth and sixth chapters explore the politics of the primary movement standing in opposition to lesbian and gay legal equality – the New Christian Right. I centre my analysis upon three of the organizations that intervened in one gay rights case – the *Mossop* litigation. Chapter 5 details the sexual politics of this movement, while chapter 6 asks what occurred when these organizations entered the legal arena. I argue that the evangelical Christianity of the right-wing coalition, which motivated and inspired their opposition to lesbian and gay equality (as well as anti-racism, feminism, and so on) was rendered invisible within the legal process. I explore why this happened, but also suggest that the effects of the New Christian Right must be assessed at a deeper level. I ask, in fact, whether the conclusions I reach in this chapter have implications for feminist and lesbian / gay legal struggle.

Chapter 7 considers the role of judges and experts within litigation. I first show the conflict between legal processes and conventions, and the external knowledges 'experts' bring to their interventions. I then go on to consider what judges do with the 'expert' evidence that *is* presented to them, and also suggest why judges reach the decisions they do in lesbian and gay rights cases. This chapter contains discussions of the relative hierarchy of external knowledges within legal discourse, the ideological politics of individual judges, and the constraints and limitations within which judges can express these politics. I conclude by assessing sociology's contribution to the 'lesbian and gay legal subject.'

Finally, in the Afterword, I conclude by exploring changes to the concept of 'family' and by considering the relationship between the lesbian and gay rights movement and other movements on the left struggling for social change. Without discounting all that has been achieved by lesbian and gay rights campaigners, I argue for a debate around the sorts of values that situate lesbian and gay liberation within a broader-based politics of social transformation.

Ethical Research Issues[11]

The 'I' in the Text

I came to this project with specific concerns about lesbian and gay legal strategies. My political perspective was informed by a variety of struggles and institutional regimes in which I had participated. Aside from having studied for university degrees in sociology and law, I had been moderately active in Toronto lesbian feminist and gay politics for over ten years – initially around violence against women, then in the pro-choice movement, and, later, around HIV / AIDS issues. I had also been peripherally involved in struggles related to antisemitism and racism. Only once was I involved with a law-reform campaign; indeed, gay rights was, for me, synonymous with a gay male liberal agenda, and law reform was something which, until law school, I rarely considered a serious vehicle for social change.

While studying for my law degree, I began to note the frequency with which human rights law-reform and rights rhetoric were evident within lesbian and gay community media and public debate. During my first year of law school, I even participated in one such struggle (see the Bill 7 episode in chapter 3), despite having many reservations. It was, therefore, contradictions and questions such as these which led me to this project.

An example of how the relation between my various selves plays out is provided in chapter 4. For most of the chapter, the 'I' in the text is that of the legal academic, applying a critical perspective to her subject-matter. However, the chapter includes a personal story, reflecting upon my own involvement in the Bill 7 struggle, and positioning myself as a 'subject' in the text (see Stanley 1990). Throughout the book, then, there is a tension between my role as academic and my own interests in the issue at hand.[12] How one negotiates the relative importance of one's own standpoint is, therefore, an important question for any writer.

Within feminist theories of epistemology, a line of thought advocates the privileging of experiential standpoints.[13] However, I am more persuaded by 'standpoint critics' who argue that identity standpoints, while perhaps being a necessary stance within some forms of political campaigning, do not reveal true or better interpretations of social phenomena within academic research (see, for example, Flax 1987 and Kline 1989b). Furthermore, such standpoints impose a homogeneity upon the category being claimed which cannot reflect or represent the diversity within it.

Another issue revolves around the question of how membership in a legal elite might effect the shape and content of my ideas. Law is extremely powerful and seductive. During the writing of this book I was asked, for example, to comment on the legal submission of a coalition of progressive organizations intervening in the *Mossop* case. In agreeing to the request I may have become caught up in the status of such a task, entranced with the potential power to influence the thinking of judges of the Supreme Court of Canada. At the same time, I questioned the whole process of having legal academics give these kinds of 'opinions' and thereby become members of a lesbian and gay legal élite – indeed, perhaps creating a new legal industry (as has been the case in the United States). My comments ultimately reflected my own discomfort with participating in the process. My decision to comment on the submission was a negotiation between various positions. I have, however, tried both to remain conscious of these contradictions and to not exclude myself and my own work from the critical comments I make.

The 'Researcher' and the 'Researched'

I have discussed above questions related to my own location within the research I have undertaken. Here, I wish to elaborate on some of these issues with respect to interviewing and publication. Although interviews do not comprise the core substance of source material for this book, the issues raised by the interview process highlight dilemmas that extend beyond it.

Feminist and other sociological literature on interviewing tends to revolve around three problematics: interviewing the 'dispossessed,' thereby highlighting the researcher's 'power over' her subjects (Oakley 1981; Roberts 1981; Opie 1982); joining 'radical' groups covertly and collecting information in secret (see Bulmer 1982); additionally, there is a small literature on interviewing the 'locally powerful,' meaning bureaucrats and professionals with local decision-making powers, usually working within key social institutions (Bell 1978; Smart 1984). The first approach, particularly its feminist manifestations, seeks to develop interviewing strategies in order to minimize power inequalities. The researcher is also encouraged to pose questions emphasizing 'empathy,' 'identification,' and 'appropriation.' Those who have written about studying the locally powerful, on the other hand, identify the *researcher's* relative *in*equality in the interviewing process, while the 'covert research' methodology literature finds its ethical dilemmas in the very nature of researching secretively, and in the problems arising from publishing studies of people who have not consented to become research subjects.

While these literatures raise important questions and research dilemmas, their applicability to the interviews I conducted for this book is not obvious. Relations of power between myself and my interviewees did not fit comfortably into any of these paradigms. When interviewees cannot be placed into a category of 'dispossessed' or 'powerful,' and especially when they express views you abhor or hold status positions well above yours (which does not necessarily mean that they are powerful within the problematic being studied), the relation between researcher and subject becomes more complex.

In the case of the lesbians and gay men I interviewed, I was both 'one of them,' thus feeling such things as empathy and solidarity, and 'one of those' – namely, an academic – thus feeling their hostility and my defensiveness. I was conscious that some individuals must have assumed my support for their positions, granted interview access, and at some level trusted me, partly based upon my ability to present myself as 'a lesbian.' Several of the contributors to the collection *Doing Feminist Research* make similar points in their own studies.

However, in interviewing fellow members of the Canadian lesbian and gay movement, in many ways I was not the powerful person in the relation. On the contrary, at that time I was a student interviewing, for the most part, lawyers, well-paid civil servants, and teachers. Furthermore, several of the lesbian and gay litigants I interviewed patronized me – in the sense of finding some of my questions irrelevant or silly and assuming my concerns were not those of 'real people.' For the most part, those I interviewed were savvy political actors who had given many interviews and knew how to handle researchers. The interviews themselves, then, are products of our respective attempts to ascertain each other's agenda, determine degrees of trustworthiness, and so on. Thus, while these individuals were, arguably, dispossessed of lesbian and gay equality, in many other ways their lives were quite privileged.

A slightly different, but related, set of concerns emerged from interviews conducted with members of the New Christian Right. Over the course of several months, I developed a friendly correspondence with certain members of conservative Christian organizations, a number of whom regularly sent me newsletters, positional statements, and other organizational information. I went on to interview two of these individuals, plus one other I had not contacted previously.

My first concern was to gain access, and thus while I did not claim to be born-again, I most certainly did not present myself as a Jewish, lesbian, socialist feminist. I was not engaging in covert research, but neither did I wish to jeopardize the project. I did not lie, but I did not tell the whole truth – I said I was a sociologist of law (which, from their perspective, was bad enough). During the interviews, I was occasionally put into the position of having to respond to a direct question about my own religious affiliation. Each time, I avoided the question, giving an ambiguous answer that revealed very little.

The tapes resulting from these interviews are products of the curious relation between me and people I have despised, feared, and fought against for most of my life (the same, of course, is true for them, vis-à-vis me). Various researchers who have interviewed conservative Christians, and even more radical right-wing groups, have written about the process by which one can develop empathy for 'the enemy' (see, for example, Aho 1990). The interviews I conducted provided me with a very different 'take' on a group of people I would previously have dismissed as religious fanatics. I could not escape the fact that they were nice *towards me*, that they did their utmost to assist my research, and that they rather poignantly expressed gratitude that 'at least someone is interested in what we have to say' (see also Klatch's discussion [1987, 17]). At the same time, I knew that the interviewees were utterly opposed to everything I believed in.

The situation was even more complicated by my gradual realization that the New Christian Right interviewees perceived themselves to be powerless in society, and people such as myself (secular humanist academics) to be far more influential in setting public agendas and determining the character of social life. This view was at odds with my own, which, historically, had attributed far greater social power to 'them.' Instead, I found I was interviewing neither the locally powerful nor any other simple élite. Not only did I not feel powerless when speaking to NCR members, my knowledge of how they constructed *me* (as an academic producer of powerful secular knowledge) meant that I instead perceived them to be rather vulnerable. I thus felt uncomfortable leading them to believe, through a sympathetic tone or smile, that I might be supportive of their cause. On the other hand, I was also motivated by an activist concern to acquire useful information, and in this sense the research resembled the covert model. To do this, I needed to establish some kind of trust or empathy during the interviewing process. And yet I found this was achieved at a personal cost, particularly when some individuals expressed the most vicious perceptions of lesbian and gay sexuality. As Rebecca Klatch (1987, 18) has noted, in the context of interviewing right-wing women, research such as this involves, for the interviewer, a 'constant process of role negotiation.'

The interviews themselves are, therefore, products of a relation between individuals wary of, yet wanting something from, the other. What the NCR respondents were prepared to say to me, and what questions I was prepared to ask of them, help to construct the interview transcript itself. As Tait (1990, 173) has suggested, interview transcripts are products of a social process, and interviewees' quoted comments must be read in this light. Furthermore, the selection of quotations is itself a politically charged process; and, yet, abuses can only be controlled, not eliminated.

Finally, there is a 'politics of publication' issue. Here, I wish to address the issue of how the publication of research implicates the relation between the academic and her subject, and creates, for the researcher, an authority from which to speak.

Before I began the research upon which this book is based, a paper of mine was published in a Canadian law journal and was subsequently reprinted in a collection of 'women and law' course materials (see Herman 1990). In this piece, I discussed, among other things, the political implications of a specific case being waged by Karen Andrews, a lesbian litigant. The construction of her case, I suggested, had dubious implications for women's liberation.

During the course of my research for this book, I arranged to interview Andrews and, towards the end of our conversation, asked her to tell me what she thought of the article. She said that it had been very strange to see herself as the subject of an academic paper and had felt that, as a person, her life had somehow been degraded and her concerns trivialized. 'I was out there, outside myself. I had become a "thing" ... I saw myself in the trenches getting my hands dirty ... [during the litigation] I had got so many vicious phone calls ... [then] I thought, this is an intellectual exercise ... who reads the Osgoode Hall Law Journal anyway?' (Andrews, interview).

In speaking with Andrews, I was at first demoralized and ready to reconsider the project as a whole. However, it was also clear that she had assumed I was someone with little or no experience in the lesbian and gay movement and had been engaged in a kind of armchair élitism.

I do not know the right way of resolving this problem. Were I to self-censor every word in this book that other lesbians might disagree with, there would be little point in continuing. On the other hand, I cannot ignore the concerns expressed by those who, like Karen Andrews, have experienced being research subjects. In my view, research must be conducted ethically, within the context of a set of values. Publication of research should be sensitive to how 'subjects' will read the text, but cannot be determined by possible or potential readings. One can never control for this anyway. Nevertheless, I have tried to keep Andrews's comments in mind.

Concluding Remarks

In this book, I have utilized three primary devices in an attempt to respond to the problematic of the researcher / researched relation. First, I have tried to indicate that my own position lies on both sides of this dichotomy. At various points in the text, I speak explicitly from my own experience in lesbian and gay politics and offer my story as one to consider. Second, wherever possible, I have included extracts from interviews where the views of lesbian and gay interviewees are at odds with my own. To some extent, then, and in some places more than others, I have attempted to create a dialogue between actors – between academics and activists. Third, I have sent my work to interviewees and others for comments. Although I made no promises to alter my text, I considered any objections seriously, and had clear reasons for including material to which interviewees took exception.[14]

2

Lesbian/Gay/Citizen

'To Be Coded Human'[1]

One starting-point to considering the relationship between lesbians, gay men, and rights reform is to explore why such reforms, and the organizations which pressed for them, appeared on the political scene. One interpretation can be drawn from the work of Chantal Mouffe. In her analysis of social movements and democracy she argues (1988, 94–5) that modern social antagonisms often result when new discursive subjects are confronted with other discursive practices which negate them. Mouffe suggests, using Enlightenment gender discourse as an example, that while women were given the opportunity to reconstitute themselves as 'equal,' this constitution was a 'contradictory interpellation' to that produced simultaneously by other, exclusionary discourses (ibid). According to her, the entrenchment of Enlightenment discourse, and its central value of 'equality,' is at the centre of Western democratic subjectivities. Mouffe's analysis is problematic in several respects; for example, many lesbians and gay men in Western democracies have complex cultural subjectivities not necessarily determined by Western liberal traditions. Nevertheless, her analysis, in my view, can provide some insight into understanding the emergence and development of a lesbian and gay rights consciousness.

As various writers have noted, twentieth-century lesbian and gay identity, as opposed to same-sex sexual activity, is historically a relatively new phenomenon.[2] The claiming of such identities was contingent upon changes to the regime of sexual regulation, particularly the medical production of homo- and hetero- sexualities towards the end of the last century. Gradually, these new subjects formed the diverse strands of what came to be known as 'lesbian and gay movements.' Adapting Mouffe's analysis, lesbians and gay men can thus be viewed as newly emergent subjects confronted by contradictory discursive interpellations. For example, as asexual citizens they possessed formal equality; as 'homosexuals' they were both denied official recognition / protection and subjected to constant and changing medical diagnoses; as lesbians and gay men they created positive, affirming community structures and culture. The development of lesbian and gay movements, thus, followed from both the production of this distinctive identity and its perceived exclusion (or inclusion as criminality) within dominant discourse.

Within capitalist democracies, legal 'equality' discourse is one of the foremost ways in which human subjecthood is recognized, or called into being. In more recent years, antidiscrimination provisions, or human rights laws, have become a significant means of ostensibly ensuring the principle of 'equal treatment.' If, as Mouffe argues, the value of equality is so intrinsically a part of Western consciousness (and this view is echoed by many others), it is not surprising that many lesbians and gay men, socialized in Canada and other similar countries, demanded inclusion within and recognition by human (including constitutional) rights regimes, one of the primary forms of liberal equality.

From the perspective of many lesbians and gay men, human rights struggles were, therefore, not about rights per se, but about what rights were thought to signify – public / official recognition, social citizenship, and identification. In this sense, then, the demand for lesbian and gay rights is a struggle for membership in the human community, and perhaps also an expression of what bell hooks (1991, 18–31) has called the 'postmodern' condition of 'yearning,' the 'urge to voice of the marginalized.'

The claim for rights has always been a significant aspect of lesbian and gay social struggle (see Marcus 1992). Over time, a distinctive rights-oriented lesbian and gay movement emerged and became an important, indeed a predominant, movement for lesbian and gay liberation. In subsequent chapters, I explore what Mouffe and others appear to underplay: the ways in which the extension of existing liberal categories to new identities not only recognizes, but regulates, contains, and constitutes them. The claiming of rights has posed significant dilemmas for lesbian and gay movements.

Human Rights Campaigns and Case Law

In Canada, human rights legislation provides protection from discrimination on specified grounds, such as 'sex,' 'race' and 'disability,' in the areas of housing, employment, service provision, and contractual relations. Each province has its own 'human rights code' which applies to matters within provincial jurisdiction, including the public and private sectors. The federal sphere has its own human rights act for matters within its jurisdiction. Claims of discrimination are initiated by individuals and investigated by a regulatory commission which endeavours to effect a settlement. Fines can be imposed, although the commissions are meant to be facilitative of good relations, not punitive towards individuals. Should the commission not conclude a satisfactory settlement – and providing it deems the complaint worthy – the claim is adjudicated by an administrative tribunal during a trial-like proceeding. Tribunal decisions can be appealed to the courts, within the principles of judicial review.

By the 1970s, human rights legislation had developed across the country.[3] Viewed as an important symbol in the struggle to combat prejudice and discrimination, this form of law inevitably drew the attention of the emerging lesbian and gay law-reform movement. Two related strategies were launched simultaneously: individual complaints based on existing grounds of discrimination (e.g., sex), and statutory reform campaigns aimed at adding a sexual orientation ground to the list of protected categories.

Early Lesbian and Gay Human Rights Case Law

Four key cases set the scene for future developments, including the decision to focus political campaigning upon the second strategy – achieving sexual-orientation amendments. In 1975, two men, in different parts of the country, officially complained that they had suffered employment discrimination because they were gay. In Saskatchewan, Doug Wilson, a graduate student and teacher who had been refused permission to supervise trainee teachers because he was a gay activist, filed a complaint with the Saskatchewan Human Rights Commission alleging he was discriminated against under the 'sex' ground in that province's human rights code. He argued that his sexual orientation was an immutable 'sex' characteristic which he had not chosen and which should not be a legitimate basis for discrimination (*Board of Governors* 1976). Before processing the application, the commission issued a ruling that 'sex' in the code included 'sexual orientation.'

Immediately, the University of Saskatchewan (the employer) applied for judicial review of the commission's ruling. The higher court found for the university, stating that 'sex' was a biological, physical condition making someone male or female, having nothing to do with 'sexual proclivity' (ibid, 388–9). This case was to have a significant effect upon ensuing lesbian and gay human rights strategies; partially as a result of this decision, the rights movement focused on achieving 'sexual orientation' amendments, rather than on struggling against judicial definitions of 'sex.'

Of equal or greater import was the case of John Damien, fired from his job as an Ontario racing steward in February 1975.[4] Having, as it was perceived, no human rights remedy, Damien filed an unfair-dismissal suit against the Ontario Racing Commission, hoping to gain redress (in the form of compensation). Damien died eleven years later, and his case, because of the Racing Commission's delaying tactics, had never reached the trial stage. However, in the early years of his legal battles, Damien's experiences galvanized a broad base of support and provided a catalyst for growing demands to amend the Ontario Human Rights Code.

Another important cased concerned the Gay Alliance Toward Equality (GATE) in Vancouver.[5] It published, among other things, a newspaper called *Gay Tide.* In November 1974, following the refusal of *The Vancouver Sun* to run a *Gay Tide* advertisement, GATE filed a complaint with the British Columbia Human Rights Commission.[6] The commission found in GATE's favour, and this decision was upheld (on technical grounds) by the B.C. Supreme Court in 1976 (*Vancouver Sun* 1976). However, the B.C. Court of Appeal subsequently overturned the lower court's judgment on the basis that the *Sun's* refusal was reasonable, given popular attitudes towards homosexuality (*Re Vancouver Sun* 1977). The case eventually found its way to the Supreme Court of Canada, where GATE ultimately lost, although on different grounds, with the Court deciding that the *Sun's* press freedom could not be curtailed by human rights statutes (*Gay Alliance* 1979). The question of gay 'rights' was left unaddressed.

Another key decision was given in *Vogel.* In this 1983 decision under the Manitoba human rights statute, the adjudicating tribunal denied the gay applicant spousal health coverage on the basis of dictionary definitions of the term 'marriage.' The court simply refused to consider Vogel's claim as sex discrimination.[7]

The reasoning in these cases explains, to a large degree, why lesbian and gay rights organizations sought to achieve sexual orientation amendments to human rights codes. For these adjudicators, sexual orientation was deemed a species apart from sex, the latter understood as conferring maleness or femaleness. The 'sex characteristic,' meaning reproductive organs, thus determined definitions of marriage – as a union of 'opposite sexes.' Sexual orientation, on the other hand, whether accepted as immutable or not, was about sexual *practice*. Lesbians and gay men could not be 'spouses' or argue 'sex' discrimination within this paradigm, despite the fact that Vogel, for example, could have received health benefits had he or his partner been a woman. Any analysis or even mention of *heterosexuality* was notably absent from these decisions.

As I discuss in chapter 7, judgments such as those given in *Board of Governors* and *Vogel*, together with the usual judicial approach in lesbian and gay child custody cases (see Arnup 1984, 1989; Gross 1986), reflect the conservative politics of the courts in question. But these cases also reveal several insights into the strategies of lesbian and gay rights reformers during this period. Doug Wilson's lawyers, for example, chose to insist that his condition (homosexuality) was immutable. By presenting 'expert' evidence 'proving' this 'truth,' they hoped to persuade others that he should not be discriminated against for something over which he had no control. Homosexuality was, in this construction, almost a disability – an affliction for which there was no cure *and* one which did not cause harm to others. This model is rooted in the assumptions of early liberal psychology. As I explain later in this chapter, this new paradigm of sexuality appeared to legitimate both decriminalization and the extension of rights to lesbian and gay men. In the 1970s and early 1980s, this was the model of homosexuality relied upon by gay rights advocates, many of whom had also been active in the movement to decriminalize gay male sex. In campaigns for statutory reform, a similar politics was expressed.

Campaigns for Statutory Reform: Early Organizing in Ontario

Lesbian and gay law reformers turned their attentions towards achieving sexual orientation amendments to human rights codes in the early 1970s. Nowhere was action more intense than in the province of Ontario. A variety of amendments to the Ontario Human Rights Code being considered by the legislature in 1972 were the focus of the first Ontario gay demonstrations specifically directed at the Code. In 1973, a step towards the desired goal was achieved when Toronto City Council passed the first policy of its kind in Canada, prohibiting discrimination on grounds of sexual orientation in city employment (Jackson and Persky 1982, 231).

The year 1975 saw the inauguration of the Coalition for Gay Rights in Ontario (CGRO, later the Coalition for Lesbian and Gay Rights in Ontario). The organization's goal was to attain 'full civil and human rights for all homosexual men and women and in this way to advance the struggle for their liberation.'[8] The organization was to consist of member gay and lesbian groups with voting rights. A steering committee was established with one representative from each group, and it was the responsibility of this committee to establish policy.

The coalition saw its primary task as that of 'struggling for the amendment of the Ontario Human Rights Code to include the term "sexual orientation".'[9] In addition to making several Human Rights Code demands, the coalition, in its founding statement, called for changes to education provision, equality for gays in health care, housing, and employment, an end to discrimination in custody and adoption determinations, as well as other related items.[10] Their seven-pronged strategy consisted of 1 / lobbying provincial MPs, 2 / presenting briefs to provincial parties, 3 / seeking out support from non-gay community groups, 4 / documenting cases of discrimination and developing attendant campaigns, 5 / periodic pickets and other forms of public action, 6 / full participation of CGRO in making gay rights an election issue at all levels, and 7 / the development of an education policy for the schools.[11]

In May 1976 two private members' bills attempting to amend the Code were defeated (Jackson and Persky 1982, 231). Nevertheless, the coalition, in June of that year, presented its brief to the Ontario legislature and continued to campaign for change. In 1977, another private member's bill was defeated; however, the CGRO could find some consolation in the recommendations of the Ontario Human Rights Code Review Committee (established in 1975), which included a sexual-orientation clause in its amendment proposals (ibid, 232).

Ontario's lesbian and gay rights reformers were further encouraged by the success of a similar amendment in Québec in 1977. An alliance of Québec gay groups had begun to lobby the National Assembly for a sexual orientation amendment to the Québec human rights charter in 1974. A formal brief was presented to the assembly by the Association Pour les Droits de la Communauté Gaie du Québec in October 1977, and in that same month the Québec Human Rights Commission endorsed a sexual-orientation amendment (ibid, 233). In December, as part of a wider package of reforms, the National Assembly passed such an amendment quietly and without much debate (see Ryder 1990, 67). The inclusion of sexual orientation in the Québec Charter was to remain an isolated, and oft cited, exampled of such protection.

Back in Ontario, 1978 witnessed another impending period of legislative debate on proposed Code amendments and the CGRO presented its second brief to Ontario MPPs.[12] This document opened by defining homosexuality as 'the sexual and emotional preference of males and females for their own gender.'[13] In sections titled 'The Origins of Homosexual Behaviour' and 'The Incidence of Homosexuality in Modern Western Societies,' the CGRO confronted various theories of homosexuality, disputing some and cautiously adopting others. The brief stressed that homosexuals had and would always exist, and attempts to change this had not been and would not be successful. The bibliography accompanying these sections listed a series of sexology studies.[14]

As before, nothing came of these events; yet, three years later, as the Code was up for revision once more, lesbian and gay rights organizations mobilized again – all to no avail. The defeat of the 1981 bill ended a somewhat demoralizing decade of human rights struggles by Ontario's lesbian and gay rights movement.[15] Sexual-orientation protection existed only in Québec. Nevertheless, despite consistent setbacks, organizations such as the CGRO regrouped, and went on to continue the (eventually successful) struggle for human rights reforms in the 1980s.

The 1970s and early 1980s campaigns reveal a law-reform movement dependent upon the public presentation of a medical model of homosexuality and the uncritical promotion of achieving social change primarily through formal political strategies. While other lesbian and gay movements were engaged in quite different forms of politics,[16] the heterosexual public was made aware of lesbians and gay men primarily through the activities of organizations such as the Coalition for Gay Rights in Ontario, as their campaigns were the most visible and interested the media more than did other forms of less conventional struggle.

The efforts of the CGRO and other lesbian and gay law-reform organizations finally paid off in 1986 with the passage of what was popularly known as Bill 7, which, among other things, added a sexual-orientation ground to the Human Rights Code of Ontario (see chapter 3). By 1993, British Columbia, Manitoba, New Brunswick, Nova Scotia, and the Yukon Territory would join Ontario and Québec in providing lesbians and gay men with formal human rights protections, and the federal government had promised to amend the Canadian Human Rights Act in the same way.[17] In the late 1980s one of the key gay rights cases, launched under this latter statute (prior to its amendment), was that of Brian Mossop.

The *Mossop* Case[18]

Brian Mossop worked for the federal government (Treasury Board) as a translator. As a federal civil servant, his employment conditions were regulated by both a collective agreement and the Canadian Human Rights Act, the federal human rights code. In the spring of 1985, the father of Mossop's partner died. Mossop attended the funeral and then applied to have his absence from work considered as bereavement leave under the collective agreement, specifically stating that his lover was male. The application was denied by the employer on the grounds that his relationship did not fall within the 'immediate family' category covered by the bereavement leave provision. Instead, Mossop was offered a paid day of holiday leave. He was not satisfied with this and, with the support of his union (the Canadian Union of Professional and Technical Employees), filed a grievance, which the Treasury Board rejected. He then laid a complaint under the Canadian Human Rights Act (CHRA).[19]

The crux of Mossop's argument before the human rights tribunal was that the collective agreement contravened section 3(1) of the act, prohibiting discrimination based on 'family status.' The agreement provided bereavement leave for 'immediate family,' including common-law couples of the 'opposite sex,' and mothers- and fathers-in-law. Mossop argued that this definition, and the resulting exclusion of same-sex families, constituted 'family status' discrimination. His case depended upon the acceptance of his relationship with his partner being defined as 'family' for the purposes of the Canadian Human Rights Act.

The principal evidence supporting this contention was the testimony of Margrit Eichler, a feminist sociologist. She argued that there was no one definition of family, that some general characteristics of families could be delineated (such as cohabitation; sharing in domestic arrangements; presence of emotional and sexual reliance; joint ownerships), and that it was more useful to describe situations as 'familial,' rather than as 'family' (*Mossop* 1989). Her conclusion, based on Mossop and his partner exhibiting most of these characteristics, was that Mossop lived in a 'familial relationship.' The adjudicator, Mary-Elizabeth Atcheson, adopted this view to support her finding of discrimination and her subsequent compensation and redress order. The Federal Court of Appeal, in reviewing Atcheson's decision, reversed her judgment (*Mossop* 1990). Adopting the conservative approach of earlier case law,[20] the court found that a sociological definition of family was inappropriate for a court of law. Legal precedent, the judges argued, must rule, and 'family' had never included homosexual couples.

The federal court's decision was then appealed to the Supreme Court of Canada, which issued its ruling in February 1993. A bare majority (4–3) held that the Court must defer to Parliament, which had clearly and explicitly refused to add a sexual-orientation ground to the Canadian Human Rights Act (at that time). Mossop, according to the majority, was attempting to receive sexual-orientation protection through the back door (the family-status ground) and the Court (despite several sympathetic nods) was not empowered to permit this.

The minority opinion, consisting of a long and impassioned judgment by Justice L'Heureux-Dubé, extended the reasoning of the tribunal. Quoting long passages from lesbian feminist authors,[21] L'Heureux-Dubé argued that lesbians and gay men formed legitimate families deserving of human rights protection. For Brian Mossop and his partner, Ken Popert, however, this case was now closed.[22]

Mossop is of interest, not solely for the politics of its judgments (see chapter 7), but also because, as with the Bill 7 struggle (see chapter 3), the litigation itself became a focus for social-movement intervention (see chapters 4–6). Coalitions of lesbian, gay, feminist, disabled, and civil libertarian groups, on the one hand, and conservative, evangelical Christian organizations, on the other, seized on the case as a forum in which to do battle over sexuality.

Finally, the *Mossop* case reflected a shift in the public presentation of lesbian and gay identity. Sociology, a discipline concerned with group relations and structural inequalities, had come to court to inform legal constructions of homosexuality. As I discuss further in chapter 3, this new paradigm was also expressed in campaigns for statutory reform, as, for example, in the Coalition for Gay Rights in Ontario abandoning its reliance on sexology to fight for Bill 7.

Constitutional Litigation

Another factor contributing to the judicial re-evaluation of gay rights was the coming into effect and growing prominence of the Canadian Charter of Rights and Freedoms. Enacted in 1982, the Charter is a constitutionally entrenched document providing individuals with a set of fundamental rights, including freedom of association and expression, equality, and several 'due process' guarantees, among other things. The judiciary is given the power to oversee that these rights are not denied unless such a denial can be 'demonstrably justifiable in a free and democratic society' (section 1). Early jurisprudence held that the Charter applies to 'government action,' meaning that it can be used only to challenge the denial of rights by actors or agencies with some degree of state nexus (*Dolphin Delivery* 1986). However, given that the provisions of human rights statutes can be found unconstitutional and that these codes *do* apply to the private sector, the Charter, indirectly, can affect the discriminatory practices of private actors.[23]

Lesbians and gay men, in common with other social movements and new identities, have focused their energies upon section 15 of the Charter (known as the 'equality section'), which came into effect in 1985. Section 15, like the statutory codes, provides protection from discrimination on specified grounds. It also offers a general guarantee of 'equality before and under the law,' and has, of course, the authority and legitimacy of its constitutionality. The grounds covered by the section are not carved in stone; it is accepted that other bases of discrimination will be identified and accepted as analogous to those enumerated (known as 'analogous grounds'). Although sexual orientation is not a specified ground, it is one such category that has been so accepted. In order to enforce Charter rights, individuals must litigate, and one of the most notable developments in the politics of Canadian social movements has been the creation of 'litigation organizations' to facilitate this process through providing funding and litigators (see, for example, Razack 1991).

The coming into effect of section 15 of the Charter signalled a new era for lesbian and gay rights litigants. The Charter, which could be used to challenge existing discriminatory *legislation*, as opposed to the discriminatory *actions* of employers, landlords, and service providers addressed by statutory human rights provision, seemed, to many lesbians and gay men, an ideal vehicle for attacking their exclusion from various social benefits schemes. Much, although not all, of the resulting litigation turned on definitions of 'family' or 'spouse' within various federal and provincial statutes.

One of the first such cases was that launched by Karen Andrews, who applied for family health coverage for herself, her partner, and their children under Ontario's Health Insurance Act (*Andrews* 1988). The government refused to extend the coverage on the basis that lesbian and gay relationships were excluded from the definition of 'spouse' upon which the coverage depended. Her legal action, which included a Human Rights Code element that was never resolved, asserted that restricting the definition of 'spouse' to heterosexual couples was contrary to several sections in the Charter, including section 15.

The judge in the case, McCrea, set the tone for conservative Charter sexuality jurisprudence generally, in 1988, by denying Andrews's claim on the basis that lesbian and gay couples do not marry and procreate. Restricting benefits to heterosexual couples was justified, given governments' important objective of 'establishing and maintaining traditional families' (ibid, 16, 194). McCrea's authorities were largely drawn from dictionaries and previous human rights case law described above, such as *Vogel* (1983).

Since the *Andrews* decision, a small but growing Charter jurisprudence has now arisen in the area of lesbian and gay equality. One of the first cases was *Veysey* (1989), in which the Federal Court of Appeal found, without much discussion, that sexual orientation was an analogous ground under section 15 and upheld the right of a gay prisoner to claim Charter protection. Interestingly, federal and provincial governments have since accepted this ruling and have chosen not to contest the basic right of lesbians and gay men to make claims under the Charter as a 'disadvantaged group.'[24]

The *Knodel* and *Egan* decisions exemplify the contradictory development of lesbian and gay rights case law (see also the discussion in chapter 7). In *Knodel*, the British Columbia trial court found that the 'opposite sex' definition of 'spouse' contained in a provincial health statute infringed the sexual orientation protection guaranteed under section 15 of the Charter. While in *Egan*, a very similar provision was found, at both trial and appeal levels, to be justified under much the same conservative reasoning as that in *Andrews* and the older *Vogel* and *North* cases. This latter approach was echoed again more recently by Southey, J, in a 'gay marriage' case (*Layland* 1993). In what can only be described as a legal contortion, the judge argued that 'the law does not prohibit marriage by homosexuals, provided it takes place between persons of the opposite sex' (ibid).

In another decision, the Ontario Court of Appeal held that the absence of 'sexual orientation' in the federal Canadian Human Rights Act (the act under which Brian Mossop claimed discrimination on grounds of 'family status') violated section 15 of the Charter.[25] The remedy imposed by the court was to rule that, henceforth, the CHRA was to be interpreted *as though it contained* the ground of sexual orientation. Although the ruling in *Haig* technically applied only in Ontario, the federal government subsequently announced that it would not appeal the decision.

Instead, the Conservative justice minister instructed the Canadian Human Rights Commission to follow the Ontario Court of Appeal's ruling in all relevant adjudications across the country.[26]

The *Haig* case manifests both the problems and perils of Charter challenges: on the one hand, the court allowed the gay litigant to circumvent the route of parliamentary reform. Those who decry the creation of an undemocratic suprajudiciary have little reason to applaud the judgment (instead, they may find *Mossop* of more comfort).[27] On the other hand, for the lesbians and gay men who for many years attempted to persuade the Conservative government to amend the CHRA, *Haig* represents the Charter's promise – the chance to force the government's hand through invoking Charter rights.

These possibilities were also represented in *Leshner*, where an Ontario human rights tribunal found that the marital status provision in the Ontario Human Rights code contravened the section 15 Charter rights of lesbians and gay men. The adjudicators then ordered the provincial government to take steps to ensure the provision of spousal pension benefits to the partners of lesbian and gay claimants.

Experts and the Law

Behind this brief history of lesbian and gay rights law reform lies the important role played by scientific evidence in shaping legal constructions of homosexuality – first, as a danger to society,[28] and then as an unfortunate affliction.[29] Within medical discourse, the transition from an approach which feared and pathologized the homosexual to one which advocated empathy and tolerance was an important intervention in legal debates over criminalization. Within child custody disputes as well, liberal psychology was deployed to show that the children of homosexuals turned out 'normal' (meaning heterosexual) and that lesbians and gay men could make 'good parents.'[30] 'Expert' psychologists scrutinized the causes and effects of homosexuality, testifying as to both its immutability and its relative harmlessness. For many lesbians and gay men, this approach represented an advance over previous constructions of homosexuality as 'sick,' 'depraved,' and 'curable' (see also Vance 1989).

Nevertheless, psychology, in both its liberal and its conservative manifestations, subjected homosexuality to interrogation and classification. The 'psy' professions (Donzelot 1980), while sympathetic to the plight of individual lesbians and gay men, none the less studied homosexuality as a 'condition.' Homosexuality's opposite – heterosexuality – remained the closeted, unspoken norm.

'Psy' constructions played an important role in lesbian and gay law-reform struggles, first, by facilitating judicial conservatism (early psychiatric constructions) and, then, but constituting the homosexual as inherently disadvantaged but deserving of empathy, tolerance, and compassion. While these 'psy' understandings of homosexuality were not dominated by legal equality paradigms, liberal psychology has been relied upon by judges and others seeking to extend equality rights to lesbians and gay men.[31]

Within lesbian and gay rights movements, the transition from criminal to human rights law reform has been accompanied by the entry of a new discourse into the debate – sociology. While homosexuality has always been subjected to sociological analysis (historically within the sociology of deviance), this branch of the discipline had not played a key role in the development of legal knowledge of homosexuality, which had, instead, tended to depend upon the 'psy' constructions. However, contestations over the legal meaning of 'family' have offered new opportunities in other areas – particularly sociology of the family, research in demographic patterns, and various feminist 'expertises.'

A similar transition also occurred within Black civil rights litigation in the United States. As Chesler, Sanders, and Kalmuss discuss (1988, 21–2), the landmark school desegregation decision in *Brown* (1954, 1955) was partly based upon a new liberal psychology that emphasized the psychological harm suffered by Black children. This approach became the new psychological paradigm, supplanting the older, conservative victim-blaming psychology as evidenced in racist decisions such as *Plessy* (1896). Liberal psychology, for the emerging civil rights movement and its leading law-reform organization, the National Association for the Advancement of Colored People, in continuing to pathologize Black and not White, was not an ideal antiracist paradigm. On the other hand, it did represent a move forward in that it could anchor a program of positive action.

By the late 1970s, liberal psychology, within school desegregation litigation, had itself been largely replaced (ibid, 24–6). Sociological explanations of structural disadvantage now competed with 'rational choice' models from political science.[32] As Chesler, Sanders, and Kalmuss document, within a twenty-five-year period, psychology experts had come to play a few less significant role in contributing to the formation of desegregation law.

I would argue that, by the late 1980s, lesbian and gay rights reform was, perhaps, beginning to undergo a similar transition. Lesbian and gay campaigners, no longer dependent upon the sympathetic pathologies of liberal psychology, began to offer different paradigms to ground their claims to equality. The *Mossop* case is one example of this new approach. By invoking the new legitimacy of feminist sociology, and rejecting the old paradigms of 'dangerous illness' or 'harmless abnormality,' *Mossop* symbolized the new era of lesbian and gay law reform in Canada. And even where adjudicators dismiss these interventions as 'upstart science,' as in *Mossop* itself (1990) or *Vogel* (1992), many conservative decision makers nevertheless now rely upon sociological, rather than psychological, expertise to counter challenges to traditional definitions of 'family,' 'spouse,' and so on. In the conclusion to chapter 7, I assess the advantages of the sociological paradigm. For now, I move on to the substance of the book – the politics of lesbian and gay rights within specific struggles.

3

The Politics of Liberal Equality

'I have no idea and frankly I do not care.'
  Bob Rae, MPP, Ontario Legislature, 2 December 1986

In chapter 2, I argued that as lesbian and gay identities emerged and consolidated the demand for and acquisition of rights were seen by many to be an intrinsic component of lesbian and gay liberation. Underlying many such demands was a desire on the part of these 'new subjects' to be 'coded human' (Ross 1990), to be identified as social citizens; inclusion within existing systems of state-based rights and status thus became a key demand. Two questions can follow from this: How was lesbian and gay equality constructed within this field of law? What are the implications of striving for inclusion within liberal equality structures? I respond to these questions by exploring the politics of Bill 7 – the struggle, in 1986, to add a sexual-orientation ground to Ontario's Human Rights Code. I first outline the events of Bill 7, and consider some of the reasons for its successful passage. I then examine the politics underlying the struggle.

My argument, in short, is that, in this specific struggle, a liberal equality paradigm was hegemonic. In other words, public debate on the sexual-orientation amendment was structured around this paradigm, and liberal legal ideology achieved an authoritative dominance that both excluded, or marginalized, other perspectives from debate and produced a consensus within which lesbian and gay equality was to be defined and permitted. I consider some of the contradictions within this ideology, including the ways in which human rights law was simultaneously articulated as significant and ineffectual. I also explore how human rights law, particularly the minority rights paradigm, constructs

homo- and hetero- sexualities, and consider the extent to which, for lesbian and gay organizations, legal strategies are pragmatic, and do not
necessarily indicate a 'buying into' of dominant values and ideologies.

The Campaign for Bill 7

The original text of Bill 7, introduced into the Ontario legislature for first
reading in 1985, contained no mention of sexual orientation. The bill was
an omnibus statute, amending a series of other pieces of legislation, in
order to render Ontario law compatible with the newly effective equality
provision of the Charter of Rights and Freedoms, section 15. This process
of Charter review was taking place across the country's provincial legislatures. In Ontario, one of the many statutes scheduled for amendment
was the Human Rights Code.

Significantly, the provincial government at this time was a minority
one, the 'left-leaning' New Democratic Party (NDP) holding the balance
of power while the Liberal party (LP) formed the government. At the
start of 1986, Bill 7 moved to the legislature's Justice Committee. A number of amendments were tabled there, including one to add sexual orientation to the list of grounds upon which discrimination was prohibited.
The amendment was proposed by Evelyn Gigantes, the NDP justice
critic.[1]

The somewhat unexpected introduction of the Gigantes amendment
prompted a measure of activity from lesbian and gay organizations. Two
figured prominently, the Coalition for Gay Rights in Ontario (CGRO), as
in earlier campaigns, and the Right to Privacy Committee, a group of
gay men predominantly active around criminal law and policing issues.[2]
The organizations quickly produced briefs, and initiated low-key lobbying efforts. The firm NDP commitment coupled with that party's new
legislative power encouraged some hopes among activists; however, the
CGRO did not expect the amendment to attract Liberal party support on
the committee.[3]

There is little evidence that the amendment caused much controversy
at the committee stage. While the Liberals did not adopt the amendment
as their own, Ian Scott, attorney general at the time, was sympathetic,
and his and other Liberal votes were cast in favour when the Justice
Committee voted in May. Two Conservative members also approved,
with two others casting negative votes. David Rayside (1988, 114) suggests the amendment was not taken particularly seriously, as few legislators believed it would reach final reading, and also that other business

assumed priority at the time. However, at least one prominent Cabinet member publicly expressed his opinion that the amendment would pass the legislature.[4] Up to this point, the amendment's progress had been smooth, with little conflict, and without a perceived need for mass mobilization in its support.[5]

It was, in some respects, the decision of the New Christian Right[6] in Ontario to make Bill 7 a rallying-point *for themselves* that led the CGRO and others to initiate a full-scale pro-amendment campaign.The anti-amendment lobby was headed by the Coalition for Family Values (CFV), an organization founded the year before in response to a positive federal parliamentary recommendation on sexual orientation.[7] Its core members were Protestant churches (particularly Pentecostals); in addition, other less visibly Christian organizations, such as REAL Women and the National Citizens' Coalition, also participated.[8] The CFV was further strengthened during the Bill 7 episode by the support of the Ontario Conference of Catholic Bishops.

By the autumn of 1986, the CFV campaign had gathered considerable momentum as the bill headed back to the legislature for second reading. The Christian coalition had launched a massive letter-writing and phone campaign, prepared briefs, and courted public opinion, relying upon materials prepared for a previous federal debate which characterized homosexuals as perverted, predatory, paedophiles.[9] However, the formal briefs submitted to politicians tended to avoid such evocations in favour of dry, legal argumentation.[10]

Towards the end of October, the amendment struggle had become highly charged and publicly visible. Both sides intensified their campaigns as the amendment appeared to be splitting the Liberal party, with rural MPPs coming under intense pressure as a result of the anti-amendment campaign.[11] As the government began to delay and equivocate, lesbian and gay activists became increasingly concerned. Both the CGRO and the Right to Privacy Committee decided to prioritize their own letter-writing and phone campaigns, as well as to plan a major public rally. The latter, held at Toronto's St Lawrence Market Hall on 20 November, attracted nearly 1,500 people. MPPs from all three parties spoke, as did representatives from the labour and women's movements, and others such as writer Margaret Atwood. This rally reflected not only the CGRO's attempts to mobilize lesbians and gay men, but also the strategies of coalition building and the recruitment of popular celebrities.[12] As the 'pro' campaign intensified, Premier David Peterson declared his support for the amendment at a Liberal party caucus meeting on 18 November (Rayside 1988, 119). Although the premier formally indicated his intention to permit a free vote, most Liberal MPPs perceived a soft whip to be cracking.[13]

By this time, the media had discovered the issue. While media interest peaked with the start of legislative debate on 25 November, a number of stories, depicting the conflict between pro- and anti-amendment forces, appeared beforehand.[14] Indeed, two major newspapers felt the issue sufficiently significant to run editorials indicating their endorsement of the amendment. *The Globe and Mail*, for example, using the language of equality and dignity, argued in the amendment's favour on 19 November.[15]

With the start of legislative debate, the struggle intensified. Despite both movements sensing by now that the amendment was likely to win approval, the political battle continued, primarily through the media. The content of MPPs' speeches was carried in detail on the front pages of the press for days.[16] Supporters of both lobbies attended the debates, cheering or heckling speakers on all sides, the conduct of legislative observers becoming as much a focus of press interest as the debate itself. On 2 December, after days of controversial and emotional speeches, the amendment passed. The entire bill itself became law two weeks later.[17] Having described the course of events, I now wish to explore some of the reasons explaining Bill 7's success.

David Rayside has carefully considered the question of why Bill 7 passed when so many other sexual-orientation amendments had failed.[18] He has identified a number of factors influencing the bill's outcome. One of these is the history of lesbian and gay organizing in Ontario (including, but not limited to, past Human Rights Code struggles) which politicized people within and without lesbian and gay communities and created organizations with resources that could be drawn upon when necessary. The importance of social movements creating formal, bureaucratic structures has also been emphasized by other writers.[19]

In addition, Rayside (1988, 217) suggests that the lobbying tactics of the lesbian and gay organizations, including a calmness of style and low-key argumentation (partially orchestrated by Rayside himself, an active CGRO member at the time), were responsible for the pro-bill forces being well received by politicians. These tactics included the decision not to hold demonstrations or marches in order not to alienate Liberal MPPs.[20] He further argues that the 'dirty' campaign waged by the Coalition for Family Values backfired by offending liberal sensitivities. As further exploration shows, this does appear to have been the case.

Rayside's views here presume a liberal consensus with respect to end-ing discrimination against lesbians and gay men. According to him (ibid, 129), survey data showed a liberalizing shift in Canadian attitudes towards homosexuality. A 1985 Gallup poll, for example, revealed 70 per cent in favour of extending human rights codes protections to lesbians and gay men. Rayside further suggests that this trend had been reflected in the media (as the largely positive editorial response during Bill 7 would seem to indicate). Arguably, the institutionalization of formal antidiscrimination measures for other groups was perceived by many liberals as needing extension to the category of 'sexual orientation.' Else-where, Rayside and Bowler (1988) have shown in more detail how this liberalizing trend occurred alongside a concurrently held view that homosexuality itself was 'morally wrong.' Thus, Canadian heterosexu-als were formally committed to the equal treatment of lesbians and gay men, while believing firmly (and equally) in the abnormality and wrongness of homosexual expressions. I consider this apparent contra-diction more closely in chapter 4.

Another factor Rayside (1988, 135–7) notes was the existence of an opportune political moment. The combination of minority government, NDP support, federal developments, and so on, contributed to the amendment's success this time around. Finally, and from Rayside's per-spective perhaps most importantly, internal party bureaucracies con-tained important amendment supporters. The unequivocal support of the NDP, particularly the determination of feminist MPP Gigantes, backed by the party's gay caucus, forced the Liberals to respond. And it was the coming-on-board of the two most prominent Liberal Cabinet members, Premier Peterson and Attorney General Scott, that ensured the amendment's passage. Rayside (ibid, 132) suggests the amendment's appeal to such persons lay in how it was framed ideologically – as a 'minority rights issue, lodged within classic liberal-democratic princi-ples.' I agree, but, as I go on to discuss, this view is not unproblematic.

While I largely concur with Rayside's assessment, I explore complica-tions related to some of his points here and in subsequent chapters. For the moment, I wish to discuss one further factor responsible, in part, for Bill 7's success. By 1986, the impact of the Charter on Canadian culture had begun to be felt. While legal cases under the equality provision (sec-tion 15) had only started to filter through the lower courts, the increased power, prestige, and authority of the Supreme Court of Canada had been demonstrated in a series of decisions under other sections.[21]

The process Mandel and Glasbeek have termed 'the legalization of politics' did not originate with the Charter.[22] I indicated in chapter 2 that, from a much earlier period, lesbian and gay rights movements sought to achieve social change through legal-rights reform. Nevertheless, the Charter's enactment signalled the increasing pre-eminence of a public discourse of individual rights and liberties. 'Charter challenge' became a new catch-phrase, entering the politics of everyday life.[23] Indeed, it was the desire to ensure that the Code's provisions did not conflict with Charter guarantees that had prompted the introduction of Bill 7 in the first place, and, hence the opportunity for Gigantes to present her amendment. While there is no way of measuring the effects of the Charter's advent upon popular consciousness, there can be little doubt that rights, as goal and rhetoric, entered Canadian political struggle as never before. This fact influenced, I suggest, not only the shift in public opinion documented by Rayside and Bowler (1988), but also the potential for the introduction and success of initiatives like the Bill 7 amendment.

Thus, a number of factors were involved in the eventual success of the Ontario amendment campaign, including the fourteen years of effort spent creating a more receptive social climate; the growing strength and sophistication of the law-reform movement; the increased visibility, vitality, and activism of lesbian and gay communities generally; and, last but not least, the advent of the Charter and the increasing prominence, authority, and significance of human rights paradigms in public debate throughout the country. I now explore these developments at a somewhat deeper level.

The Hegemony of (Legal) Liberalism

The process of interaction between pre-existing legal frameworks and social-movement identity politics is complex. Most human rights regimes are premised upon a particular understanding of social life – namely, that society contains a variety of diverse minority-like populations, each of which suffers a kind of antiquated prejudice no longer tolerable in liberal democracies. Within this framework, the state acts as a neutral protector, facilitating the eradication of individual aberrations through the passage and enforcement of public rights documents. The preamble of Ontario's Human Rights Code, for example, speaks of 'the inherent dignity and the equal and inalienable rights of all members of the human family'; it is Ontario public policy to create 'a climate of understanding and mutual respect.'

This legislation attempts to resolve social problems, for example, racism and sexism, through encoding individuals as discrete categories, whose difficulties can be alleviated through providing freedom from discrimination on specified grounds: race, ancestry, place of origin, colour, ethnic origin, citizenship, creed, sex, sexual orientation, age, marital status, family status[24] and handicap. The goals of the preamble are presumably facilitated by providing a 'right to equal treatment' and a 'right to freedom from harassment' with respect to goods and services, housing, employment, and membership in professional associations (sections 1, 2, 4, and 5). This, then, was one of the legal frameworks the Canadian lesbian and gay movement confronted as it grew and began to express demands beyond the repeal of Criminal Code sanctions. However, the choice to struggle for inclusion in these regimes necessitated a self-definition compatible with pre-existing concepts.

The model currently hegemonic within human rights–type struggles is one of a homogeneous minority population. As applied to sexuality, the model represents society as having always contained a majority of heterosexuals and a minority of homosexuals. Often, this is made explicit through reliance on the concept of immutability – that sexual orientation is fixed genetically or in early childhood, and is only waiting to be discovered. There have always been and will always be those who sexually prefer their own sex. This preference, occurring without any conscious agency on the part of the individual, should not, liberal argument goes, be a basis for discrimination. When liberals acknowledge that biology may not be the sole determinant of sexuality, they tend to draw an analogy between sexual orientation and religious orientation – as a deep-seated, fundamental aspect of identity that can be changed only at great cost, if at all.

Legal liberalism, upon which human rights laws are premised, thus assumes a series of truths: society is pluralistic, there are majorities and minorities, true democracy necessitates the protection of minorities from the tyranny of majorities, and true minorities share characteristics that differentiate them from the majority norm. The majority must exhibit qualities of tolerance, understanding, and compassion, ultimately evidenced by their willingness to extend legal protection to identified minorities. Even in periods when antidiscrimination laws are rolled back, as in the United States in the 1980s, and real incidents of abuse escalate, this ideology continues to dominate. Even neoconservative politicians have tended to pay it, at least, lip-service.[25]

The pre-eminence of the minority paradigm was clearly evident during the Bill 7 struggle. The Coalition for Gay Rights brief, for example, exhorted MPPs to be true to the 'liberal tradition.'

Most Canadians appreciate the difference between acceptance and tolerance – and most are prepared to be tolerant. Citizens of our country tend to believe that all people, even those whose views and practices they cannot accept, should be treated equally by the law. The law should not try to force acceptance, but it should enshrine tolerance ... We are convinced that people's experiences can change their prejudiced attitudes; tolerance is often transformed into acceptance by the realization that a person one is close to belongs to a denigrated minority. We need the minimal protection afforded by inclusion in the Code in order to be able to share our lives more honestly and to show homophobic people that their beliefs about us are not true.[26]

The brief's introduction also refers a number of times to the Charter and the values it is perceived to represent.[27] Citing a paper prepared by then Ontario attorney general Ian Scott, the CGRO outlines the factors that might make a group of people a legitimate 'analogous ground' under the Charter – namely, that the group has received human rights protection elsewhere, is subject to a pattern of discrimination (the main subject of the brief), and is not economically based.[28] The CGRO also borrows two further factors.

That the major characteristic defining the group not be easily changeable by the individual – recent medical and psychological research concludes overwhelmingly that it is not easy to change one's homosexual orientation.
   That the group be a discrete and cohesive class – though not all its members are necessarily visible, the lesbian and gay community has a well established group identity distinguishable in part by networks of friends, an alternative social-service support system, and shared social, cultural, commercial and political activities.[29]

Here, the brief explicitly presents a homogenous, immutable minority.
   During legislative debate on the amendment, liberal and social democratic MPPs took up these themes of pluralism, tolerance, and society's commitment to fighting discrimination against minorities. Ian Scott, in introducing the amendment and being the first to speak on its behalf, argued that no one should be deprived of services or discriminated against as a result of his or her membership in a class (Hansard, 25 Nov. 1986, 3620). People, he went on, should be considered on their merit and

willingness to obey the law (ibid). Society, Scott argued, was pluralistic, and opinions as to the morality of certain behaviours were a private and personal matter (ibid, 3623).[30] He urged his fellow MPPs to consider 'how we have honoured the human rights of our fellow citizens' (ibid, 3622).

Themes of tolerance and pluralism were echoed by many who spoke in the amendment's defence. Robert Nixon, Liberal House leader and veteran of over thirty years in the Ontario legislature, spoke of government's duty to enshrine and extend human rights for all citizens, and to eliminate prejudice in all its forms (Ontario Hansard, 26 Nov. 1986, 3690–1). In a speech detailing various incidents of discrimination he had observed, David Reville, NDP MPP, eloquently urged the legislature to exhibit tolerance and moral fortitude (ibid, 1 Dec. 1986, 3788–90). Liberals Caplan, Wrye, and Peterson, and Conservatives Fish, Gillies, and Grossman, echoed these sentiments, extolling the virtues of a Canadian society committed to ending the persecution of minorities.[31]

Bob Rae, the social democratic leader of the Ontario NDP (and provincial premier following the 1990 election), offered the fullest amendment defence rooted in elements of liberal ideology. His speech brings together ideas of tolerance, rights, harm, privacy, and pluralism, and typifies the liberal approach.

We start with the affirmation that it is a question of rights ... rights are not given by the state. Rights are not delivered to individuals as a matter of utilitarian convenience. Rights are not given; they are recognized in law because they are innate to what it means to be human ... I speak as a democratic socialist and as someone for whom liberty is a fundamental value ...

... the other value which I think we are attempting to affirm in this amendment is a value to which I ascribe a great deal of importance, and that is the value of privacy. I have literally no idea whether the vast majority of the people with whom I deal day to day are gay or not. I have no idea and frankly I do not care, because I do not think it is any of my business in the work that I do as a legislator. It is not relevant ...

We are a pluralist society ... the purpose of law is not the expression of private outrage but rather the expression of public tolerance. (ibid, 2 Dec. 1986, 3850–2)

Provincial legislators varied in the extent to which these values were viewed as already dominant in society or in the necessary process of being extended. Their common position was that the appropriate role of government was to foster these principles, and that, indeed, a consensus existed that doing so was desirable. Further, there was an assumption that government, through its legislative powers, had the *ability* to create a society where everyone was truly treated equally.

Few of those who spoke in the amendment's favour chose to discuss sexuality explicitly. Indeed, their emphasis on privacy precluded such explicitness. Those who did venture into discussions as to the causes of homosexuality tended to hold views based on its genetic origins.[32] Their speeches contrasted sharply with those of speakers against the amendment. While I consider how social conservatives construct sexuality more fully in chapter 5, the Bill 7 episode reveals the extent to which liberal ideology abandons discussions of sexuality to the right. Twenty-six MPPs spoke against the amendment, and, often using rhetoric taken directly from materials produced by the Coalition for Family Values, almost everyone offered his or her views as to what homosexuality was, and what purpose heterosexuality and the family served in society.[33] Many of these politicians expressed the view that homosexuality was a *choice* that threatened societal stability.[34]

One voice did attempt to inject a feminist analysis into the debate. Evelyn Gigantes, the MPP responsible for the amendment, responded in her speech to right-wing rhetoric by arguing that *heterosexual* men were largely responsible for the abuse of children, linking the right's obsession with gay paedophilia to the privileging of abuse of boys over the sexual abuse of many more girls by heterosexual men (Ontario Hansard, 25 Nov. 1986, 3626–7). She described right-wing Bill 7 propaganda as 'semipornographic' and exposed the contradiction embodied in the view that heterosexuality is simultaneously natural and threatened (ibid, 3627). Gigantes also explicitly addressed the sources of homophobia.

I feel deeply offended by the understanding that some men will organize in religious and business groups to say that men who are not like them are traitors to a system where sex is a rightful means of oppression. Some of those men are hypocrites. Some are not telling the truth. Some know they are not heterosexual. Some of those women are strangers to what is best in the female sex, directness and honesty.

There are 125 elected representatives in the Ontario Legislature: 10 are women. If the sexual numbers and the social power were reversed, I believe the clauses of section 18 relating to sexual orientation might not even be necessary. Women do not feel threatened by homosexual people, male or female. It is the maleness of economic and social domination of our society that is threatened by this reform; not the womanness or the childness, but the maleness that so profits by its domination through being male.

... it is my humble opinion that the hatred and victimization of homosexual people is part of a male-dominated system, dealing with men who do not join as if they were traitors. There is no task that I have undertaken that has made me feel more radical than this one. (ibid, 3629)

Gigantes's speech is remarkable, not only for its content, but for the fact that it was like no other speech, and, indeed, no other reported contribution from any amendment campaigners.

For the most part, the CGRO brief and the speeches of supportive MPPs shared a common language and ideology – legal liberalism. However, parliamentary briefs and legislative debates are rather élite forums. While the galleries tended to be full during the Bill 7 debate, most Ontarians would have read about the speeches in their daily newspapers. How were the ideas discussed above translated into media copy?

While I am not offering a comprehensive press analysis of this struggle, I do wish to consider briefly the question of how the Bill 7 episode was represented in the mainstream media, particularly in the three major Toronto-based newspapers. As I have suggested, while there was some coverage of the amendment prior to its discussion in the House, the press did not become fully interested in the amendment until the 'anti' campaign intensified and legislative debate began. Major newspapers thus became participants in the bill's interpretation at the height of its controversy. In this respect, one could argue that the press was quickly compelled to take sides, and this is, indeed, what happened. By the end of November, *The Toronto Star* and *The Globe and Mail* were identified as being amendment supporters. The *Star*'s coverage was the most explicitly in favour of the bill;[35] while the *Globe*'s reporters were somewhat more neutral, their paper's editorial board was not.[36] *The Toronto Sun*, in keeping with its reactionary, populist stance, came out against the amendment.[37]

During the period of debate, three points in particular are worth making about press participation. First, up to the time of the amendment's passage, there was virtually no reported comment from CGRO activists or any other lesbian and gay spokespeople. Second, the campaign and views of the Coalition for Family Values (CFV) did receive a great deal of publicity;[38] however, in *The Star* and *The Globe and Mail* the CFV was portrayed as extreme, vindictive, and 'out of touch.'[39] Thus, while the opinions of the anti-amendment lobby were widely disseminated, much of this took place within a context of condemning these views and the tactics employed by those holding them.

Third, the only perspective publicly endorsing the amendment's passage was that embodied by liberalism. The editorials of *The Toronto Star*, *The Globe and Mail*, and *The Ottawa Citizen*, for example, all used the language of tolerance and pluralism, and spoke of Canada's 'great history' as a human rights leader. The writers further insisted that the amendment was simply a way of extending basic liberal values to a group suffering discrimination and did not signify in any way a radical restructuring of society. Even *The Toronto Sun*'s editorial decrying the amendment's passage insisted upon that paper's support for equality and its condemnation of persecution.[40]

Thus, a short review of press coverage shows that the values expressed by liberal politicians during legislative debate were the same as those providing justification for the amendment in the major newspapers. The defenders of the amendment were not lesbians and gay men themselves, or their representatives, but rather, politicians, reporters, and editors.[41] The lesbian and gay movement had almost no entry into what was communicated to the public through the press.[42]

This process of exclusion (and, as I discuss below, self-censorship) ensured that the minority lesbian and gay subject dominating the Bill 7 stage rendered invisible an alternative, feminist construction of, for example, 'compulsory heterosexuality' (Rich 1981). Indeed, with the exception of Evelyn Gigantes's speech in the House (which appears to have been ignored by the media), heterosexuality remained an unstated, unquestioned norm against which others were implicitly measured and perceived to be 'different.' This obfuscated an understanding of the relationship between sexuality and gender, while further entrenching, and hence leaving unchallenged, principles of liberal equality ideology. Instead, lesbians and gay men were to be allowed into the 'human family' through the paternalistic benevolence of political patriarchs.

The Politics of Liberal Equality

The hegemony of liberal paradigms within the Bill 7 struggle was, I would argue, politically problematic for several reasons. To begin with, the minority framework is a model of questionable value to any social group; in relation to lesbians and gay men it seems particularly inappropriate. If, as many feminists and others contend, sexuality is socially constructed, and there is no necessary or natural link between reproductive capacities, gender categories, and sexual desire, then representing lesbians and gay men as an immutable minority may restrict rather than broaden social understandings of sexuality. Lesbians and gay men are granted legitimacy, not on the basis that there might be something problematic with gender roles and sexual hierarchies, but on the basis that they constitute a fixed group of 'others' who need and deserve protection.[43] Arguably, then, human rights frameworks thus regulate new identities in ways that contain their challenge to dominant social relations.[44]

Second, another consequence of the human rights strategy is that it tends to entrench the liberal public / private divide by locating the source of lesbian and gay oppression in the public spheres of employment, housing, and service provision addressed by the legislation. The CGRO brief regarding Bill 7 represents the areas of employment and housing provision as key sites of discrimination (as they must be in order to publicly justify a sexual-orientation amendment to legislation that applies only in a limited realm).[45] Interestingly, the CGRO brief also lists child custody as one of the areas where discrimination against lesbians and gay men occurs;[46] however, Ontario's Human Rights Code has no jurisdiction over the expression of judicial homophobia in custody judgments.[47]

Judy Fudge (1989) has contended, in the context of women's rights, that too much attention paid to achieving inclusion within laws which reinforce the public / private divide may in fact further obscure private sphere relations, a key site of women's oppression. Feminists who critically analyse notions of political citizenship make a similar point (see, for example, Pateman 1989). I would extend this analysis and argue that, in the context of sexuality struggles, a focus on public-sphere discrimination leaves unsaid and therefore unaddressed one of the primary sites of the construction and enforcement of heterosexuality – home and family relations.[48]

A third drawback to the liberal equality paradigm is how it serves to obfuscate divisions within social movements, perhaps marginalizing important political issues in the process. In the Bill 7 campaign, the CGRO presented the heterosexual public with a homogenous whole, a group of women and men self-defined as lesbian and gay, who suffered the same discrimination. There was no question that both lesbians and gay men deserved the same protections. Ironically, with the exception of organizations like the CGRO, many gay men and lesbians preferred to work separately,[49] and political battles often raged between them. Liberal equality discourse not only minimizes divisions within the minority, however; it also renders it nearly impossible for linkages to be made between individuals' different minority memberships – each is seen to be discrete and capable of individual resolution (see Crenshaw 1989; Iyer 1993). In the case of the so-called lesbian and gay minority, this has the effect of ensuring that lesbians' experience as 'women,' 'Jewish,' 'Black,' and so on is submerged.

Fourth, the very goal of the pro-amendment campaign meant that the Human Rights Code itself remained unquestioned – not only was it considered to be a legitimate way of addressing systemic oppression, but also the mechanisms and procedures of the Code could not seriously be challenged within such a strategy. The experiences of classes of people previously included in the legislation, for example, under the grounds of 'sex' or 'race,' have not been positive. Particularly in the area of race discrimination, the Code has not proved to be an effective weapon at all. The Code's individual complaints (and perpetrator) model, coupled with the commission's mandate to conciliate and effect a compromise, have not been perceived by human rights 'consumers' to have aided in eradicating racism in Ontario.[50] The experience of many people who have filed complaints is one of massive delay, bureaucratic bungling, and poor results.[51] These and other criticisms have been made of antidiscriminatory structures in the United States and Britain (see Freeman 1982; Fitzpatrick 1987). Further, as Kristen Bumiller (1988) has documented, many people who could file complaints, for a variety of reasons, do not.

Bumiller (1988, 61), drawing upon Foucault's work, has argued that modern antidiscriminatory law is continuous with older mechanisms of social regulation. It functions this way by constructing a 'classification of identities' – categories of persons who are, in some way, 'lesser than' an unstated norm (ibid, 69). She suggests that American civil rights legislation produces subjects that are not able to effectively engage in social struggle. The 'victims' of antidiscriminatory provision are passive onlookers, who play little or no role in redressing the abuse they have experienced. Indeed, the form of law in this area produces individuals who decline to identify their problem as a legal one, blame themselves for what they have suffered, and create non-legal strategies of resistance that succeed in further entrenching their victim status. Bumiller concludes that antidiscriminatory law is another form of modern discipline, producing self-policing identities, and ensuring the channelling of resistance in ways that do not radically shift the balance of power.

While Bumiller's analysis tends, as do many Foucauldian approaches, to reify an all-powerful discourse,[52] she nevertheless provides an important insight into understanding human rights law. These legal regimes produce and enshrine fragmented identities; people are forced to compartmentalize their complex subjectivities in order to make a claim. Often, as Bumiller notes (ibid, 82–107), the result is not to make a claim at all. Instead, individuals construct their problem as trivial, view human rights law as ineffective anyway, and often get more satisfaction from 'sacrificing' themselves (by not complaining) than by 'losing control' through entanglement in bureaucratic procedures. Ultimately, all of this serves to channel and diffuse social protest by reinforcing the victimization of the legislation's alleged beneficiaries (ibid, 39, 49–51).

One study considering lesbian perceptions of human rights in Ontario would seem to confirm Bumiller's research. Didi Khayatt (1990, 1992) found that, while lesbian teachers felt human rights were important psychologically, few were under illusions as to what the Code provided in the way of redress. Teachers did not feel that a sexual orientation amendment would enable them to come out more easily and, while they tended to believe the Code would be helpful if they lost their job due to discrimination, most felt that the work atmosphere, should they be reinstated, would be intolerable. As the reports of the Ontario Human Rights Commission show, extremely few complaints based on sexual orientation have been made.[53]

During the Bill 7 struggle, lesbian and gay campaigners were not unaware of these issues; indeed, the CGRO brief makes explicit reference to some of these concerns:

Prejudice and oppression are not automatically eradicated by legal protection, as is shown by the experiences of women and people in our community oppressed by racism or religious intolerance. Long after sexual orientation is added to the Human Rights Code, we can expect discrimination against us to continue. Getting rid of deep-rooted anti-gay attitudes will require more fundamental social change than is to be achieved by expanding the interpretation and enforcement of the law.[54]

Thus, at the same time as campaigners and supporters expressed the importance of amending the Code, enhancing its status as an agent of social change, a message was also being given out that the amendment's effects would be negligible. This is most clearly revealed in the political speeches of amendment supporters during legislative debate. Member after member minimized the significance of the amendment, arguing that its achievement would barely cause a ripple of change in social life, at the same time as they insisted that the amendment must pass if Ontario society was truly to reflect liberal values. MPPs Scott, Johnston, Reville, Mackenzie, Wrye, Rae, and Peterson discussed at length what the amendment would *not* do.[55] Much of this denial was to counter the right's doomsday rhetoric; nevertheless, these politicians were also expressing the commonly held view that human rights laws make little difference to people's day-to-day lives. Indeed, at one stage Attorney General Scott advised lesbians and gay men to engage in Charter litigation if they wanted to achieve substantive new rights; the Code, he suggested, was not the appropriate instrument.[56]

However, for the Coalition for Gay Rights in Ontario, amending the Code was seen to be necessary not because doing so would end discrimination against lesbians and gay men, but because doing so would signal that society was formally condemning homophobia. The amendment was viewed as a significantly symbolic gesture.[57] Following its passage, David Rayside, a CGRO spokesperson, in one of the few CGRO contributions making it into the mainstream press, was quoted as saying that although the amendment would do little to change people's daily lives: 'I think this kind of legislation sends out a signal. And I think it's a much longer term process. It's not evident in the courts and tribunals. It happens in the hearts and minds of people. And that can take a decade, two decades, half a century.'[58] Three days later, however, other CGRO activists were quoted making quite different comments. John Argue, also active in the NDP Gay Caucus, argued the amendment would ensure the extension of health benefits to same-sex couples, and Tom Warner predicted that 'there will be complaints in a wide range of areas,' including child custody law.[59] At the same time, Attorney General Ian Scott was insisting that the Code could not be used to challenge existing law, including child custody.[60]

Paradoxically, or, perhaps, ironically, the choice to struggle for inclusion within human rights regimes legitimated legislative frameworks that even amendment supporters seemed to deride. This contributed to the enhancement of the Code as a favoured instrument of social change, marginalizing the experience of those already all too familiar with its inadequacies. At the same time, a 'no major impact' rhetoric was deployed strategically, partly to quiet opposition and partly as an honest assessment of the Code's importance. Contradictory and conflicting messages, as to the point of law reform, were thus communicated, and the campaigners' intended goals somewhat undermined. Finally, the constant repetition by liberals that Canada was a country with a 'great human rights record' served to perpetuate this myth and render the experience of those who would dispute it of no account.[61]

I have thus far argued that the goal of achieving inclusion within existing human rights structures, and the resulting hegemony of liberalism, renders more legitimate the legislation itself and its attendant ideologies. It also has these effects with respect to law in general. For example, the CGRO brief implied that part of a solution to the discrimination and violence it detailed necessarily required *legislation*. The politics of the pro-amendment campaign succeeded in reifying law, the Code in particular, as an answer to social problems (see Smart 1989, 161). While within lesbian and gay communities, the amendment was viewed by most people as a first step of largely symbolic value,[62] and, as I have shown, the brief itself partially makes this point, the wider public received contradictory messages. While some activists and their lawyers implied that the amendment's passage assured the impending release of various benefits, liberal politicians argued the bill would have little practical effect.

Some might question whether it is wise to distil for public consumption a model of sexuality and a view of formal institutions (like law), not particularly dominant within lesbian and gay communities. Others have argued that, as a first step, particularly in a neoconservative climate, it is *necessary* to do so (Cicchino, Deming, and Nicholson 1991, 628). Could the members of the CGRO have chosen to challenge the legal assumptions, rather than accommodate them, and provide for Ontario's public a justification for human rights protection not reliant on traditional liberal ideologies?[63] Why was the voice of a heterosexual feminist MPP the only one to link homophobia to male domination? If she could do this standing on the floor of the Ontario legislature surrounded by more than one hundred men, was there not, perhaps, more room to communicate a progressive sexual politics than amendment campaigners allowed?

Chris Bearchell, a long-time Toronto lesbian activist and CGRO campaigner during Bill 7, deems such questions irrelevant (interview). Communicating a radical sexual politics to the public was not the CGRO's priority. She argues that the point of the campaign was to organize and politicize lesbians and gay men, not heterosexual outsiders. The CGRO used the Code struggle to draw lesbians and gay men into a political battle, to educate them, and to facilitate a province-wide lesbian and gay network. According to Bearchell, radical rhetoric is not effective at moving lesbians and gay men to the left; people's politics shift through their engagement in grass-roots struggles and through their relationship to a community.

Other CGRO activists might not concur with Bearchell's views as to the point of the CGRO campaign. Nevertheless, her comments are important in terms of pointing out the divergent concerns of academics and activists. Much of this chapter has been an inquiry into the dominance of liberal ideology in public debate around sexuality, particularly in the context of Bill 7. One of my concerns was that oppositional gay and feminist sexual politics were seemingly structured out of the legal process in this instance. Yet, as Bearchell's comments suggest, the CGRO itself made little effort to inject an alternative perspective into the debate, choosing instead to rely, for pragmatic reasons, upon liberal rhetoric. It may be, therefore, inaccurate to suggest that alternative perspectives were excluded *at the stage of public debate*; in fact, communicating an alternative sexual politics may have been deemed either impossible or unimportant by the CGRO itself at an earlier stage – hence, the lone parliamentary voice of Evelyn Gigantes.

The intentions of the CGRO, or any other sector of the lesbian and gay community, are not unimportant. However, my concern is precisely with *un*intended implications, and under considered effects. By choosing, for whatever reasons, non-threatening rhetoric and 'acceptable' campaign strategies, lesbian and gay communities, I have argued, leave unchallenged liberal principles and contribute to the entrenchment of problematic concepts such as the minority rights paradigm. At the same time as some lesbians and gay men were being politicized into a lobbying campaign, the identity they were being asked to take on was that of the 'minority' subject of liberal human rights law. In contrast, perhaps, to Bearchell, I do not view politicization as an inherently progressive process; the support of lesbians and gay men for human rights protection for ourselves says very little about the character of our political commitments in other areas.

Furthermore, the decision not to infuse the debate with alternative ideas about sexuality was, as I have noted, an abandonment of the field to liberals and the right. The effects of pragmatic political struggle are seen not solely in terms of what was communicated to the heterosexual public but also in terms of what was communicated to lesbians and gay men in the mainstream media. The CGRO's choice to be a voice of lesbian and gay liberalism implicitly meant that the organization was not speaking for feminist, socialist, and other progressive lesbians and gay men. Thus, while some apolitical people may have been gathered into the process, others, such as me at the time, became increasingly marginalized from the 'public face' of the lesbian and gay movement.

Concluding Remarks: The Possibilities of a 'Minority' Politics

I have argued that the demand to include sexual orientation within a list of protected grounds in human rights law often succeeded in entrenching a minority rights paradigm with respect to lesbian and gay sexuality. This, in turn, strengthened a belief in the immutable nature of sexuality, and thus left unquestioned the inevitability, normalcy, and 'majority' status of *heterosexuality*. In the Bill 7 example, the mobilization of lesbians and gay men, to the extent it took place, was short term and tended to exclude the expression of more radical perspectives. For example, oppositional analyses of sexuality were marginalized, and radical activists may have been alienated by the campaign's embracing of liberal politics. From these observations, one might conclude that I see nothing but gloom and doom in struggles to include sexual orientation provisions within existing human rights regimes.

However, Bill 7 was but one example of such a reform initiative. Other similar struggles may afford different opportunities and achieve contradictory results. I have no doubt that this is the case. There are also, however, other ways to complicate the analysis of Bill 7 I have set out above. Does including the category 'lesbians and gay men' within the concept of 'minority' succeed in shifting the very meaning of 'minority' and, as a result, challenge the 'naturalness' of its 'majority opposite'? The minority paradigm is most frequently expressed within liberal discourse. Such discourse, I have argued, often assumes a hegemony within struggles for lesbian and gay rights reform and is, therefore, the understanding that I shall focus upon.

The dominant liberal understanding of 'minority,' affirmed by human rights law, is of a group of people with a shared culture and history. The deployment of the term reveals its necessary opposite – majority. Within human rights regimes, minorities are peoples different from the majority norm, who have been afforded official protection from bigotry towards them. As applied to sexuality, the minority paradigm has constructed lesbians and gay men as a homogenous group, one permanently consisting of small numbers of people with little or no control over the characteristic that defines them as a minority – sexual orientation. Within liberal approaches to minority, the 'naturalness,' inevitability (for the majority), and (implied) superiority of heterosexuality are not questioned. Furthermore, the minority paradigm does not tend to consider sexuality as a field of *regulation* and, hence, social construction.

I would argue that, at first glance, these dominant understandings of minority have *not* been seriously undermined by lesbian and gay rights reform in Canada. The inclusion of sexual orientation within existing human rights legislation has simply extended a liberal paradigm to lesbian and gay identities without subverting it. At the same time, this inclusion has facilitated the expression of immutability arguments within the mainstream lesbian and gay rights movement. Rather than making people question what we mean by 'minority,' struggles such as Bill 7 succeed in entrenching biological explanations and binary oppositions.

Lesbian and gay rights activists are increasingly jettisoning 'psy' discourses for those of sociology (and history); however, little disruption to the minority / majority opposition has occurred as a result. Although it is no longer popular to talk about the 'lesbian and gay minority' as sick, perverted, and / or pathetic, it is still considered appropriate to use uncritically the term 'minority.' There are simply 'new' defining characteristics of the minority: geographical space; social and cultural institutions, and a 'history of persecution.' Heterosexuality, and the forces which render it nearly unavoidable, are not obviously undermined as a result. Does this, however, have to be the case?

I would suggest that, while there is nothing inherent within antidiscriminatory legislation that necessitates expressing a minority paradigm, the form these kinds of laws take, as I have noted in this chapter, facilitate its adoption. Nevertheless, lesbian and gay rights campaigners, rather than strategically accommodating liberal themes, could instead choose to articulate different rationales, justifications, and arguments. The ability, or practicality, of doing this will vary according to circumstances.

For early 'homophile rights' activists, relying then upon the insights of liberal psychology, the demand for inclusion within liberal conceptual paradigms was a radical one (D'Emilio 1983, 244; see also Marcus 1992). The idea of suggesting that these lesbian and gay rights pioneers should have exhorted society to overthrow heterosexuality seems fatuous. Arguably, however, we have moved on from there. The ground paved by these earlier activists has enabled 1990s lesbian and gay rights reformers, perhaps, to contribute towards a paradigm shift in our understandings of sexuality. This will not be appropriate for all societies and cultures everywhere; for some, conventional reforms must come first and, for others, neither of these routes may be appropriate.

However, in countries such as Canada, where conventional rights reforms have had some success in shaping new social climates, new agendas may be desirable. A strategy to *dis*articulate minority from hegemonic liberal discourse might help to challenge dominant understandings of 'minority' as a concept, together with the accompanying 'naturalness' of the 'norm.' If the lesbian and gay minority were represented less in terms of *sexual difference*, and more in terms of a *political opposition*, then the meaning of 'minority' in this context might indeed be shifted. Unfortunately, from my perspective, this is unlikely to happen. In North America, the mainstream lesbian and gay rights movement has, to a large extent, institutionalized a liberal approach to reform. Law reform tends to be an activity largely engaged in by professional lobbyists who advocate an interest group model (see Merrett 1991). Many of these reformers publicly argue that lesbian and gay rights are exactly about 'the right to be different,' and not about 'troubling' heterosexuality or heterosexuals.

Although I have thus far suggested that achieving a right to be different succeeds in affirming dominant liberal paradigms, the extension of these paradigms to new identities may have several positive effects as well. There are, for example, benefits in terms of the distribution of resources. Given that, in countries such as Canada, some resources are directed towards groups which have officially achieved minority status, lesbians and gay men are able to draw on these for community projects. Furthermore, the social identity of minority may facilitate resistance, mobilization, and opposition by fostering a certain consciousness and solidarity among identity holders (see also Weeks 1985, 195–201).

If the addition of sexual orientation to human rights laws, on whatever terms, signals an increasing social acceptance of homosexuality, this might, in turn, have an important impact upon young men and women contemplating their own sexual identities. In other words, as Brian Mossop suggests in chapter 4, the official visibility of lesbian and gay identity might lead to more people coming out. If this were so, the meaning of 'minority,' as applied to homosexuality, might indeed shift as heterosexuality's claims to universal truth were undermined. As well, other related effects such as the increasing confidence and strength of those already claiming lesbian or gay identities, and the corresponding panic of conservative Christians forced to explain and justify 'God's Plan' (see chaper 5) are possible. In the long term, then, it may be possible to argue that the fixity of the minority / majority opposition is in fact cracked by the extension of the liberal minority paradigm to lesbians and gay men.

Finally, in responding to the concerns of theorists who question the appropriateness of a gay rights strategy for lesbians (see Eaton 1991; Robson 1990b, 1992), it may be worth here considering a point made by Judith Butler (1991), writing in a somewhat different context. She has observed, as have many others, that in public discourses 'the lesbian' has been notably absent. While sex between men was certainly given an entirely negative construction, at least male homosexuality was *present* in public debate, law, and other discourses. This, Butler argues, has offered to gay men a site from which to resist. 'To be prohibited explicitly is to occupy a discursive site from which something like a reverse-discourse can be articulated; to be implicitly proscribed is not even to qualify as an object of prohibition ... It is one thing to be erased by discourse, and yet another to be present in discourse as an abiding falsehood' (ibid, 20). Human rights laws, perhaps, offer to lesbians the opportunity to articulate a form of resistance. In debating our inclusion within this gender-neutral form of law, in contesting the paradigms of sexuality deployed to gain 'our rights,' lesbians are perhaps able to participate in public sexuality debates as never before. In chapter 4, I extend some of these ideas to consider the role of rights rhetoric in social struggle.

4

Beyond the Rights Debate

In chapter 2, I began by suggesting that the struggle to amend Ontario's Human Rights Code was one about inclusion within liberal equality discourse, rather than about rights per se. Here, I wish to consider how rights rhetoric was deployed by various agents in the struggle over Bill 7, as well as by actors involved in the *Mossop* litigation.[1] I have suggested that liberal ideology achieved authoritative dominance on the Bill 7 stage. Rights is arguably one of the most significant rhetorics of liberal equality. The claim of a 'right' and the rhetorical deployment of phrases such as 'we have a right to ...,' are evocative, persuasive symbols in contemporary social struggle. In this chapter, then, I focus specifically on rights rhetoric as a tool that social movements wield while engaging in political action. However, the use of rights rhetoric has been a frequent subject of criticism by legal scholars.

Bill 7 and the Rights Debate

Most progressive legal theorists agree that rights (as objectives and discourse) are potentially problematic. The main point of disagreement, as I read it, is between those who characterize rights as abstract, individualistic, *dis*empowering, and obfuscatory,[2] and those who say rights struggles *may* be these things, but they can *also*, perhaps simultaneously, be *em*powering, necessary, foci for resistance.[3] From either a marxist or poststructuralist position, rights critics argue that current rights struggles are either examples of a depoliticized culture or questionable invocations of dangerous discourse. Rights defenders, on the other hand, some of whom also espouse socialist and post-structuralist perspectives, emphasize the positive effects of rights struggles upon social-movement mobilization and individual consciousness, while tending to marginalize the structural and discursive constraints noted by the rights critics.[4]

In explorations of struggles such as Bill 7, a number of questions are raised by this literature. How helpful is it to characterize this conflict as one about rights? Certainly, rights rhetoric was deployed by all parties; however, can this dimension alone be said to constitute the substance of the struggle? Bill 7 was partly an act to amend the Ontario Human *Rights* Code; does this fact reveal something significant about the struggle's essence? Are the implications of rights struggles inherently negative, or does the language of rights, as some argue (Minnow 1990), assist in the building of an 'interpretive community,' an arena of shared understandings facilitating political communication? Or do rights claims, as others contend (Fudge and Glasbeek 1992), obscure fundamental relations while depoliticizing social struggle?

First, with respect to Bill 7, one must question the usefulness of those analyses which are litigation-centred, those which proceed on the basis that the achievement of abstract rights per se was the goal, and those which focus on the individualistic character of rights claims. The fight for Bill 7 needs to be analytically separated from questions to do with Code utilization; furthermore, I have argued that the CGRO and its constituency desired positive social recognition (not abstract rights). In addition, the pro-amendment forces advocated for rights on a collective, not an individual basis. The anti-amendment forces countered this, not so much by asserting the individual rights of others (although this was done by the tabloid press)[5] but through implying that legislative protection condoned the sexual (and immoral) 'lifestyle' of a political group by giving them 'special rights.' For both sides, Bill 7 clearly invoked the collective 'lesbians and gay men' (or 'homosexuals'), rather than the individual lesbian or gay supplicant.

Furthermore, while the 'pro' campaign masked one reality of the lesbian and gay movement (in the sense of minimizing underlying political divisions and presenting a homogenous community), it could not be characterized as abstract.[6] For example, incident after incident of discrimination and often brutal violence was detailed in the CGRO brief. The liberal press picked this up, focusing on the theme of discrimination; its editorials used rights rhetoric to address questions relating to the necessary eradication of unacceptable prejudice in liberal democracies. At issue for the amendment supporters were not rights per se, but, rather, questions to do with 'what is right,' particularly with respect to the extension of tolerance and other liberal values, and the role of the state in facilitating these.

Similarly, the Coalition for Family Values deployed the language of rights strategically. They and their supporters argued that lesbians and gay men wanted special rights.[7] For them, the amendment signified official condoning of a lifestyle choice.[8] In their legislative briefs, conservatives worked to distance homosexuality from other categories receiving human rights protection. For example, unlike 'true' minorities, conservatives argued, 'homosexuals' are neither economically disadvantaged and politically powerless, nor the victims of immutable characteristics beyond their control.[9] In their less official materials, the CFV and others described homosexuality as a predatory lifestyle, posing a danger to young children, and expressed through practices such as paedophilia, necrophilia, and bestiality (further discussed in chapter 5). Human rights protection, then, would make it impossible for 'good people' to protest against such practices by giving homosexual practitioners 'special rights.' 'Gay rights', in this context then, actually meant unwarranted *privileges*.

It thus seems unhelpful to draw an analogy between the appearance of rights rhetoric in the Bill 7 episode and that existing in, for example, abortion debates. Bill 7 was not about a conflict of rights requiring some kind of political balancing.[10] Such a conflict is a potential result of human rights *adjudication*; for example, a situation where a gay man files a complaint based on a newspaper's refusal to run his explicitly same-sex personal ad may well centre on the man's 'right to be free from discrimination based on sexual orientation' as balanced against the paper's 'right to freedom of the press.'[11] While it may be appropriate to question lesbian and gay human rights strategies on the basis that *Code utilization* may lead to a 'duelling rights' showdown (although this seems a criticism of institutional practice rather than a comment on the 'nature' of language), the political struggle over *amending* the Ontario Human Rights Code did not itself raise these issues.

Carol Smart, another rights critic, makes a different point to the ones above. She suggests that rights achievements bring increased state surveillance as claimants must 'conform to specification [as] a prerequisite for exercising such rights' (1989, 162). State agencies must collect information, ensuring individuals fit the category under which they are claiming. I would argue, however, that not *all* rights claims necessarily bring increased surveillance. The law reform achieved by lesbians and gay men through Bill 7 does not appear to do so; proving one's sexual orientation (or race or sex) is not a prerequisite for redress under the Code. What one must prove is *discrimination* on the basis of a listed factor which it is assumed the claimant possesses. One need not reveal the intimate details of one's life, only those relevant to the allegations at hand (legal relevancy is, of course, a highly problematic concept).

However, with respect to other kinds of legal claims, for example, a gay couple's claim to be a 'family,' Smart's warning becomes more meaningful. As I noted in chapter 2, and explore further in chapter 7, expert constructions of homosexuality play an important role in categorizing and constituting lesbian and gay families. Nevertheless, even when lesbian and gay rights struggles *do* bring increased surveillance, they may also offer points from which to resist.[12]

Another aspect of the rights critique is the suggestion that individuals and social movements are fooled by the promise of rights. Rights become reified in political struggle, by a duped or mystified constituency labouring under a kind of false consciousness (see Gabel, 1980). Michael Mandel (1989, 308), for example, refers to Charter rights as a 'hoax,' while Judy Fudge (1989, 459) indicates that Charter-using feminists 'accept' prevailing discourse, 'assume' the state is an instrument, and 'see' the courts as autonomous and rights-claims as self-executing. While I accept and am persuaded by many of the arguments made by these writers, I find this view of social-movement struggle to be somewhat unhelpful – at least with respect to lesbian and gay political activity.

During the Bill 7 episode, a comparison, for example, between the CGRO brief and Bill 7 editorials, and commentary from CGRO activists in the radical lesbian and gay press reveals the extent to which liberal pluralist discourse was deployed strategically, and did not indicate a duped or mystified lesbian and gay community.[13] In fact, one of the principal architects of the CGRO campaign, partially responsible for its careful, liberal, muted tones, was a man who, in a later article, described himself as holding socialist-feminist beliefs. David Rayside (1988) has provided a sophisticated, political defence of human rights strategies within a committed left-wing perspective. Another CGRO activist, Chris Bearchell, expressed in an interview having had a similar perspective and strategy. There is no reason to doubt that many other lesbians and gay men reached similar conclusions after much deliberation, either being genuinely persuaded that rights campaigns were defensible theoretically, or that they were, simply, necessary, pragmatic steps.

Within lesbian and gay rights movements, few, if any, people believed that winning Bill 7 would achieve equality, much less liberation. The human rights code strategy was always one among many; it was viewed as a necessary step, as much a symbolic hurdle as a material benefactor. 'The law' was resorted to because it was there, the structure existed; and, as modern lesbian and gay identity emerged and consolidated, analogies between lesbian and gay experience and other oppressions were made. The admonitions of some theorists not to expect serious change from law reform seems, in the case of Bill 7, to be misplaced. While the public rhetoric of the pro-amendment forces suggested that discrimination against lesbians and gay men would end with their incorporation into human rights legislation, few were so naïve as to seriously believe this (see Khayatt 1990; Ross 1990). The discourse deployed was strategic and hopeful, not indicative of a wistful, trusting, submissive approach to law or belief in law's neutrality, objectivity, and so on.[14] In order to more fully explore the rights perspectives of social movement activists, I consider below the views of several actors involved in lesbian and gay rights litigation.

Conservative Christian Perspectives

As I discuss in chapters 5 and 6, conservative Christian activists have become increasingly involved in trying to stem the tide of lesbian and gay equality. Here, I wish briefly to consider some of their views on rights.

For Don Hutchinson, a captain in the Salvation Army of Canada and its legal adviser, rights rhetoric and claims are quite problematic. Rights move the focus away from a discussion of *privileges* (which is what so-called rights 'really are') and *responsibilities*, which is what people ought to have. 'I don't like the word "rights" because it implies that I can take something away from you. I prefer privileges and responsibilities ... When we put it in the context of rights, we start to get into a battle between you and me about what I can do, and what you can do, as opposed to what the society we live in permits us to do. The question of rights tends to focus on individuals' (interview).

Hutchinson associates the dominance of a culture of rights to the role of lawyers in formal politics. 'We live in a very rights-oriented society which has partially come about because our principal legislators are people who were involved in the adversarial system, who have a very different perspective on life.' He argues that, 'when we start to focus on rights, we start to move away from a focus on needs' (interview).

Judy Anderson, president of REAL Women, has similar views: 'I'd like to see a Charter of responsibilities rather than a Charter of Rights ... the Charter of Rights pits group against group, ideology against ideology ... rights have become paramount to everybody ... the Charter creates a more selfish society, [it's] win / lose and makes society more polarized, makes people less willing to compromise' (interview). Anderson's opinion of other human rights legislation is also largely negative. While she believes in the idea of having human rights laws, she characterizes the Ontario Human Rights Commission as 'social engineers' and 'Big Brother,' telling me in an interview a story about a friend who has been, unjustly in her view, charged with race discrimination under the Code and intimidated.

Hutchinson and Anderson's opinions on rights, at times, appear similar to those of the rights critics discussed above. While progressive theorists tend not to engage in a discourse of privileges and responsibilities, they do identify social life as being overly rights-oriented and litigious. Some, in keeping with Don Hutchinson's views, also prefer to focus on notions of needs, rather than rights. Others, like Anderson, have discussed the problems inherent in a means of adjudication which insists on a winner-take-all resolution. In a subsequent chapter, I discuss how conservative Christian leaders associate the Charter and the Supreme Court with an assault on local democracy – yet another point at which they and the rights critics converge.

Lesbian and Gay Perspectives

In interviewing lesbian and gay rights litigants and lawyers, I found that few concerned themselves with the meanings of rights per se, or with many of the issues with which theorists occupy themselves. Instead, people cared about the extent to which they received publicity and were able to publicly communicate their lesbian or gay politics, and / or mobilize others. For many, impact on a personal level was not attributable to qualities intrinsic to rights rhetoric or claims, but was simply a consequence of being engaged in public political struggle.

Karen Andrews, for example, went to court to have her household declared a legal family for the purposes of receiving dental coverage, not for rights in the abstract (interview; see also Andrews 1989). She found her experience with the legal process to be 'a productive use of anger,' despite losing the judgment and having her grounds for appeal rendered moot. She believes that her case made people think about lesbian and gay issues and caused them to have to look at pictures of a lesbian couple, which appeared on the front page of their newspaper, for the first time. According to Andrews, the litigation process was a success, regardless of outcome, as she was able to appear regularly in the media and be a prominent public spokesperson (ibid).

Brian Mossop and Ken Popert (of the *Mossop* litigation) agree with this assessment. For them, their legal case was simply a 'way of getting yourself on radio or television, so you can say things and millions of people can hear it' (Mossop interview).

There are only a limited number of ways in a society like ours that you can gain access to the mass media, one of them is to hold demonstrations, one of them is to launch some kind of legal case. The media defines the forums in which it's possible to find the platforms ...

It's very useful now we have the Charter of Rights, it's a legitimate subject, no one questions, as they might have before the Charter, whether there is such a thing as 'rights' ... Rights gives you a language. (Popert interview)

Somewhat unsurprisingly, Andrews, Mossop, and Popert were quite dismissive of academic opinion condemning rights struggles. Karen Andrews finds academics to be disrespectful of social activists and believes they write little of relevance to 'real people' (interview). According to Ken Popert, 'it's only lawyers and academics who actually are fooled and think that rhetoric is the only thing going on. Most people understand what the real questions are, even though it's being cast in a different way' (interview).

Brian Mossop argues that when he and Popert appeared on radio shows about their case, callers wanted to talk about *homosexuality*, not rights, or law, or litigation. The ability to do this, gain access to the media to talk about homosexuality, was the whole point of the action.

The main audience is the youngest generation of people who are listening, people who maybe have not come out yet ... who are worried about what life holds in store for them. We go on the radio and say – here we are, we're a gay couple ... it doesn't have to be all that bad ... maybe you could consider telling one of your parents ... the whole point is for people to come out earlier and earlier and earlier. (Mossop interview)

For these gay litigants, a case which they lost on appeal (*Mossop*, 1990, 1993) has been largely successful. In response to an interview question about how radical analyses of sexuality are excluded from legal processes, Ken Popert stated that he didn't 'particularly care what is said in factums, or in court.'

Certainly, this is not true for all those involved in lesbian and gay legal struggle. Karen Andrews, while critical of academic endeavours, nevertheless expressed interest in legal arguments made on her behalf (interview). The coalition of progressive organizations intervening in the *Mossop* case (see chapter 2) took great care with the writing of their legal submissions. For Gwen Brodsky, the coalition's lawyer, getting the right language, tone, and politics was crucial (interview).

Brodsky, too, has little time for the rights critics. She believes such writers are far removed from the concerns of 'disadvantaged people.' In contrast to much critical theory on the Charter, for example, Brodsky argues that its advent has encouraged social movements to build coalitions and think about what equality *means* in the concrete:

The possibility of increasing rights, to take steps to secure more rights, has helped the community-based organizations to mature, and has given them a focus that they didn't have before. It has created both the opportunity and the necessity to try and figure out what's being talked about in any given circumstance where equality is the essential objective. Ten years ago, I don't think there were conversations in community organizations about what equality *meant*. The lobbying was more ad hoc, there was not much opportunity to figure out unifying themes. (interview)

Interestingly, Brodsky closely ties these developments to the Court Challenges Programme which provided public funding to groups seeking to challenge discriminatory laws:

if there hadn't been any money available through the court challenges programme to allow groups to undertake litigation, and to have national consultations to formulate their positions in the litigation, the Charter would not have had the effect I'm talking about *at all* ... to the extent those funds exist, they have fuelled an interest among the community organizations to better understand their own positions ... and that's empowering, to even have the sense that there's a chance of success in an effort to secure increased rights.[15]

Brodsky believes the factum-writing process to be an important one for the social-movement organizations involved. What the judges think of it, while important, is not the only issue. Preparing a legal submission on behalf of diverse interests has been, according to her, a growing and learning experience for all participants.

It's a very different experience to try and do litigation that is respectful of the clients, is an empowering experience for them, does place control in their hands, that's a very different thing from the traditional model of litigation ... really listening for hours and hours, going away and redrafting a factum 12, 15, 20 times, sending it out to 10, 15, maybe 20 people, who then send it out to their boards, subcommittees ... it grows and advances as we work, in the process of talking about what our position ought to be, how to express it, the different co-intervenors have heard one and other ... the factum really will be a collective effort. In a situation like this, you just don't release it until you have something that people are prepared to say is theirs. All of them. To claim it. (interview)

For these groups and their legal counsel, the goal is not 'to get on the radio,' but to share knowledge and experience collectively, and, eventually, write a document that all can feel is 'theirs' – that does not advocate equality for some, at the expense of others.[16]

Brodsky's comments suggest that critical scholars have perhaps devoted insufficient attention to the positive role of federal funding programs in facilitating social-movement networking. Progressive writers often focus on how state funding constrains and co-opts actors and movements (see, for example, Findlay 1987, 1988; Schraeder 1990); however, Brodsky argues that this was not the case with the Court Challenges Programme. Administrators usually acted in an arm's-length fashion and did not attempt to control or police the organizations they funded. However, at the time I interviewed her – in 1991 – Gwen Brodsky also noted that ministry bureaucrats were increasingly attempting to assert control over the program, one recent change having been to curtail meeting funds allocated to legal coalitions. According to Brodsky, many of the positive effects facilitated by social-movement Charter litigation would therefore no longer be possible.

Most rights defenders are not uncritical, naïve believers in the power of rights claims to solve substantive social inequalities. Rather, they argue that rights documents are here to stay (for some time, anyway), and that there are positive ways to work within existing rights regimes.

Where the Charter is concerned, I prefer to think of myself as a thoughtful realist. I believe that the Charter can have a positive role in struggles for progressive social change, but that in order for its potential to be achieved Charter litigation needs to be: rooted in community-based politics, combined with other political strategies, and regarded critically by its users. The Charter has the power to effect change, whether that change be regressive or progressive; that is why I have devoted energy to arguing in favour of progressive interpretations, public funding for access to Charter rights by members of disadvantaged groups, and increased accountability on the part of government respondents in Charter cases. I also believe in the value of allowing the voices of marginalized groups to be heard. (Brodsky, personal communication to author)

At this point, I would like to offer an experience of my own as example. During the Bill 7 struggle, I was a member of (although not an activist within) the Coalition for Gay Rights in Ontario. I responded positively to their calls for letter-writing and phone calls to MPPs, encouraging family and friends to do the same. I attended the rally at St Lawrence Market on 20 November (see chapter 3). At the same time, I was rather ambivalent about the merits of the demand – indeed, then, I tended to believe, along with the rights critics, that such struggles were diversionary and possibly harmful to 'real' social change. Nevertheless, I felt that it was incumbent upon me, as a member of Ontario's 'lesbian and gay community,' to show solidarity with this lesbian and gay struggle, despite my reservations.

When legislative debate began, I decided to stop off on my way home to have a look and listen. I returned nearly every afternoon, fascinated and appalled. What I remember most were the speeches of Conservative party back-benchers, filled with hatred and disgust, directed, as I experienced it, at me.[17] Describing what I heard the next morning, my straight law school friends (I was in my first year) would say, 'How could you bear to sit through that?'; and yet, somehow addicted to the spectacle, I went back each day for more.

Not being a party to 'insider' knowledge, I had no way of telling (the media were ambiguous) whether the amendment would pass or fail. When the vote was called, and the amendment's passage announced, the portion of the gallery where I sat erupted into applause, many of us hugging and congratulating each other. Was I duped into believing that this victory meant I was now a liberated lesbian? I do not think so; although there is no doubt that the Bill 7 experience moved me, in various ways. I cannot say that I felt 'empowered'; I knew the Code would be a most ineffective instrument. I did not feel that my participation as a 'constituent' of a social-movement organization left me particularly powerful as an individual; although I did get some sense that the lesbian and gay movement as a whole had been strengthened through the process of obtaining a 'victory,' whatever its content. I did, however, feel a strong sense of self-affirmation. Bill 7's passage gave me increased confidence; its defeat would have felt demoralizing, on both a personal and a collective level.

Rights Are Neither 'Good' Nor 'Bad'

Does all this then mean that, as some argue, rights rhetoric necessarily serves important *positive* functions within political struggle? Alan Hunt (1990), for example, suggests that the language of rights claims is the kind of universal discourse necessary to construct a new moral order. In contrast to Fudge, who warns that rights rhetoric can also be used by conservative forces (1989, 449), Hunt finds the competing claims raised by rights demands to be a factor in the latter's favour, as this compels a serious public debate over which and whose rights should be prioritized. This argument, as previously noted, is only marginally applicable to the Bill 7 episode where the expression of competing rights claims was rare. While the potential for a serious debate exists hypothetically, within the Bill 7 struggle no such engagement took place. Discussions of whose rights should have priority, for example a lesbian landlord's or a homophobic tenant's, were rarely found.

I would agree with Hunt, however, that one cannot condemn a legal strategy solely upon its ability to be successfully deployed by opponents. The fact that rights rhetoric can be used by either side in a struggle is a fact neither in, nor against, its favour. Surely all strategies for change are potentially available to all those seeking it. This, in my view, says little about the efficacy of the strategy at any given moment, for any given movement. Words and strategies have no *inherent* meaning; while there are *dominant* meanings, struggles between social movements are exactly about and over the power to interpret social relations. In the case of lesbians, gay men, and their opponents the meaning of 'family,' 'spouse,' 'normal,' and indeed 'woman' and 'man' are at stake. Certainly, not all social movements have equal resources to engage in these battles and this is a point somewhat neglected by the rights defenders. Yet, the fact of resource inequality says little about the intrinsic value of any particular goal. If rights rhetoric mobilizes a progressive movement around a given issue, it seems tangential to counter argue that right-wing movements *could* use rights to mobilize themselves. At the same time, it seems injudicious to suggest that such countermovements are

inherently facilitative of communication and justice, or that all movements have an equal capacity to mobilize and make successful public
interventions.

Hunt goes on to espouse a perspective, drawn from Laclau and
Mouffe (1985), that argues that new social movements 're-combine' elements of existing discourse in constructing a 'new' liberatory one. Thus,
it is only natural that social movements use rights rhetoric (Hunt [1990]
speaks of making rights claims); the point is that rights are rearticulated
in ways that transform them. In arguing his politics of 'rights without
illusions' (not dissimilar to Scheingold's position over twenty years
ago),[18] Hunt finds further encouragement in the fact that rights struggles
play a role in constituting social actors and their identities. With respect
to Bill 7, it is worth exploring each of these assertions in turn.

First, were rights and other elements re-combined within pro-amendment discourse in ways that could be said to be counterhegemonic? I
argued in chapters 2 and 3 that 'rights' was used synonymously with
'equality,' and that equality was implied to be achievable through inclusion within existing legal frameworks. It seems dubious whether this
articulation was counterhegemonic. On the contrary, I have suggested
that this approach entrenched principles and structures of liberal equality without challenging the paradigm's limitations (discussed in chapter
3).

The anti-amendment forces, on the other hand, articulated rights *away*
from equality; gay rights was synonymous with paedophilia and bestiality. Within a political climate increasingly responsive to lesbian and gay
rights claims, the articulation of the Coalition for Family Values more
clearly played an oppositional role. The fact that mainstream liberal politicians were sympathetic to the CGRO, and appalled by the extremism
of the anti-amendment lobby also suggests this interpretation. Indeed, at
the time, two *Conservative* party MPPs took the unprecedented step of
speaking out to the press about their disgust with the CFV campaign.[19]
It could thus be argued that there is nothing inherently progressive
about engaging in counterhegemonic opposition – it depends on what
(or whose) hegemony one is both fighting against and attempting to create.

There is also no reason why progressive social movements *necessarily*
rearticulate rights in such a way as to challenge status-quo social relations. On the contrary, many social movements deploy rights rhetoric
conventionally; indeed, doing so often plays an important role in the
short-term success of particular campaigns. Certainly, this seems to

have been the case with the Bill 7 sexual-orientation amendment campaign.

Furthermore, the perspective of many rights defenders would seem to reify discursive struggle, finding it capable of achieving almost anything – most of which is somehow assumed to be progressive. While the rights critics tend, in my view, to be overly dismissive and apocalyptic, the rights defenders take insufficient account of the limits and constraints within which progressive social movements work (see Fudge 1978, 1989). Not all social actors have access to similar resources, means of communication, and so on. In addition, 'discursive elements' cannot simply be, as Martha Minow (1990, 306–7) seems to suggest, 're-invented' and disseminated at will. As Carol Smart (1989) has shown, powerful, oppressive discourses such as law can play a 'colonizing' role, 're-combining' the expressions of progressive movements in unprogressive ways. And, as Joel Bakan (1991) has persuasively argued, institutional constraints can render the best intentions ineffective.

Hunt finds further encouragement from the fact that rights claims assist in the construction of subjects and identities. I have no argument with this; however, why should this process be seen as an unqualified 'good'? Surely questions to do with what kinds of subjects and identities oriented to what end must be posed. In the previous chapter, I suggested that the form of many lesbian and gay rights claims entrenches the binary opposition between hetero- and homo- sexualities rather than seeking to transcend it. Human rights regimes pose, like criminal law, their own dilemmas of regulation. Is the minority model of homosexuality that dominated the Bill 7 struggle a positive, progressive one? Should we celebrate equally the rightwing's construction of the 'defender of civilization and family' during this struggle? Not all social movements are to be applauded simply because they are social movements, new or not.

Martha Minow, another rights defender, suggests that the language of rights has a particular resonance, that rights rhetoric is so much a part of the fabric of social life that its deployment can achieve a kind of shared understanding. Rights rhetoric 'makes those in power at least listen.'[20] She argues that 'the langauge of rights thus draws each claimant into the community and grants each a basic opportunity to participate in the process of communal debate' (1990, 296). How helpful is this analysis?

Neil Milner (1986), in applying the views of Minow and others to his studies of two organizations involved in struggles over psychiatric patient rights in the United States, argues that 'rights talk' produced contradictory effects. On the one hand, an organization of patients' families expressed an antirights discourse, arguing that patients were incapable of exercising rights, and that a rights model masked the reality of family caregiving (by giving patients rights against the state, which then undermined family decision making) (ibid, 653–8). And yet, this same organization used 'rights talk' to build their *own* communal identity; Milner argues that the families appropriated rights language to ground their own collective claim to recognition as caregivers.

Organizations representing patient interests had, at the same time, their own rights dilemmas. On the one hand, groups argued for a general patient's right to choose and refuse treatments, based on the individual's capacity to make treatment decisions. At the same time, many of the same organizations advocated a different approach vis-à-vis electroshock 'therapy' – namely, special safeguards, or even banning, based on a model which constructed the patient as a victim of coercive practices who could *not* exercise free choice (ibid, 664–6).

Milner (1986, 670; 1989, 123) reaches several conclusions as a result of his detailed studies. While he suggests that the rhetoric of patients' rights may build an interpretive community, he argues that these dominant understandings can then undermine popular struggles which highlight power inequalities, such as the antishock campaigns. He also suggests that the rights talk favoured by lawyers imposed a legal model upon the patients' movement, fostering conflict between activists and lawyers (1986, 665–6). Milner ultimately argues that rights language is a complex tool; its effects are not predictable.

Returning to Bill 7, it seems apparent that the articulation of lesbian and gay rights with liberal equality principles did succeed in building a kind of interpretive community. In the Bill 7 struggle, a liberal consensus was achieved among both mainstream politicians and the press that homosexuals deserved jobs and housing. As Rayside and Bowler (1988) have suggested, this consensus may extend to a majority of the Canadian public. If one takes the view that a consensus formally condemning discrimination is a prerequisite for more substantial shifts in practice and opinion, then this achievement is no small success. However, it can be just as easily argued that the interpretive community that Bill 7 and similar struggles establish is an élite one. A community of politicians and press editorial boards may not necessarily be the one an oppositional lesbian and gay movement wishes to build – especially when the wider public continues to maintain a simultaneous belief in the 'unnaturalness' of homosexuality. Just as we must ask 'what identities,' we must also ask what or whose 'community' are we talking about?[21]

Bill 7 further demonstrates that the New Christian Right may have succeeded in building their own interpretive community. There is little evidence that each community engaged with each other in any meaningful way, nor is there any reason to think that they would. As I have argued, it is doubtful whether those who respond positively to a general call for lesbian and gay rights, while maintaining disgust with homosexual expressions, are actually being gathered into a community at all. Simply because rights rhetoric is powerful, and tends to get the best response, does not mean that anything terribly significant has happened.

One might also ask, how deep are the understandings a community may have? At what point do those with power *stop* listening (Minow 1990, 297)? There is reason to suggest that dialogue (ibid, 296) (assuming there was one) breaks down as soon as rights are given concrete *meaning*. While a majority of Canadians support equal rights for lesbians and gay men, it is unlikely that this community will appear quite so coherent when these rights are seen to be operationalized in adoption and fostering procedures, alternative insemination policies, affirmative action programs, and so on. Practical issues such as these are often shifted to the margins when rights rhetoric is deployed.

In interviews, Don Hutchinson, Judy Anderson, and Jim Sclater, three New Christian Right activists, each expressed the opinion that lesbians and gay men deserved 'basic human rights.' However, when pressed, they were largely unable to specify exactly what *kinds* of rights they supported. Furthermore, each also approved, in principle, of human rights codes. However, in conversation with me, they clearly did not accept the ways in which the codes had been used; in other words, they expressed agreement with human rights in the abstract, but did not wish to see any actual change in the lives of human rights beneficiaries.[22] There seems little advantage to creating shared understandings at such abstract levels. Indeed, one could argue that rights rhetoric and legal frameworks actually *inhibit* serious dialogue (see also Fudge 1989; Milner 1986, 670) – this certainly seems to have been the case with Bill 7 where concrete issues were discussed only in order to reassure the heterosexual public that the Human Rights Code amendment would have no effect upon them (see chapter 3).

Other rights defenders, and I include here theorists such as Patricia Williams and Elizabeth Schneider, have suggested that, for 'Black' people and 'women' in the United States, the expression of demands in the form of rights, the use of rights rhetoric, has been empowering and self-affirming (P. Williams 1987; Schneider 1986). Rights claims, for Williams, are important symbolic expressions for those who have historically been denied 'self'-ownership (P. Williams 1987; see also Matsuda 1987; R. Williams 1987). Interestingly, many of the writers making these points were active themselves within social movements and, thus, speak from their own senses / feelings about how that experience affected them and their colleagues. Such a perspective is meant to be a corrective to the perceived excessive negativity of the Critical Legal Studies and marxist rights critique. Speaking in a different context, bell hooks has written that 'the civil rights movement made it possible for me to be talking' (1991, 219).

Despite my own difficulties with the left-wing critique of law / rights / litigation, I would none the less question to what extent these rights defenders have responded to the substance of the critique. It is not enough to simply say that rights assertion is self-affirming.[23] One must ask, what 'self' we are talking about. And, who is doing the 'talking' on our behalf? The lesbian and gay 'self' publicly expressed through struggles like Bill 7 is largely the construct of liberal medical discourse – the abnormal member of an immutable sexual minority who deserves tolerance and protection, rather than repression and discrimination. As I suggested in chapter 3, I do not believe that this 'subject' is one to celebrate unquestioningly.

Rights, Mobilization, and Communication

I now wish to explore the effects of legal struggle in examples, particularly with respect to issues of mobilization and communication. It could be argued, for example, that Bill 7 mobilized the pro-family movement more effectively than it did the lesbian and gay movement. Certainly, the Coalition for Family Values was able to initiate a greater letter-writing and phone campaign and succeeded in having the amendment discussed across a network of conservative churches. Furthermore, as I showed in chapter 3, their statements were given ample publicity by politicians during debate, and by the media. The CFV's leader, the Rev. Hudson Hilsden, became a prominent spokesperson for the anti-amendment lobby – indeed, of all social-movement actors he as an individual had the most visible role.

This was not the case for the 'pro' campaign. While Chris Bearchell contends that lesbian and gay communities were mobilized as well (interview), it is difficult to argue that this occurred to the same extent at the grass-roots level.[24] At the same time, I have suggested that feminist and radical gay analyses of sexuality were not publicly communicated.[25] In these respects then, the anti-amendment campaign was more successful, despite losing the short-term battle. However, I have also suggested that the CFV's campaign backfired. While their words made it into print, often they appeared within a critical context which undermined their authority. Thus, the illiberal CFV contributions had little practical effect in terms of shifting the terms of debate.

Other effects were shared by the two movements. For example, each gained valuable experience, established provincial networks, and forged links between formal organizations and their constituencies. Both the CFV and the CGRO had some success in politicizing previously inactive sympathizers. And each established ties with other social movements and organizations, although the CGRO was, arguably, more successful at linking with a wider range of interests, in part because the CGRO was, unlike the CFV, a single, formal entity with a defined set of goals and practices.

For the CGRO and its constituency, the Bill 7 victory was, on one level, empowering and strengthening. However, losses often have the effect of retrenching social movements, and further provide a stark 'enemy' upon which losers can focus future battles. Bill 7 was only one instance of a conservative Christian gay rights intervention; in subsequent years there have been many more (see chapter 6). Wins, on the other hand, can cause complacency, apathy, and the disintegration of coalitions that no longer have a clear purpose.

I have thus far suggested areas in which the New Christian Right, as a social movement, may have either surpassed or equalled the achievements of the lesbian and gay movement, irrespective of the amendment's passage (much of this analysis might also apply to pro- and antichoice struggles in the 1980s). I would argue that in only one area did the CGRO establish a gain that the CFV did not, and this situation resulted from something quite unpredictable. During the Bill 7 campaign, important support for lesbian and gay equality was achieved within both the Liberal party, and the NDP. The Coalition for Family Values, for its part, garnered substantial support from the Conservatives. However, the coming to power of a Liberal minority government shortly before Bill 7's introduction signalled the end of more than forty years of uninterrupted Tory reign in Ontario. Four years later, the Liberals were to be replaced by the first-ever NDP government. Without these political shifts, Bill 7 might never have passed, and the inroads made into estab-

lished parties by lesbian and gay organizations rendered of no consequence. Such events are unpredictable 'chaos' phenomena that send
contained theories and strategies awry.

Without engaging in too much repetition, I could make a similar set of
arguments about litigation efforts. However, in this example, I would
suggest that the lesbian and gay participants fared significantly better
than their Christian activist counterparts. If we compare the experiences
of Karen Andrews, and Brian Mossop and Ken Popert, with that of Judy
Anderson of REAL Women, the former feel that they have far more successfully communicated their sexual politics to the public. In contrast to
the Bill 7 episode, where the CFV had the only visible spokesperson on
the public stage, these instances of litigation have provided lesbians and
gay men with opportunities to speak on behalf of their communities.

However, this is, of course, not unproblematic. Just as the Rev. Hilsden
may not have at all times spoken on behalf of the Ontario Conference of
Catholic Bishops during Bill 7 (see chapter 3), so too it may be that the
lesbians and gay men the media select as newsworthy do not represent
at all the diverse interests, identities, values, and politics of lesbian and
gay communities. The fact that a lesbian's picture is on the front page of
The Toronto Star says little about who she is politically or whether lesbian
communities appreciate her words.

I am suggesting, then, that while Bill 7 politicized and mobilized lesbian and gay communities, there was no concurrent effect of communicating a progressive sexual politics to that or any other group of people.
And, while litigation has provided a platform for individuals to speak
out about sexuality, and organizational leaders to network,[26] it has not
acted as a catalyst for wider mobilization. At the same time, the conservative Christian countermovement has achieved its own, related successes. It would thus appear that both rights critics and rights defenders
have had their fears and hopes realized.

Finally, it is important to remember that political mobilization can
occur at an individual level, and that individuals are what make up
'movements.' Take, for example, the experience of Karen Thompson,
whose seven-year-long battle for legal guardianship over Sharon Kowalski, her brain-injured partner, became a key symbol in the fight for lesbian and gay equality in the United States (see Thompson and
Andrzejewski 1988). In writing about her experiences as a closeted lesbian in small-town America, Thompson explains how her life was irrevocably changed, and radicalized, through her attempts to have the
courts recognize her, rather than Kowalski's parents, as the most suitable

legal guardian. Towards the end of her largely autobiographical book, cowritten with Julie Andrzejewski, Thompson writes a symbolic letter to the hospitalized lover that she has not been allowed to visit for many years. In it, she expresses some of the effects her legal battles have had upon her own political development.

I want you to understand how fighting for our right to live our own lives and make our decisions has transformed me from the conservative, private person you knew into an activist and feminist. Activist and feminist: probably you know more than anybody how these words used to frighten me. I see that same fear in other people, who are more afraid of me as an activist and feminist than as a lesbian ...

... in fighting for us, I have also begun to feel the pain of others who have also experienced oppression. And I have learned about the connections between different forms of prejudice and the people who profit from others misery. I have learned how people with power can manipulate and twist 'facts' to blame those who are victims. I have experienced being called aggressive, crazy and vindictive when our rights were being violated and I sought to protect them ...

... My commitment to you hasn't wavered, even though years have passed since I've seen you. If success means that you are free, then so far I have failed. But if success means that thousands of people have opened their minds or obtained legal protection as a result of our struggle, you and I have already made a difference in the world. Sharon, I will continue to fight for us and for all the others who have been or could be separated by this same injustice. And I hope and pray that some day we will be fighting side by side – that we'll have the chance for a love that shares all we've learned. (ibid, 219–20)

Karen Thompson and Sharon Kowalski won their case in 1991, the court finally recognizing their 'family of affinity.'[27]

Power, Interpretation, and Social Change

It may be a self-evident observation that we are critical of things we do not get much out of and encouraged by things we do. In the area of labour law, for example, it is generally accepted that the Charter has *not* advanced the rights of workers; indeed, the courts have used the Charter to delegitimize certain labour activities, such as secondary picketing, by not protecting them under Charter grounds. Various writers have noted and been critical of the capacity of the Charter to effect any positive change in the social conditions of working life.[28]

In addition, it would be difficult to argue that Charter litigation, and its attendant rights rhetoric, has assisted in the mobilization of the working class or in communicating class analyses to the wider public. At the same time, the courts have used the Charter to fill out the legal personality of corporations, giving them the right to defend religious freedom, and so on. In very few ways, if any, has the Charter effected any erosion of corporate power or profit. Hence, the almost universal Charter denunciation by marxist legal theorists.

On the other hand, a majority of feminist lawyers clearly view the Charter's advent as a good thing for women. While some academics, notably those writing within a marxist tradition, remain critical in this area as well, most others are 'cautiously optimistic' – not only about results, but, as Gwen Brodsky argued above, with the capacity of Charter litigation to mobilize social movements, and open up avenues of communication, not only between movements and 'the public' but also between movements themselves. Many activists within lesbian and gay movements agree.

No doubt, if cases involving complaints of sex discrimination were decided differently, if feminists felt they were not getting anywhere with Charter litigation, the overall assessment would be quite different. Conversely, as Judy Anderson of REAL Women remarked in an interview, under different circumstances, should REAL Women perceive cases to be going *its* way, they might not be offering criticisms 'so loudly.'

As I argued at the beginning of this chapter, the debate is not so much about rights, or charters, or codes, but about underlying political analyses and visions and about the power relations that shape the terms of equality. For socialists, it is not the Charter that is the problem, but the prevailing liberal ideology of courts and legislatures. This is how I read the point made by Joel Bakan (1991) in his reply to those who write about how the Charter could *potentially* be interpreted; quoting an old Yiddish aphorism Bakan notes, 'if my grandmother had wheels she would have been a trolleycar.' Certainly, socialists *could* give rights documents any number of interpretations – however, the Charter is in different hands (see also chapter 7).[29]

However, it could also be argued that feminism, at least certain 'brands' of feminism, have colonized liberal ideology with much greater success than have marxist class perspectives. This would not be the case for all capitalist democracies, but it may well be true for Canada, where the state has been for some years, formally at least, a partisan player in feminist politics, providing funding and ministry resources, and making public statements about the need to combat women's oppression. They way 'women' and 'oppression' have been defined is, without doubt, not to the satisfaction of many feminists (see T. Williams 1990); nevertheless, the dominant definitions certainly owe more to the feminist movement than to, for example, REAL Women and its conservative Christian brethren, or even, indeed, to traditional liberal ideas of womanhood.

To illustrate this point more specifically, in the *Mossop* case, a strategic decision was made by the Salvation Army (who largely controlled the litigation for the New Christian Right coalition) *not* to argue the case as one about gay rights. When interviewed, both Don Hutchinson, the Army's legal adviser, and Ian Binnie, the coalition's lawyer, consistently maintained that the case was about the definition of 'family' and not about 'gay rights.' At the same time, both Hutchinson and Judy Anderson, of REAL Women, repeated several times in interviews that they had no wish to 'gay bash' or to be *perceived* as 'gay bashers.' What can we take from this?

First, it seems clear that some Christian activists feel that gay rights has gained a certain institutional legitimacy; publicly, some sections of conservative Christianity have acknowledged that, at this time in Canada, it is not acceptable to deny lesbians and gay men some ambiguously defined measure of human rights. Indeed, the Salvation Army categorically did not wish to fight the *Mossop* case using rights rhetoric at all (Hutchinson and Binnie interviews). The impact of a 'culture of rights' has, thus, imposed constraints upon the expression of conservative Christian politics. Even within the Bill 7 struggle, the Coalition for Family Values felt compelled to state it supported 'basic rights and freedoms' for 'homosexuals.'[30]

And, yet, at the same time, rights rhetoric can play a more positive role for the right. Helvacioglu (1991) has argued that, in the United States, the New Christian Right has turned to a strategy of local protest in which rights rhetoric is increasingly deployed. This, Helvacioglu suggests, may prove more profitable for conservative Christian activists than illiberal outbursts – particularly given the social power of rights claims and a constitutional history of protecting religious minorities, (ibid, 121).[31] In Canada, it seems evident that past attempts to shock and appall Canadians with tales of homosexual depravity have been largely unsuccessful. It thus seems probable that the Canadian New Christian Right will soon learn to rearticulate its demands in a different register. However, will the same process occur for them as has occurred for their opponents? As I explain in the following chapter, conservative Christians prefer to constitute themselves as the 'moral majority'; however, by claiming their own 'rights,' they implicitly accept the liberal paradigm which constitutes them as a minority in need of 'protection.' In other words, what will be the contradictory effects upon their social movement for conservative Christians deploying a politics of liberalism? And, how 'effective' might such strategies prove?

Concluding Remarks

In the case of lesbian and gay rights claims in Canada, in the 1980s, the relative strength of the lesbian and gay rights movement, and its support from other movements, meant that rights-related law-reform strategies were viewed by participants as having been largely successful, even when actual litigation was not. How lasting, however, are these effects? If, as Fudge (1989) and Milner (1986) have argued, rights rhetoric inhibits consideration of substantive political issues and is capable of being used to advantage by any social group in a specific instance, the gains won may easily be eroded. The experience of abortion rights in the United States is a case in point, where state governments can swing from liberalization to criminalization over a relatively short period of time.

Furthermore, human rights legislation is only one legal regime among many. Governments may enshrine lesbian and gay rights in one statute, while at the same time ensuring the continued privileging of the heterosexual nuclear unit in family, tax, pensions, property, and other areas of law. Adding grounds to pre-existing human rights documents is relatively easy; giving those rights real meaning in terms of the distribution of resources is quite another. As I argued above, the support of 'the public' for lesbian and gay rights also erodes as specific demands are formulated. And I have suggested that demands for inclusion within pre-existing human rights frameworks are complicated by how the 'minority subject' is constructed within liberal equality discourse, that liberalism's hegemony in this area makes it nearly impossible to challenge prevailing norms around gender and *hetero*sexuality.

On the one hand, I agree with Brian Mossop and Ken Popert that rights are not the issue. Rather, the agenda of lesbian and gay rights activists is to get on the radio, mobilize, and other such things, not acquire rights. And, to a large and growing extent, rights claims and rhetoric have proved successful in this way for lesbians and gay men in Canada. Furthermore, Brian Mossop would disagree that he has been unable to discuss substantive issues. As I illustrated above, his litigation has allowed him the opportunity to appear on phone-in shows to talk, not about rights, but about homosexuality and coming out.

In the process of engaging in legal struggle, I would further argue that notions of normality, equality, rights, and so on do shift. This is evident in the Bill 7 story itself, where over a period of fifteen years the Coalition for Gay Rights in Ontario, and the lesbian and gay movement as a whole, achieved a significant impact upon defining the terms of human rights. It is not trite to make the observation that hateful comments about lesbians and gay men that could be said publicly fifteen years ago cannot be as easily said now. This is important and not something to be derided or dismissed.

Shifts in meaning over time are also evident in other areas. Law initially offered (male) 'homosexuals' no private realm whatsoever. The Wolfenden reforms, won through the campaigning of early 'homophile rights' organizations, constructed a narrow arena in which homosexual (usually male) sex was to be decriminalized. More recently, demands for lesbian and gay rights in the areas of adoption and fostering, reproductive technologies, and a whole host of other 'family sphere' areas, have confronted the liberal Wolfenden consensus (Cooper and Herman 1991). The public / private distinction is no longer as tenable. In the area of sexuality, then, this element of liberal discourse has indeed been transformed; in fact, it has been rendered tangential to many social-policy discussions.[32]

The analyses and strategies adopted by lesbians and gay men in legal arenas are, to some extent, shaped by the activities of their formidable opponents. In the next two chapters, I turn my attention to the movement leading the opposition to lesbian and gay legal equality in Canada – the New Christian Right (NCR). I have discussed some aspects of conservative Christian activism in these last two chapters. I now wish to deepen this analysis by first providing a detailed interpretation of this movement's conception of gender and sexuality (chapter 5), then, considering the intervention of three NCR organizations in the *Mossop* case (chapter 6). I conclude chapter 6 by assessing the relative 'effectivity' of the NCR in Canada.

5

'Normalcy on the Defensive':[1] New Christian Right Sexual Politics

According to 1991 census data, just over 80 per cent of Canadians claim a Protestant or Catholic religious identity (Canada 1993). Within the last ten years, the conservative, evangelical, Protestant brand of Christianity has experienced, on the whole, a significant growth in membership (ibid). At the same time, the numbers of those claiming 'no religion' has also increased formidably (ibid). Arguably, then, Canadian society, with respect to religion, is becoming increasingly polarized between those who 'believe' fervently and those who choose to disassociate themselves from established faiths.

It is the 'born again,' conservative, evangelical Protestants who, together with many conservative Catholics, have provided the 'army' (to use their terminology) in the fight against lesbian and gay equality. At its heart, their struggle is against the increasing secularization of Canadian society. Lesbian and gay rights, in their view, epitomizes this trend and is one of the most significant threats to the reaffirmation of Canada as a Christian nation.

In this chapter, I accord a rather high degree of determinism to conservative Christian theology in shaping the character of anti–lesbian and gay rights activism. By focusing upon the role that conservative Christianity plays in relation to lesbian and gay law reform, I suggest that this theology lies at the root of the most vocal opposition to lesbian and gay equality. This focus is not intended to suggest that other factors are not also important; rather, my aim is to counterbalance many feminist analyses of the new right, which may mention, but tend not to explore or highlight, the impact of *Christianity* on the activities of right-wing actors.[2]

Yet it is New *Christian* Right activists who have led the opposition to the gay rights struggles which form the substance of this book. For example, during the Bill 7 episode, the Coalition for Family Values was composed almost entirely of Christian organizations, while during legislative debates almost every MPP speaking against the amendment indicated that his or her opposition was also based upon Christian tenets. One legislator, for example, stated that 'God laid down the laws years ago ... it is quite clear that homosexuality is wrong ... woman was made for man and man for woman, and no other mix works ... If I were to vote for this amendment, I would be going against everything I believe in and have been taught.'[3] In the *Mossop* case as well, as I go on to show in this and the following chapter, the key organizations fighting Mossop's claim were and are members of Canada's New Christian Right (NCR).

To date, little detailed research on the NCR in Canada has been undertaken.[4] Lorna Erwin (1988b), whose research provides one of the few sources, has shown that members of Canadian NCR organizations maintain an impressively coherent position on 'moral issues.' Furthermore, their membership is extremely homogeneous, in social position and moral outlook. Ninety-four per cent of the respondents to Lorna Erwin's pro-family movement study named religion as one of the most important factors in their lives. An astounding 99 per cent attend church at least once a week and over 90 per cent expressed concerns about feminism and gay rights, identifying these movements as 'serious threats' to the family (ibid).

The NCR membership is also extremely socially homogeneous. The majority of respondents were relatively well off, educated, middle-class professionals (ibid). This pattern is consistent with U.S. research indicating that the stereotypical portrait of the evangelical Christian as a poorly educated, rural Southerner is far from the case these days. As Lechner (1990) has argued, NCR activists are very much 'modern subjects' reacting against the secularization of the modernity which produced them.

Erwin's results constitute one of the few sources of knowledge on the Canadian New Christian Right. However, her data ought not to provide conclusions regarding the belief systems of Canadian conservative Christians generally. For example, Reginald Bibby, who has conducted the most comprehensive surveys of religious attitudes available in Canada, found that, while conservative Christians did disproportionately disapprove of premarital sex, homosexuality, and communism,[5] in contrast to the 90 per cent of pro-family organization respondents who viewed gay rights as a 'serious threat' (Erwin 1988b) over 50 per cent of conservative Christian individuals indicated to Bibby that they *approved* of gay rights (Bibby 1987). Bibby's studies also indicate that conservative Christians are no more (or less) racist than the general population, no less disapproving of working women, and no less in favour of universal rights to health care and adequate income than Canadians overall.[6]

My discussion, then, is about the Canadian New Christian Right and not about conservative Christianity generally. I explore the sexual politics of three organizations active in the NCR coalition that came together to adopt a strategy of legal intervention following the human rights tribunal's pro–gay rights decision in *Mossop* (see chapter 2). Individually, and then together, they chose to hire lawyers and apply for official intervenor status; when this was granted, they prepared legal submissions arguing against the tribunal's 'sociological' definition of family. Despite the differences between the individual organizations, and there are many, they are none the less united by their adherence to a profoundly conservative expression of Christian sexual politics.

Background to the New Christian Right

Theology

New Christian Right activists are, as I mentioned above, evangelical,[7] conservative Christians. They are largely, although not exclusively, Protestant.[8] I use the phrase 'conservative Christianity' following Steve Bruce (1984, 4–8), who suggests two primary characteristics distinguishing this faith. First, and perhaps foremost, is an insistence on the literal truth of the Bible (particularly the Gospels), a belief known as 'biblical inerrancy.' While liberal Christians allow for the possibility of interpretation and the cultural construction of biblical meanings, conservatives find such a thought abhorrent. For them, each word is God's Truth.[9] Hence, for example, their efforts to compel the teaching of creationism in public schools (see La Follette 1983; Peshkin 1986; Rose 1988).

Second, conservative Christians believe that the Bible prophesies the Second Coming of Christ and the arrival of the 'millennium' (not necessarily in that order). There are various versions of this scenario, more popularly known as Armageddon. Broadly, in order for Christ to reappear, the Jews must return to Palestine, whereupon the Beast (see below) and the Antichrist will engage in battle (the 'great tribulation'). Just before the battle begins, the saved Christians will be 'raptured' up from earth to meet Christ. Once the forces of darkness have all been eliminated, Christ and the 'saved' – now called saints – will return to reign on earth for 1,000 years.[10]

At various points, key figures have predicted the date upon which the 'great tribulation' would begin. For example, the creation of Israel was said to constitute 'the Jews' return,' while 'the Beast' was represented by the Soviet Union (Diamond 1989, 131). Armageddon would thus begin with a nuclear attack (in modern scenarios) upon Israel by the former USSR (Chandler 1984, 43–4). In a different version, the Beast is represented by Arabs, Africans, Asians, and Russians, who first fight it out among themselves (again, in Israel). All Jews, with the exception of 144,000 who convert to Christianity,[11] are killed (along with many other unsaved) in the process. As the 'saved' Christians are raptured away, the 144,000 converted Jews take on their missionary work as the final battle looms. Western civilization, led by the Antichrist, meets the Asian Beast, led by China, and all-out destruction ensues. Eventually, Christ and the raptured army of saints descend to usher in the millennium.[12]

Conservative Christian eschatology informs many of the political positions adopted by the NCR movement. For example, the American NCR's enthusiastic support for Israel, particularly in light of continued NCR antisemitism (Bruce 1990), makes little sense without an understanding of the role Jewish people play in Armageddon (as Christian missionaries). Similarly, the NCR's pro-defence stance is linked to the preordained role the United States is destined to play in leading Western forces against the Beast from the East. However, it is also important to recognize that theology is not, despite NCR protestations, a static, unchanging world-view. The assignment of different nations to play the Beast and Antichrist roles, and the construction of a dependency upon specific weapons technology, is a historically contingent process. Biblical inerrancy and dispensationalist eschatology, then, are the 'religious lens' through which conservative Christians view the world (Klatch 1987).

Politics

Before moving on to a consideration of the New Christian Right organizations involved in the *Mossop* challenge, I wish to broadly outline what could be considered the North American NCR 'platform.'[13] While different analysts emphasize particular constituents, the NCR agenda can be said to consist of the following positions: anti-abortion; anti–affirmative action; anti-communism; anti-feminism; anti–gun control; anti–lesbian/gay; anti-welfare; pro-defence; pro-family; pro–foreign intervention.[14]

Many, but not all, of these 'issue positions' overlap with a general New Right agenda; the American NCR was one of the most vocal proponents of the nuclear arms race, accompanied by strident anti-Soviet rhetoric (recall that both nuclear weapons and the former USSR play key roles in the inevitable battles of Armageddon). Further, as Diamond (1989, 147) has shown, NCR organizations have actively supported right-wing groups and even death squads in Central America, the Philippines, and southern Africa. NCR leaders have been among the severest critics of welfare state programs, including affirmative action policies.[15] With some exceptions, the Canadian organizations I go on to discuss adopt most of these positions.

Organizations

I have set out above the basic theological and political contours of the New Christian Right in North America. Now, I wish to localize this analysis, focusing upon specific organizations active in Canada today. I have chosen to examine three of these – the Salvation Army of Canada, REAL Women, and the Focus on the Family (Canada) Association. Each organization is particularly active in anti–lesbian and gay initiatives; I have chosen them specifically for their involvement as legal intervenors in *Mossop*.[16] The organizations which comprise the *Mossop* coalition share the aspirations of their American cousins. Indeed, organizations such as Focus on the Family and REAL Women take their inspiration, and in the former case their funding, from similar American manifestations.[17] Furthermore, each of these organizations, like its American counterpart, is primarily urban-based and professionally dominated. While their politics very much embody a reaction against 'modernist thinking,' their own leadership, strategies, and structures are products of the society they wish to transform (see Lechner 1990).

The Salvation Army
The Salvation Army, with a history of 'social purity' activism, (see Valverde 1991), has a mission, among other things, to 'preach the Gospel of Jesus Christ.'[18] According to Don Hutchinson, the Army's legal adviser and key figure in the NCR *Mossop* intervention, 'the long-term goal would be that the whole world come under the sway of Jesus Christ, I can't apologize for that' (interview).

Nevertheless, as I go on to show, the Army remains, to some extent, a reluctant member of the 'New Christian Right movement.' Salvationists share few non–family-related policies with other NCR organizations, and leaders wish to maintain the Army's identity as distinct from those with whom it joins in 'short-term coalitions.'[19]

Focus on the Family Association (Canada)
Focus on the Family Association (FFA), a branch of a much larger American Christian corporation, is a relative newcomer to the Canadian political scene. Focus's 'statement of faith' reads:

We believe the Bible to be the only infallible, authoritative Word of God. We believe that there is only one God, eternally existent in three persons: Father, Son and Holy Spirit. We believe in the deity of our Lord Jesus Christ, in His virgin Birth, in His sinless life, in His miracles, in His vicarious and atoning death through His shed blood, in His bodily resurrection, in His ascension to the right hand of the Father, and in His personal return to power and glory. We believe that for the salvation of lost and sinful man, regeneration by the Holy Spirit is absolutely essential.[20]

The organization's structures, resources, and strategies are modelled on FFA's American parent, which, in turn, emerged out of the explosion of 'new' Christian groups in the 1970s.[21] Focus on the Family advises parents and their children on how to maintain Christian life in a secular world[22] and, increasingly, seeks to influence the public policy-making process.[23] The organization publishes a wide variety of magazines geared to different audiences and has established a network of radio stations across the continent.[24] Focus on the Family (Canada) is headquartered in Vancouver, where it also operates a storefront Christian bookshop.

REAL Women of Canada
REAL Women (RW) is an all-Canadian organization, formed in 1984 as part of a right-wing backlash to the perceived gains of those RW terms 'radical feminists' (Anderson interview; see also Erwin 1988a). The organization's activities consist predominantly of contesting every demand made by their feminist adversaries;[25] they have also maintained a vociferous opposition to lesbian and gay rights.[26]

REAL Women is also an organization of the New *Christian* Right, a connection often overlooked as the organization itself chooses not to publicize this fact. Nevertheless, Lorna Erwin's research (1988b) indicates that conservative Christianity is the common bond of REAL

Women supporters. Consider also, the words of Judy Anderson, at the time of the interview president of the organization:

... [for] those of us who are Christians,[27] religious faith is very important ... [but] one of the last things I'm going to do unless asked about it is talk about my faith ... Christianity is low man on the totem pole, anyone can give a kick at Christianity and get away with it ... an amazing amount of people would totally dismiss me, oh, she's just a Christian, she's just a fundamentalist, so, I don't go out there and talk about my faith – why would I? It's the whipping boy now ... we're pretty careful about putting our faith on the front burner ... we're all going to be pretty careful about where and when we talk in those terms.[28]

I do not consider these three organizations as a monolithic bloc; on the contrary, in the ensuing pages I have tried to distinguish their perspectives and politics as often as possible. Nevertheless, their vehement, oppositional position to lesbian and gay equality facilitated their coming together as a 'legal coalition'; this opposition, rooted in their theology, is their common bond.

Sexual Politics

There are four themes I move on to consider. First, the NCR conceptualization of 'the family' as the fundamental, God-given unit of society, including a narrow and limited definition of what the family can be. Intimately related to this is the NCR's construction of traditional gender roles as preordained and absolutely imperative to social well-being. Second, the construction of homosexuality as sinful, diseased behaviour. The NCR's analysis is focused on the perceived activities of gay men; 'the lesbian' is almost completely absent from these discussions. Third, the depiction of a homosexual 'fifth column,' an 'enemy within' conspiring to subvert the family and, ultimately, 'take over' the nation itself. The furthering of the 'homosexual agenda' is related to the perceived power of the 'secular humanist' (or radical feminist) conspiracy generally. Fourth, the articulation of children with risk, vulnerability, and moral health. Ultimately related to their views on family, children are constituted as simultaneously pure and extremely vulnerable to a process of corruption. The fear of losing children (to the secularist culture) lies deep within NCR discourses.[29]

Underlying and emerging within these themes is the NCR's construction of sexuality itself, as something fluid, changeable, and vulnerable to persuasion. The organizations considered here take pains to deny any biological factors in producing homosexuality; indeed, they attribute such explanations to gay rights opportunists seeking state protection. The NCR's perspective on sexuality is intimately related to its construction of gender. Male and female 'opposites,' whose purpose is to procreate within marriage, are viewed as God-given Truths. NCR opposition to lesbian and gay equality cannot be understood without taking account of how this opposition is rooted in their desire to strengthen, model, and reproduce patriarchal gender relations; and, further, how the inspiration and authority for this desire is taken, literally, from the conservative Christian tradition.

'The Family'

While coalition members give different emphases to other themes, all consistently reiterate the primacy of the family.[30] According to Focus on the Family, 'the family is a God-ordained institution and not just something that evolved in the human race.'[31] 'The family,' states the Salvation Army, is 'the primary social unit in society.'[32] According to Judy Anderson, (then) REAL Women president, the family is 'the cornerstone, the basic building block of society' (interview).

Above all, what defines 'the family' is marriage. It is not an abstract conception of family that is God-given. According to the Salvation Army, 'God's intention for mankind is that society should be ordered on the basis of lifelong, legally sanctioned, heterosexual unions. Such unions (marriage) lead to the formation of social units (families) which are essential to human personal development and therefore to the stability of the community.'[33] For Focus on the Family, marriage is for life; that is God's Plan. 'We believe that the institution of marriage is a permanent, life-long relationship between a man and a woman, regardless of trials, sickness, financial reverses or emotional stresses that may ensue.'[34] These ideas are consistently reiterated throughout the materials of REAL Women as well. As Erwin has documented (1988b), the Canadian pro-family movement is fundamentally concerned with perceived threats to marriage, such as divorce, alcoholism, and, of course, homosexuality.

This rigid prescription of gender roles is characteristic of NCR family discourse generally.[35] The organizations of the *Mossop* coalition, for the most part, do not diverge from this pattern. According to Jim Sclater of Focus on the Family, 'we know that God designed women to have a nurturing effect on children, male and female, we know that men are supposed to have not only a nurturing effect but to demonstrate the more aggressive role of the hunter, down through various civilizations' (interview). In keeping with this, a Focus on the Family magazine directs women to 'make the home a haven' for their husbands, and be his 'helpmate.'[36] Erwin's survey data show that an overwhelming majority of REAL Women respondents believe that women should not undertake full-time employment, that motherhood has been devalued by feminism, and that liberal divorce laws and public childcare provision undermine the family.[37] Women and men, according to REAL Women, Focus on the Family, and the NCR generally, are not the same and thus 'equality' is an inappropriate goal.[38]

At the same time, however, the NCR explicitly urges Christian women to action; they are *not* to become completely 'family focused.' On the contrary, the publications of Focus and REAL Women exhort women to 'take up arms' in the struggle. One American Focus magazine distributed in Canada explains how you can 'lobby Congress from your kitchen.'[39] Dobson and Bauer (1990, 261) do not idly state that *'women are the key'* to Christian battles. The REAL Women organization's own success is necessarily predicated upon the politicization and activation of women cadres.[40]

The NCR's construction of gender and the family is thus a contradictory one. On the one hand, underlying the NCR's anti–lesbian and gay agenda is a conception of God-ordained family structure, based on lifelong marriage between a man and a woman, both of whom know their place. At the same time, the 'subservient' woman is constituted through Christian rhetoric as a political actor, an important member of the 'army of saints,' her role being to assist in the preservation of the God-ordained family unit. How, then, does the NCR represent homosexuality as a threat to 'the family's' moral order?

'The Homosexual'

Consider the following statement, released for public consumption by REAL Women during a 1986 federal parliamentary debate on lesbian and gay equality.

The homosexual seeks sex in the young age group. As he ages, when he begins to lose his attractiveness, he resorts to buying sex. That need has given rise to a subculture or [sic] prostitution of boys and younger men in inner cities ...

... Many homosexuals, because they cannot procreate, must recruit – often the young. They promote recruiting 'straights.' With new legislation such seduction becomes permissible and acceptable.[41]

One of the first notable aspects of this analysis is that it is entirely male-focused. REAL Women conjures up the familiar spectre of the sick, depraved, predator seeking out young boys to 'buy' (presumably, 'the homosexual' is too ugly and disgusting to get sex for free) in order to engage in assorted perversions. The reader's mind is immediately filled with images of filth and rotting flesh, a kind of Dorian Gray picture of ugliness and depravity. Their victims, in contrast, are innocent, pure, young boys.

These activities do not, however, take place on a purely individual level. A 'subculture of prostitution' exists, implying a network of homosexual paedophilia in the heart of the inner cities. Inner cities, themselves, seem to represent the corruption of innocent (male) youth.[42] A logical chain of 'self-evident' assertions is established in the excerpt: homosexual men seek sex with young boys; as homosexuals age they 'lose their attractiveness'; they then must 'buy' sex with young boys, initiating the boys into a 'culture of prostitution.'

Related to REAL Women's construction of the predatory paedophile is the organization's implication that homosexuals are insinuating themselves into the fabric of traditional society. Their 'diseased tentacles' are grasping at young men, not simply for sex, but in order to 'recruit' them. Here, REAL Women evokes both anticommunist and antisemitic imagery. Homosexuals seek recruits for an ever-expanding network of subversion and, at the same time, their self-reproduction threatens a 'take over,' a rat-like infestation and germ spreading reminiscent of Nazi propaganda films.[43]

Interestingly, homosexuals recruit because they 'cannot procreate.' Leaving aside the biological inaccuracies, REAL Women seems to be suggesting that heterosexuals do not need to recruit because they do procreate. Homosexuals require, RW argues, a 'pool' of other homosexuals to have sex with, hence they recruit, encouraging others to become homosexual – this is their means of reproduction. The implication that can be taken is that sexuality is *political* – it can be inculcated, like any other ideology. I discuss this point further, in relation to child sexuality, below.

Lesbians are notably absent from the discussion. It is, in this case, unlikely that 'he' was meant to imply 'he and she.' The image is a familiar one, often evoked with respect to gay men.[44] More recently, as Ross (1988) has shown, REAL Women has increasingly directed its fury at lesbian feminists. One of the organization's chief villains has been the federal Secretary of State Women's Programme, which has, from time to time, provided minimal funding to lesbian groups. REAL Women's efforts to stop this happening, and win its own grants, has encouraged the production of a specifically anti-lesbian rhetoric. However, Judy Anderson, when interviewed, explicitly *excluded* lesbians from any potential threat to children posed by homosexuality.

Themes of sex, disease, and depravity are most clearly expressed by Focus on the Family. Indeed, this organization's fascination with the explicit details of homosexual sexual practices is profound. I will use two texts as illustration: an American Focus publication entitled *The Homosexual Agenda* and my interview with Jim Sclater, national director of public policy for the Canadian branch.

Brad Hayton's *The Homosexual Agenda: Changing Your Community and Nation* (n.d.) is primarily a community action manual for Christian activists in the United States. The publication, also distributed by the Canadian branch, is directed at individuals who have likely not as yet been involved in anti-gay campaigning, and Hayton offers helpful suggestions on drafting letters, influencing school boards, conducting meetings, and selecting appropriate prayers. The bulk of the manual contains a series of 'secular' arguments and 'facts' about homosexuality that activists can write in their letters, say on radio shows, and generally arm themselves with.

You know that homosexuality is wrong, and you believe it is wrong because the Bible says so. 'Because the Bible says so' is the bottom-line argument for the Christian. And yet using the Bible does not always convince your representative, city councilman, or friend of the soundness of your opinion. They probably don't believe in the Bible. You need other arguments for your beliefs – arguments that they are more likely to hear and accept. (Hayton n.d., 9)[45]

After briefly reviewing arguments about conflicting rights, Hayton narrows his discussion to the theme which dominates the book – disease. According to Hayton, 'homosexuals have many more sexually transmitted diseases than heterosexuals' (ibid, 12). Referring to several articles from reputable medical journals, Hayton argues that '"Gay rights" laws merely protect and promote STDs ... In the case of AIDS, it is a licence to kill' (ibid). Citing newspaper articles from 1979 and 1980, he states that, in San Francisco, the incidence of sexually transmitted diseases increased after the passage of gay rights laws. The footnotes to this section of the manual explicitly discuss syphilis, rectal infection, 'gay bowel syndrome,' gonorrhoea, herpes, and assorted other conditions to which homosexuals are presumably prey. Again, the primary, almost the sole, object of scrutiny is the gay man, although this is rarely made explicit.

The manual then goes on to claim that homosexuals molest children regularly, and, in a statement of 'fact' I have not seen reported elsewhere in NCR literature, that 'out of all the mass murders in the U.S. over the past 17 years, homosexuals killed at least 68% of the victims, were implicated in at least 41% of the sets of crimes, committed 70% of the 10 worst murder sets, and were involved in five of the eight murder sets perpetrated by two or more people' (ibid, 15). The authority for this claim is a publication entitled 'Murder, Violence and Homosexuality,' published by the Institute for the Scientific Investigation of Sexuality, a right-wing Christian research facility.

Quickly, however, Hayton returns to his favourite theme – the specific sexual practices which 'cause' specific diseases. Male homosexuals have higher incidences of every possible disease than their heterosexual counterparts, including lice (ibid, 16). Lesbians make an appearance here as well.

In comparison to heterosexual females, lesbians are 19 times more apt to have had syphilis, 2 times more apt to have had genital warts, 4 times more apt to have had scabies, 7 times more apt to have had an infection from vaginal contact, 29 times more apt to have had an oral infection from vaginal contact, and 12 times more apt to have ever had an oral infection from penile contact. (ibid)[46]

Hayton then moves on to detail the specific behaviours that 'cause' these conditions. Readers are advised that 'only adults' should read on as 'graphically detailed homosexual behaviour' is depicted. We are then presented with a series of homosexual sexual practices (some differentiation between the practices of men and women is occasionally made): 'the insertion of the penis into the rectum of sex partners' causing 'fecal material' to 'enter through the urethra'; 'inserting the tongue into or licking the anus'; 'eating and / or rubbing themselves with the faeces of partners' ('homosexual men ingest, on the average, the fecal material of 23 different men per year'); 'urinating or defecating on their partners'; 'sadomasochism'; 'handballing or fisting where the hand and arm are inserted into the anus up the rectum'; and 'drinking urine.' This is only a selection of what Hayton offers the reader as 'information' and 'argument' (ibid). Most of this section is not footnoted. Hayton continues by giving statistics on the number of sex partners 'homosexuals' have in an average year (hundreds), concluding that 'sodomy laws protect communities and the nation from disease' (ibid, 16–17).

A subsequent section on 'the homosexual agenda in education' begins by disputing the data about how many homosexuals there are in the United States (the 1 in 10 figure), but quickly lapses back into discussions about 'anal intercourse, eating faeces, drinking urine, engaging in fisting, and pouring urine over one another' (ibid, 22). Another section, about 'domestic partnership' legislation, discusses a number of issues, including parental rights, role modelling, and so on, but again concludes with 'data' about child molestation, 'fecal and urine ingestion, sadomasochism, fisting, fellatio, etc.' (ibid, 27). The manual's final section, '"Gay Pride" Demonstrations / Parades,' once again details all these things, and the accompanying question and answer sheet does so over again.

For Jim Sclater, public policy director of the Canadian Focus branch, homosexuals are typical of an 'everything goes' society that has extended 'sexual licence' well beyond acceptable limits. 'You wouldn't believe,' Sclater constantly repeated in an interview, 'what these people get up to'.

... homosexuality is destructive of the image of God that was put into the person and is medically destructive. My own doctor, years ago, said that if anybody were to see the wreckage of human flesh that comes into his office as a result of homosexual, particularly male, practices they wouldn't be very impressed with it as a lifestyle ... it's a chemical addiction, any sexual activity generates that chemical and people don't want to go for long without it ... they need another hit.

Sclater's focus on the health aspects of homosexual behaviour is typical of the organization which has, strategically, chosen to develop this line of argument instead of the deeper biblical prohibitions that shape their selection of authoritative 'scientific data.' It was Sclater who gladly provided me with a copy of Brad Hayton's *The Homosexual Agenda*.

I have presented the perspective of Focus on the Family in some detail for two key reasons, first, as an illustration of a predominant theme in NCR literature – that of homosexual disease and depravity. Various writers have considered how sexuality and the body have been conceived and regulated in different historical periods; the articulation of sex with disease, death, cities, and sin is not new.[47] More recently, much theoretical work has been done on the cultural production of a specifically AIDS-related medical-moral discourse.[48] For many conservative Christians, AIDS was a portent, a sign of the great tribulation to come (Palmer 1990). In the popular, and particularly the Christian, imagination AIDS has signified the revenge of God, the contamination of the race and the pollution of the nation. AIDS-inspired rhetoric of disease and blood has provided a modern expression of old metaphors.[49]

In representing this theme of imminent contamination, the New Christian Right has available to it Christianity's historical construction of devils, within which Jews form the first, and forever recurring, leitmotif. In different historical periods, this 'enemy' also takes other forms – witches, communists, homosexuals, and so on.[50] Often, adversaries display characteristics common to several Christian devils; for example, the association of Jewish men with effeminacy, or the articulation of communists with homosexuals and Jews during the McCarthy witch-hunts. Indeed, much of the rhetoric deployed by the NCR against 'homosexuals' (and communists before them) is directly traceable to Christian anti-semitic discourses. As Mosse (1985) and Gilman (1985, 1988) have shown, Jews were historically associated with disease, corruption, child abuse, madness, criminality, filth, sexual degeneracy, and urban decay (among other things).[51]

Within the Christian tradition, the power of 'devil construction' is immense. It binds Christian communities together in a common purpose; in addition, as Murray Edelman has noted (1988, 68–87), the identification of 'enemies' is central to the *self*-identities of those pointing the finger. Just as there can be no 'saved' if there are no 'unsaved,' the 'diseased, depraved homosexual' is a *necessary* figure for the self-constitution of morally pure, Christian soldiers.[52]

New Christian Right activists are no doubt aware of the resonances this rhetoric has within collective consciousness; while the authors of these texts no doubt believe their own claims, Hayton, Sclater, and others also explicitly acknowledge that their deployment and rearticulation of this old discourse is strategic. They perceive it as a way of communicating, a language to convey their politics to a wider audience.

In addition to presenting this continuity of loathing, I have also sought to show the extent to which lesbian and gay lives – or, more accurately, perceptions, speculations, and imaginings about lesbian and gay lives – play a pornographic role in NCR discourse. The relish with which these activities are related, and endlessly repeated, in graphic detail, complete with explicit descriptions of various body fluids (and solids), reveals the ways in which, arguably, conservative Christians express their own sexual needs and fantasies, and in so doing, produce pornographic text.

This is not a novel point. Various writers have noted how, for example, the details of 'lesbian sex' are related by fascinated judges during lesbian custody decisions (see Eaton 199). Others (for example, Smart 1989) have deconstructed the rape trial as a form of pornography for the attending male voyeurs. NCR authors, while seemingly intending to induce shocked horror in their audiences, at the same time provide their constituency with 'approved' pornography – objectifying, degrading, and explicitly sexualizing lesbians and gay men in the process.

Alone among the three, the Salvation Army refrains from participating in this 'devil construction,' perhaps because the Army's history has ensured that its perspective on 'the city' is a more sensitive one, attuned more to the social factors that shape individual behaviour. It has refused to become publicly embroiled in what, according to Don Hutchinson, their legal adviser, might be perceived as 'gay bashing' (interivew). The Army consistently reiterates the biblical prohibitions – the Christian basis of their opposition to certain elements of the lesbian and gay rights agenda. Images of debauchery, disease, orifices and their contents, and sex itself are notably absent from their texts.

Secular Humanism and the Homosexual 'Enemy Within'

Nothing short of a great Civil War of Values rages today throughout North America. Two sides with vastly differing and incompatible worldviews are locked in a bitter conflict that permeates every level of society. Bloody battles are being fought on a thousand fronts, both inside and outside of government. Open any daily newspaper and you'll find accounts of the latest Gettysburg, Waterloo, Normandy, or Stalingrad.

Instead of fighting for territory or military conquest, however, the struggle now is for the hearts and minds of the people. It is a war over *ideas*. And someday soon, I believe, a winner will emerge and the loser will fade from memory. (Dobson and Bauer 1990, 19–20; emphasis in original)

The theme of antichristian conspiracy has a long history – from the betrayal of Jesus, to the more modern Protocols of the Elders of Zion, and continued in recent years through Cold War rhetoric. It is, of course, the 'devils,' described above, who conspire together to further satanic agendas. Conservative Christians, despite their relative religious hegemony and imperialist conquests, have created a self-culture of heroic resistance to conspiratorial attack – historically from Jews, Muslims, and communists, among others. For the NCR, the 'secular humanist conspiracy' is a central ideological tenet.[53] For evangelicals, secular humanists are any people who do not accept biblical truth and the divinity of Jesus (among other things) – thus, the phrase is *not* used solely to refer to atheists. Rather, secular humanists can be, and often are, other Christians – those who deny the literal truth of the bibles, 'revisionists' who reinterpret doctrine, and so on. They are, of course, anyone who seeks to upset God-given categories of gender and sexuality as well. In recent years, the chief villains have appeared as 'radical feminists' and 'homosexual activists.'

A recent book by James Dobson, the American founder of Focus on the Family, and co-authored with Gary Bauer, an ex–Reagan adviser, details the extent of the secular humanist conspiracy, and the role of the lesbian and gay movement within it.[54] Following the Civil War of Values quote reproduced above, Dobson argues that Christian tradition and belief (upon which the United States was founded) have, in the last thirty years, come under increasing attack from a value system advocating a 'new morality' – namely, 'secular humanism' – where 'prohibitions dissolved, rules changed, restrictions faded, and guilt subsided' (Dobson and Bauer 1990, 20–1).

It would be inaccurate to call the social reorientation of American thought and behaviour a 'conspiracy' *per se*, because it was not centrally coordinated. No high level czars determined society's course in some mysterious smoke-filled room. On the other hand, we are convinced that those who despise the Judeo-Christian system of values – and there are many – worked on a hundred independent fronts to produce a common objective.

As the civil war grows more heated in recent years, they have laboured much more closely to accomplish their goals. Can there be any doubt that the ACLU, National Organization for Women, the National Abortion Rights Action League, People for the American Way, political liberals, and others have joined forces to drive for final victory? (ibid, 108–9)

Throughout the text, 'secular humanists' are referred to as a 'cultural elite' that has established itself in order to produce cultural expressions that invade and destroy 'the homeland' (ibid, 43). 'With continual propaganda injected into the culture, the centre finally caves in. Good people become afraid or unwilling to stand in front of what appears to be an onrushing train. Tradition yields – the old beliefs recede. What was unacceptable and offensive becomes the norm.'[55] In this way, Focus's activists identify, as does REAL Women, large urban centres as sources of contagion. Nationalist and antimodernist rhetoric are mixed to tell a story of increasing moral crisis, intended to inspire Christians to action. However, the battle won't be easy as 'thus far only a courageous minority has been willing to defend the beloved homeland with their lives' (Dobson and Bauer 1990, 22–3).

The word 'homeland' has familiar ethnocentric connotations within ideologies of nationalism;[56] elsewhere in the book, not-so-subtle racist language and imagery are used when discussing 'the Black family,' drug use, and urban poverty (ibid, 29). The word also conjures up the 'land of the home' – the family – for it is here, particularly in the realm of child and adolescent sexuality, that the authors perceive one of the greatest threats to the Christian mission. I pursue this point further below.

In attempting to defend the homeland, the realm of culture, as a terrain of ideological struggle, is identified as key. Dobson and Bauer's book contains an entire chapter devoted to 'The Battle Over Words.' 'Words,' they argue, 'do matter, [they] are the currency of discourse'; words are the 'bullets' of 'war' used to 'advance the modernist agenda' (ibid, 217–18).

More recently, and no doubt partially as a result of the decreasing significance of the 'Soviet threat,' the NCR is focusing its energies and its fears upon the lesbian and gay movement, one of, in their view, the key players in the conspiracy.

Today there are few political and social movements as aggressive, powerful, or successful as 'gay rights' advocates. Homosexuality is no longer considered a dysfunction but rather an orientation or a 'sexual preference.' If you oppose homosexuality or condemn it from a moral perspective, you risk being labelled 'homophobic' – a 'sickness' described as a fear or loathing of homosexuality. (ibid, 107)

In the authors' view, the lesbian and gay movement has had tremendous linguistic success. Their cultural advances in redefining and reinterpreting traditional concepts have been enormous.

This brings us to yet another verbal phenomenon – the recreation of new words – new weapons to be used in the civil war. If homosexuality is not considered abnormal, something else called homophobia is ...

... This redefinition of an old word – homosexuality – and the creation of a new word – homophobia – is not a minor event or a mere curiosity. Through these semantic changes, normalcy is put on the defensive. (ibid, 223)

Dobson and Bauer's analysis here is reminiscent of 'post-modern' approaches to social struggle, which emphasize the significance of language. Unlike many marxist critics, who minimize the significance of linguistic 'reforms' (see chapter 4), these conservative Christians argue that current social struggles are nothing more, nor less, than contests over meanings and interpretations. Thus, the success of 'homosexual activists' has, for Dobson and Bauer, 'real,' material consequences.

In 'proving' the 'homosexual conspiracy,' Focus on the Family points to the perceived infiltration of the 'homosexual agenda' into schools, media, and government.[57] In newsletters directed at their own readership, quoting heavily from American publications like Dobson and Bauer's book discussed above, the Canadian branch draws attention to an immediate and serious threat. Focus goes so far as to argue that 'virtually all materials presented in the public school system endorse the gay and lesbian lifestyle as a legitimate option.'[58] The organization's president argues that a 'conspiracy' exists to 'separate the students totally from the values inculcated in their homes.'[59] Focus's political magazine *Citizen* consistently links 'homosexual activism' with 'radical feminism' – together these two currently pose the greatest conspiratorial threat.[60]

The view that major institutions are run by a cultural élite is echoed by REAL Women's Judy Anderson. For this organization, key conspirators are clearly identified as 'radical feminists.'

... feminism has a lot of clout politically these days, the media certainly supports feminism almost 100% ... we can't even get our point of view into the media most of the time ... CBC [Canadian Broadcasting Corporation] won't touch us with a ten-foot pole ... Mossop has his cheerleaders in the media, 99% of the media are on his side ... the CBC is just one left-wing, socialist, feminist point of view, newspapers are little better. (Anderson interview)

Feminist ideology has infiltrated into government and the courts as well. Thus, REAL Women attributes its public funding difficulties to the placement of 'radical feminists' in key governmental positions.

... the Secretary of State's Women's Programme is mainly run by feminists ... LEAF [Women's Legal Education and Action Fund] gets all the money, we're strapped for cash always ... the radical feminists got $11 million dollars from the Secretary of State last year, we got $6,900 ... one ideology is given amazing amounts of government funding to promote their agenda through the courts and people like us are out in the cold ... feminists have gotten control of funding at all sorts of levels and they're pretty keen to hold onto it ... the Prime Minister's appointments secretary is in that network, his access is very much cut off to people like us. (ibid)[61]

The courts, as well, have replaced legal analysis with sociological trea-tises best exemplified by the feminist ideology of Bertha Wilson.[62]

I have to give the radical feminists credit, they saw all this, they were involved in bringing the Charter in, men lay down and put their legs in the air – said, okay, you can have what you want – they got section 15 in there behind closed doors, I have to give them credit politically, it has changed the face of society, they got into the seat of power and grabbed it. (ibid)[63]

For Anderson, 'radical feminists' have achieved levels of power REAL Women members can only dream about. The membership's experiences with funding applications and news coverage have taken on a life of their own; 'radical feminist' power is identified as the cause of the orga-nization's political marginalization, media 'trashing,' and legal losses. The 'radical feminists' have been constructed as the primary enemy; during my interview with Judy Anderson, we were ostensibly discuss-ing the *Mossop* case, however very little of Anderson's anger was directed at the lesbian and gay rights movement. For her, feminism and gay rights seemed one and the same: 'A number of LEAF lawyers are lesbians, they're free to be lesbians, but I think there's a bit of a conflict of interest with their cases, getting my tax dollars to intervene in some-thing very close to their own backyard.' Anderson seemed able to con-sider lesbian activism only in the context of LEAF, an organization which, along with the National Action Committee,[64] is one of REAL Women's chief 'radical feminist' power-holders and conspirators (LEAF did not intervene in *Mossop*).

Focus on the Family, on the other hand, does not personalize the con-spiratorial politics to such an extent. Perhaps because the organization has a significant pastoral component, which REAL Women does not, and stable funding sources from its readership and sponsors, which

REAL Women may not, Focus does not appear as *personally* threatened (as an organization) by 'secular humanism' as REAL Women does by 'radical feminism.' For the FFA, the conspiracy's greatest threat is to children, and it is to that theme that I turn below.

The Salvation Army is, once again, a relative non-contributor to the theme of conspiracy. Don Hutchinson, when interviewed, was careful not to imbue the federal Justice Department with conspiratorial motivations with respect to its involvement in *Mossop*, and at no point did he indicate that the media or the courts were under the influence of a particular 'cultural elite.' Hutchinson did, however, express the view that it was publicly acceptable to vilify Christianity (I discuss this further in the following chapter). Furthermore, while not using the war terminology of Focus on the Family, Hutchinson none the less does believe that there are 'two value systems in conflict.' However, rather than suggesting conspiratorial theories as to why one is pre-eminent, he is more aware that lesbians and gay men may feel equally unable to adequately influence public policy in their interests.

Unlike Anderson or Sclater, Hutchinson, speaking for the Salvation Army, is far more sensitive to how many others in society perceive Christianity – as a 'powerful oppressor' (see also chapter 6). For Focus and REAL Women, the 'conspiracy' is powerful and deliberate, and often included within it are groups of people who themselves usually feel as marginalized, despised, and ignored as these evangelical Christians. Hutchinson is more willing to acknowledge this explicitly, going so far as to recognize that Brian Mossop's reasons for engaging in gay rights litigation were based on experiences Hutchinson himself has never had to 'endure' (Hutchinson interview). Having said this, however, it should be remembered that Hutchinson's comments to me in an interview do not necessarily represent the views of the Army's membership. For example, an editorial on the *Mossop* case in the Army's newsletter did appear to raise the spectre of a possible conspiracy between the 'homosexual agenda' and public institutions.[65]

Whether the conspiracy is called 'secular humanism,' 'radical feminism,' or 'homosexual activism,' both Focus on the Family and REAL Women clearly believe that it dominates all the major social institutions; the marginalization of their own perspective leaves them feeling, as Anderson put it, 'down a dark hole' (interview). As is characteristic of those who believe there is only one Truth, most views or actions which do not support the tenets of conservative Christianity are taken as being indicative of the conspiracy's power.

In this book, I do not wish to investigate the truth or falsity of this perception; I do not think that conservative Christians lie when they describe the world they see. What is important is the role conspiracy theories play in social-movement politics, and the particular continuities the NCR constructions have with Christian fears historically. The NCR's secular humanist, or radical feminist, conspiracy fulfils an important role: it finds the source of perceived problems in an identifiable 'enemy' (see Edelman 1988), and proposes an all-out battle to the death as solution. NCR constituencies are thus (the leadership hopes) simultaneously terrified, mobilized, and activated. Concurrently, the family, marriage, and gender distinctions are built up, buttressed, and fortified.

Indeed, the family, the 'homeland,' increasingly becomes the bulwark, the last stand against utter destruction. As 'the conspiracy' controls 'the state,' only 'the family' can lead the battle. Like the economic new right, conservative Christians condemn big government; for the latter movement, however, their condemnation is related to the state's perceived advancement of the secular humanist agenda, its intrusion into the family sphere, and its perceived usurpation of church and familial authority. In other words, a new right commitment to laissez-faire capitalism is only part of their motivation.

Fields (1991) has argued, drawing from Habermas (1987b), that the New Christian Right is a new social movement, like many others, attempting to assert the values, structures, and traditions of civil society against encroaching state and professional domination. Such a perspective is helpful to understanding how the NCR associates lesbian and gay legal rights with state interference and the undermining of familial authority. The advancement of lesbian and gay equality is articulated with other developments, such as desegregation and affirmative action, as part and parcel of government out of control, of state interference in the domains of church and family.[66] For example, both Don Hutchinson and Judy Anderson, during the course of my separate interviews with them, discussed what they perceived to be the excessive politicization of race relations.[67]

It is here, in the expression of a general 'antistatist' politics, that conservative Christians meet the economic new right. However, it would be misleading to suggest that the NCR is antistatist per se. On the contrary, evangelicals desire nothing less than the establishment of a *Christian* society with individual behaviour governed by the perceived teachings of Jesus and the apostles. It is the *secular* state which they oppose, and, in the understanding that the Second Coming might be some way off, they have opted for the next-best solution of asserting local autonomy and decrying state interference – all, in the name of the children.

'The Child'

Late that evening ... I quietly slipped into each of my children's bedrooms to watch them as they slept. My wife, Carol, and I always performed this ritual when our children were very young, just as millions of other parents do. We would tiptoe in, pull up the covers, check for a fevered brow and just reassure ourselves they were alive and well.

But that night I was looking for a different kind of reassurance – one I couldn't find merely with my eyes or ears or touch. I wanted to know that the world my children would grow up in would still embrace and honour the love and commitment between a man and a woman united before God in marriage. I wanted to know that they could have their own children and raise them in a free society that knew the difference between virtue and vice, good and evil, right and wrong.

That night, more than ever, I realized that it wasn't just invisible microbes that threatened the health of my children and the next generation of Americans. Their futures, and our hopes and dreams, were also threatened by an invisible ideology that seemed each day to encroach upon our society, pushing aside the truths that have guided civilized men and women throughout the centuries.

No number of death threats, no amount of media criticism, no amount of pressure would stop me from fighting for these children, or for the millions of others who depend on us to leave them a legacy of freedom and hope. (Bauer, in Dobson and Bauer 1990, 118)

For the New Christian Right, the secular humanist conspiracy is directed at 'the hearts and minds of children' (Dobson and Bauer 1990). If 'they' can steal the children, 'they' will, and by controlling the next generation, have won:

Children are the prize to the winners of the second great civil war. Those who control what young people are taught and what they experience – what they see, hear, think, and believe – will determine the future course of the nation. Given that influence, the predominant value system of an entire culture can be overhauled in one generation, or certainly in two, by those with unlimited access to children. (ibid, 35)

The hottest and most dangerous confrontation to date – and the battle that may well establish the eventual winner – is being fought over child and adolescent sexuality and the policies relevant to it. It is here that the secular humanists have made their most audacious invasion of the homeland. (ibid, 43)

... child and adolescent sexuality are seen as critical to the survival of the Judeo-Christian ethic, and indeed, to the continuance of Western civilization itself. We human beings are sexual creatures. God made us that way. We recognize our sex assignment as boys or girls from our earliest moments of self-awareness, and that identification will influence everything we do to the end of our lives ...

It follows, then, that stability in society is dependent on the healthy expression of our sexual nature. If this energy within us is siphoned off in the pursuit of pleasure; if it is squandered in non-exclusive relationships; if it is perverted in same-sex activities, then the culture is deprived of the working, saving, sacrificing, caring, building, growing, reproducing units known as families.

Robbed of sexual standards, society will unravel like a ball of twine ... (ibid, 54–5)

Focus on the Family's founders here articulate child sexuality itself as the 'homeland.' Schools, day cares, virtually any publicly funded institution become centres of anti-Christian indoctrination, encouraging, indeed compelling, children, specifically boys (although this is unstated), to 'spill their seed' in the pursuit of pleasure.

Dobson and Bauer take an approach that differs from the disease-ridden rhetoric of Brad Hayton (discussed earlier); monogamous heterosexual marriage is here represented as the linchpin of capitalism. Sexual regulation is essential to the reproduction of the workforce itself. Foucault's analysis of sexuality as a regulatory regime is here confirmed in the articulation of child (hetero)sexuality with economic prosperity and the need for a disciplined workforce.[68] However, what is ultimately 'at stake' for NCR activists 'is nothing less than the *faith* of our children. Our ultimate objective in living must be the spiritual welfare of our sons and daughters' (ibid, 53). Once again, the bottom-line fear is children's loss of Christian belief.

The need to keep 'homosexuals' away from children is at the heart of much anti–lesbian and gay activity. The chief victim of the homosexual fifth column is the child; this theme constantly recurs in conservative Christian discourse. Human rights protection will legitimize this sinister 'seduction.' Both Focus on the Family and REAL Women express profound fears about losing children to an alien culture. Underlying these fears is the view that children's sexuality hangs in the balance; without the 'right' influences, they will renounce 'God's design' (heterosexuality) in the pursuit of pleasure (homosexuality).

Children, above all, are innocent; however, their sexuality, while God-given, is, for reasons rarely explained (perhaps to do with temptation doctrine), seemingly easily capable of being corrupted. One of the secular arguments that NCR activists consistently deploy is that of the need to model appropriate gender behaviour. Jim Sclater, for example, argues,

> We know that young guys have to see what a male looks like or they won't figure it out for themselves. There's a period, particularly for male adolescents, where they're not sure what direction they're going. We think it's important that families be constituted by a father and a mother. We know that God designed women to have a nurturing effect on children, male and female, we know that men are supposed to have not only a nurturing effect but to demonstrate the more aggressive role of the hunter, down through civilizations. Without that, that's the classic development of homosexuality where the mother is the main figure. That's been proven over and over and over again. Where the father is absent, even when he's present. That can be very confusing for a male child. (interview)

The modelling argument is presented constantly in NCR opinion;[69] I do not wish to discuss its finer points. What is interesting for my purposes is the extent to which the fear of inappropriate modelling is rooted in a belief in the precariousness of childhood sexuality. Parents might wake up one morning and find that their children have been hijacked by homosexual body snatchers. They will then have to watch in agony as their children embark on lives of unbelievable sexual degeneracy, probably culminating in their early death from AIDS.

REAL Women, as I have discussed, also represents the heterosexual, child or adult, as a person capable of being seduced, and thus not at all fixed in his or her sexuality. At the same time, the suggestion is made that homosexual behaviour, despite its assorted horrors, is indeed extremely seductive, and therefore desirable. The appeal of homosexuality, the implied 'once bitten forever smitten' logic, is evident. Despite articulating homosexuality with death and disease, the NCR paradoxically and simultaneously constitutes it as pleasurable and addictive. Jim Sclater argues that people, particularly men, need restraining; too much 'sexual licence' and too little Gospel leads men to pursue sexual pleasure at whatever cost (interview).

In contrast to Nazis, neo-Nazis, and fascists generally, the modern NCR tends not to attribute homosexuality to genetic causes.[70] To do so, given biblical prohibitions and punishments, might entail advocating practices such as sterilization, imprisonment, or even death for lesbians and gay men. The mainstream NCR is distinguished from the extreme right by virtue of its relative acceptance of *concepts* of equality, universal citizenship, and rights. The organizations studied here are not overtly racist, in the sense of preaching race superiority (although they do express a strong element of anti–affirmative action backlash), and tend not to indulge in biological explanations for structured inequality (although other sections of the NCR may do so). Indeed, Judy Anderson, Don Hutchinson, and Jim Sclater expressed, to varying degrees, their support for basic human rights, including those for lesbians and gay men.[71]

NCR activists also express the view, as do many sexuality theorists, that homosexuality *and heterosexuality* are sets of practices, rather than innate essences: 'There is no credible scientific evidence to support homosexual claims that "gayness" is either genetically determined or immutable.'[72] Judy Anderson argues that sexual orientation and 'lifestyle' are two separate issues: 'I'm married, I've been attracted to other people in my seventeen years of marriage, I made a choice, I'm either true to my husband, and my vows – I make a choice ... we're talking lifestyle' (interview).

For NCR activists, it must be difficult to imagine that children could possibly be *born* homosexual – that is not God's plan. God created male and female, to complement each other, and created heterosexual union through marriage as the forum through which this complementarity is to be expressed (Hutchinson interview). For Don Hutchinson of the Army, and in contrast to the *public* utterances of Focus and REAL Women, the key issue is 'what is and what is not sin' (ibid). While humans suffer recurring punishments as a result of sin, 'deformities' must be acknowledged as just that – indications of the fall from grace, not 'celebrated' in 'pride days' and condoned by the state.[73] Jim Sclater argues,

... we all know that there is a huge spectrum of homosexual roles, let alone a spectrum of activity. There's the effeminate male, the classic concept of the homosexual, but that's only one tiny portion of it. Or the butch gal, or whatever – just one tiny segment of the lifestyle. All humans are on some spectrum between male and female, in birth certain hormonal things can create hermaphrodites. It is a spectrum, where you fit is partly determined by genetics or hormones, but there's no genetic marker or key that's ever been found that would dispose a person to gay or lesbian lifestyle. The hormonal thing has never been proven in humans.

Just as there are accidents in birth, not everyone is born perfectly or at the right end of the scale, the Christian answer to that is that all of creation is suffering under the Fall, we have fallen away from God's perfect design and the whole universe is suffering ... homosexuality may occur in some ... the Christian answer is if it occurs because they're too close to one end of the spectrum by hormonal causes or whatever, to us that's in the same category as someone being born with a clubfoot ... it's not God's design. (interview)

Those who may be somehow near the 'wrong' end of the sexuality spectrum, and who insist on living 'the homosexual lifestyle,' must therefore be prevented from proselytizing their lifestyle to others, in the same way that 'we' would not allow people with clubfeet or alcoholism to encourage others to adopt their disability. Those needing the greatest protection are those with the most malleable sexual identities – children.

One way for the New Christian Right to offer such protection is to stem the tide of lesbian and gay legal equality. How successful have they been at doing this? In chapter 6, I explore the Canadian NCR's attempt to challenge gay rights in the *Mossop* case. I consider the relationship between their insider sexual politics and their public legal argumentation, and conclude the chapter by assessing NCR effectivity at a broader level.

6

The Saints Go Litigating

Courts, Lawyers, and the Legal Process

Perceptions of Law and the Charter

Evangelical Christians have never shied away from engaging in political struggle. On the contrary, influencing social policy has always been at the forefront of their agenda. Historically, such activism took place around a number of different issues (see, for example, Hertzke 1988). In the last decades of the twentieth century, their activities have centred on constructing countermovements to those waged by socialists, feminists, antiracists, peace activists, and lesbian and gay communities – the new threats to 'Christian society.' As James Sclater expressed it:

This is not the time to pull back and say that we seem to be relatively ineffective in our attempts and therefore we must 'leave the outcome to God.' I believe that He has called our organizations into being in order to speak effectively into our culture and to prayerfully put our best efforts into stemming the tide of anti-family ideals and material. May He strengthen all of us as we attempt to be faithful to that calling.[1]

In the United States, the relationship between the NCR and legal processes is a contradictory one. Initially, the perceived 'liberal excesses' of the Warren and Burger courts played a key role in motivating the NCR's activism, particularly its decision to focus on electoral politics. The litigation experiences of the NCR – for example, around creationism or school prayer – were not positive ones. The 'legal system,' far from being viewed as a friend, was perceived as being controlled by the secular humanist conspiracy. In 1981, a document produced by one of the foundational American NCR organizations, Religious Roundtable, in tones possibly reminiscent of rhetoric that one might imagine fuelled the medieval crusades, reflected the general view. 'The born-again Ayatollahs of Paganism, enrobed as federal court judges, with unchecked power, in violation of the Constitution, have established their religion of Paganism upon us, imposing its barbarism and corruptions, demanding the modern materialist gods of consumerism and careerism be sated with children's blood' (quoted in Jorstad 1987, 34; see also ibid, 226–7). Yet gradually, the American NCR began to realize that they could influence the composition of the courts, wresting them away from the Godless 'barbarians.' The judicial appointment process, therefore, became a prime site of NCR activity, the goal being to fill the courts with conservative judges eager to find the 'original intent' of the constitutional 'Founding Fathers.'[2]

In contrast to the highly legalized culture of the United States, conservative Christians in Canada have been slow to mobilize around law-related issues. However, within an increasingly Charter-litigious society, this is quickly changing. In the mid-1980s, the National Citizens' Coalition (NCC), a right-wing business lobby with ties to the conservative Christian movement, funded Charter litigants attempting to overturn progressive labour law. During the same period, the NCC, along with the Pentecostals, REAL Women, and others, participated in the campaign against Bill 7 in Ontario (see chapter 3). The NCR has also been moderately active in election-related activities.[3]

More recently, as lesbians and gay men increasingly engage in human rights litigation, under the statutory codes and the Charter, so too have the evangelicals explored the possibilities of legal intervention. At the 1991 pro-family conference in Ottawa, a workshop was held on how to develop the newly incorporated Foundation for Legal Education and Justice, an umbrella body to fund and strategize around legal intervention.[4] According to Jim Sclater, this organization will be 'less overtly Christian,' and, in so being, will hope to attract the support and funding of other organizations that 'do not necessarily agree with all of our family agenda' (interview).

In explaining their decision to litigate, NCR leaders point to the increasing use of Canadian courts by other interest groups seeking to further political agendas. Don Hutchinson argues,

... we live in a very litigious society now, a lot of people are becoming more aware of their rights before the courts. A number of special interest groups have proceeded before the courts to seek changes in how certain issues are viewed which Parliament might not have been prepared to grant. So too the church has become more aware that its positions can also be presented before the courts ... a number of religious groups, and in this particular instance [the *Mossop* coalition] you could classify the groups as evangelical Christian groups, have gained a realization that we have the ability to stand before the courts and make presentations in the same way that other special interest groups do, and try and preserve and promote our point of view. (interview)

More than the other organizations, REAL Women has identified participation in Charter litigation as a key campaigning strategy. Judy Anderson, president of REAL Women, argues that 'courts are now the main avenue for social change since the Charter' (interview). However, for Anderson, participation in litigation is hindered by the 'radical feminists' who control the funding sources. For example, the Court Challenges Programme, a federally funded, arm's-length body that awarded Charter litigation funds to applicant groups, refused REAL Women funding on the basis that the organization sought to restrict, rather than enhance, equality. The program was, for Anderson, part of the 'radical feminist' conspiracy: 'all the people who administer the funds are quite partisan' (ibid).[5]

REAL Women's construction of a bias in Charter-litigation funding is also found in various right-wing media commentaries.[6] They also rely on the work of two Canadian political scientists who co-authored a study claiming that a 'court party' has arisen in Canada.[7] They argue that left-wingers, feminists, and others with similar politics have succeeded in obtaining federal funding in order to fuel social change through the courts. The authors maintain that these forces, frustrated in their attempts to install a socialist government through democratic processes, have created their own political 'court party.' The conclusion of these academics – that democratic process is being fundamentally subverted by left-wing judicial activism – has provided welcome 'evidence' for the NCR, who have quoted liberally from the study.[8]

Partially as a result of this perceived bias, REAL Women views the Charter as an unqualified evil which they argue about only because they have to: 'instead, we say, get rid of the Charter' (Anderson interview). For Anderson, the Charter is undemocratic, providing a few people with 'no accountability to the public' the opportunity to 'in one fell swoop change the whole force of Canadian jurisprudence and social norms' (ibid). Echoing many of the Charter criticisms made by marxist legal academics, Judy Anderson argues for 'more grass-roots participation' (ibid). Anderson's comments are based upon her perception that the Supreme Court of Canada has adopted the 'radical feminist' agenda. When asked whether, should the Court be staffed by judges more to her liking, she would still have the same views about the Charter, she replied that, while the process would continue to be undemocratic, 'if things were going our way we might not be saying it quite so loudly' (ibid). Nevertheless, were it not for the funding problems, REAL Women would happily make litigation 'one of our primary strategies' (ibid).

Don Hutchinson of the Salvation Army has a similar critique of Charter-based legal struggle, arguing that a 'rights-oriented' culture loses sight of the importance of social responsibility and the blessing of being granted privileges (interview).[9] However, for the Army, litigation is increasingly being seen as another way of expressing a political message. The *Mossop* coalition, Hutchinson argues, was a 'wise investment,' a form of 'stewardship,' 'what the Salvation Army does is invest in people's lives' (ibid).

Law is one of the many ways to indicate your concern. Our primary concern is to share the gospel, in our words and in our deeds. That sharing and coming to positional statements on a number of issues on which there is a biblical perspective takes place in a number of different ways ... lobbying the government ... appearing before the courts ... the Sunday morning Holiness meeting ... providing soup to people commonly referred to as street people ... ministering to teenagers. (ibid)

The Army now 'budgets' for litigation and Hutchinson insists that no other area of Army service suffers as a result.[10]

These three NCR organizations all, to varying degrees and for diverse reasons, share the belief that we live in a overly rights-focused culture. Courts and judges are hopelessly biased against 'traditional morality'; the Charter (and, by implication, all human rights frameworks) has been a tremendously successful tool in the hands of 'the left.' Because of this, they too are forced to participate in activist litigation.

Creating the NCR Coalition

The impetus to form a Christian intervention coalition in *Mossop* came initially from Jim Sclater and Focus on the Family.[11] Following the publication of the tribunal decision in *Mossop*, and the indication that the government would appeal, Focus decided the issue was significant, and that they, and others, should get involved in some way. Jim Sclater called the Justice Department and spoke to Barbara McIsaac, senior counsel on *Mossop*, who indicated, he states, that the 'government didn't have much of a case' (interview). Focus, who believed that a strong argument against the redefinition of 'family' to include gay couples could surely be made, began to contact fellow Christian activists.

After discovering that a number of other organizations were already involved in legal interventions, and thus could not play a leading role in *Mossop*, Sclater, who had been referred to the prestigious Bay Street firm McCarthy Tétreault, decided that Focus's resources permitted them to act as instigator. Focus and REAL Women had worked together in the past, and were at that time involved in setting up the Legal Defence Fund; RW was thus a natural partner for Focus to contact. The Salvation Army became involved through McCarthy Tétreault; the firm was the Army's general counsel, and had relayed to them Focus's interest in *Mossop*. Eventually, the other two members, the Pentecostal Assemblies of Canada and the Evangelical Fellowship of Canada, both with active histories in opposing lesbian and gay equality, joined up as well. As various interviewees expressed it, activists wished to have a mix of organizations 'known' to the courts as intervenors (e.g., REAL Women) but also with long, respectable histories (e.g., the Salvation Army).

The intervening organizations never met as a group, although there was some phone contact between individual leaderships, and Focus and REAL Women met at their pro-family conference in the spring of 1991. While Don Hutchinson of the Army stated he was 'aware of the doctrinal beliefs of the other organizations' (interview), it was clear to me, in conversation, that his knowledge of Focus on the Family, in particular, was extremely limited.[12] It was, however, the organizations' 'faith' which provided, for Hutchinson, the key common ground (ibid).

Despite not being able to meet and discuss the case, both Don Hutchinson and Jim Sclater expressed satisfaction with how McCarthy's handled the matter. Hutchinson and Ian Binnie, counsel from McCarthy's, had worked together to ensure that the legal submissions did not engage in 'gay bashing'; each took great pains to insist that the case had 'nothing to do with gay rights' (Hutchinson interview). Of all the organizations, then, it is the Salvation Army that played the most instrumental role vis-à-vis the legal submissions. Don Hutchinson felt that the factum was 'a good reflection of our [i.e., the Army's] position' (ibid). Jim

Sclater, on the other hand, acknowledged in an interview having very little input into the drafting of the factum, as did Judy Anderson (although neither expressed dissatisfaction).

In contrast to the EGALE et al. coalition,[13] which was partially funded by the Court Challenges Programme (thereby confirming the NCR 'court party' and conspiracy theses), this intervention was funded by the organizations themselves; McCarthy's agreed on a ceiling for each intervention (for example, at the Federal Court, it was approximately $17,000). According to Jim Sclater, primary funding came from the Salvation Army, with the Pentecostals and the Evangelical Fellowship assuming a certain amount as well (Sclater interview). Don Hutchinson, of the Army, insisted that the Army's share was not being funded out of publicly raised monies; when pressed to say where the money came from, he suggested that sources included income from Army property and investments (clearly sources which were, at some point, raised through public donation or state subsidy).

Interestingly, then, the Salvation Army, a somewhat reluctant and anomalous member of Canada's New Christian Right, was the directing hand behind the submissions, and provided, it seems, the bulk of the funding. Indeed, the Army, despite its divergence from much of the sexual ideology represented in the previous chapter, could be said to have publicly 'fronted' the litigation. Their participation had contradictory implications. On the one hand, the Army's name, as Ian Binnie himself noted when interviewed, provided the coalition with public credibility they might not otherwise have had. The Army is well known and well respected. Their reputation for a more 'caring' Christianity mutes the 'new right' politics of Focus and REAL Women. At the same time, their overt Christianity, in the context of the two other organizations not being 'known' as conservative evangelicals, risked the coalition itself being publicly considered as a group of 'Christian fundamentalists.'

For the Army itself, the contradictions ought to be more severe. Based on shared biblical understandings of homosexuality, they joined with groups politically far to the right of themselves, funding and legitimizing these others in the process. Don Hutchinson was sensitive about this, repeating that the coalition was a 'short-term thing' only, and that the Army had no desire to 'gay bash' (interview). Nevertheless, their participation with the other organizations will no doubt have a more long-term effect upon the Army's politics and future moral activism. Unfortunately, other than expressing vague reservations about REAL Women's politics (and indicating he knew very little about Focus's), Hutchinson was not willing to discuss this dilemma further.

The Process of Legal Translation

Here, I consider the ways in which the sexual politics of Focus on the Family, REAL Women, and the Salvation Army were expressed, or not, within the coalition's legal submissions in *Mossop*. In agreeing to intervene as one party, coalition members consented to representation by one law firm and, while able to submit separate affidavits, to the presentation of a joint factum (statement of argument and authorities). The documents I refer to include affidavits of organizational leaders and the Federal Court of Appeal factum.

The phenomenon of third-party intervention is a relatively new one in Canada, achieving increasing prominence in the post-Charter era.[14] In the United States, third-party briefs filed by an *amicus curiae* (friend of the court) are common, and have been a significant form of social-movement legal struggle. In Canada, there is no 'right' to intervene. Applicants must establish, through submissions, that they possess a relevant perspective that will prove valuable to the court and will not be presented by the parties themselves. In practice, this burden may not be a heavy one (depending on the case), and it has become commonplace, for example, for LEAF, the feminist legal action organization, to intervene in significant cases affecting 'women's rights' (see Razack 1991). Such activities on the part of lesbian and gay organizations, and by the right in Canada, have been less noticeable (the latter has tended to fund individual litigants).

In *Mossop*, the NCR coalition thus had to achieve intervenor status before being able to make their argument to the court. The documents produced to enable this were affidavits from organizational leaders, and the Application for Leave to Intervene. The former establish the individual credentials and expertise of the coalition partners, the latter condenses the information and argument the coalition believes constitutes a unique and important contribution to the debate. While, formally, each organization must establish its own 'right' to intervene, unknown organizations, or those with dubious credentials, facilitate the process through the involvement of well-known and well-respected groups, such as, in this case, the Salvation Army. Once an organization has been granted status, the Application for Leave will form the basis of the factum – the submission that presents the coalition's argument to the court.

I now go on to explore a selection of the materials offered in the Federal Court of Appeal – the forum in which the NCR coalition made its initial intervention.

The Affidavit of Lt-Col. William Speck, Salvation Army of Canada (in the Federal Court of Appeal)

William Speck, the officer responsible for the Army's intervention before Don Hutchinson's involvement (Speck has since retired), purported in his affidavit to establish the basis for granting intervenor status to the Salvation Army. The document begins by setting out the history of the organization; its bulk consists of repeated statements about Salvationists' view of 'the family,' interspersed with references to the Army's service role vis-à-vis 'broken' families. The affidavit does not suggest that 'the family' and marriage are God-ordained; instead, Speck argues that children receive advantages through being raised within 'traditional' families.

Indeed, the words 'God' and 'Jesus' do not appear at all; as an aside, Speck refers once to the Army's goal of 'promoting Christian values' (para. 7). There is, therefore, no context provided or explanation given for the Army's perspective on familial and sexual issues. While it could be argued that most readers would know that the Army is a Christian organization, a decision was clearly made to find 'secular' substantiation for the Army's religiously motivated intervention. The affidavit suggests that Salvationists' primary concern is with the welfare of children (paras. 12–15). While this is certainly *one* of their concerns, it is not the principle that motivated their attack on homosexuality – namely, *sin* (see chapter 5).

One of the most revealing passages from the affidavit is the following.

The Salvation Army recognizes the inherent difficulties in defining with precision the term 'family' in today's society, and in adopting a single or unified vision of the limits of what may constitute a 'family'. As a result, we do not necessarily disagree with the approach of the Human Rights Tribunal in this case of examining the function of families in today's society rather than focusing entirely on family structure.

Nevertheless, we were profoundly distressed to learn that the federal government had neither adduced relevant evidence nor submitted pertinent argument in opposition to the Complainant's 'functional' approach. (paras. 13–14).

The tone and argument of this passage could not be further from those expressed in an editorial in *War Cry,* the Army's newspaper, following the tribunal decision. The editorial in the May 1989 issue argued that the adjudicator had 'grossly offended most people and ignored the whole of human history' in its 'attempt to legislate immorality.' The writer suggested that a 'homosexual rights' domino effect would occur – 'life as we know it has been changed irrevocably.' Far from pleading for 'relevant evidence' to be 'adduced,' the *War Cry* went on to call for the dismantling of 'unregulated bodies' (meaning the federal Human Rights Commission) that were engaged in 'undermining the foundations of this society.'

Despite *Mossop* being about the legal recognition of a gay male couple, and despite the Salvation Army's own views as to the immorality of and danger posed by homosexual practices, Speck's affidavit mentions homosexuality itself only once, on the final page. The Army neither explains that homosexuality is contrary to God's plan nor that 'the marriage of one man with one woman is a sacred institution ordained by God.'[15] Instead, the affidavit simply reiterates the importance of 'the family' for the welfare of children and society as a whole, emphasizing the 'reproductive function' of traditional families.[16]

The 'reproductive function' is not something explicitly argued within Salvationist politics. It could be assumed that the Army would agree that traditional families serve a 'reproductive function' which, given their understanding, lesbian and gay families do not; however, the Army's positional statements on 'homosexuality' and 'family' do not make this argument.[17] It thus seems probable that its incorporation within William Speck's affidavit was urged by legal counsel, aware that past 'gay rights' cases had centred upon this distinction (see chapter 2). Similarly, the deployment of the 'child welfare' principle was encouraged by lawyers, confident that such rhetoric would be a language the court would understand. When interviewed, Ian Binnie, the coalition's lawyer, quite confidently told me what could, and could not, be heard by judges.

The Affidavit of Constance Gwendolyn Landolt, Vice-President, REAL Women of Canada (in the Federal Court of Appeal)

Gwen Landolt, long-time REAL Women vice-president and herself a lawyer, began her affidavit somewhat defensively. Paragraph 2 claims the organization is 'inter-denominational,' while 3 and 4 emphatically announce REAL Women's commitment to women's equality. Landolt suggests that the differences between REAL Women and other women's equality groups lies only in the means used for social change.

REAL Women's primary argument is similar to that of the Salvation Army's. The traditional family is the most important social unit, defined through the marriage of a man and a woman. Marriage, RW argues, is a 'social' as well as a personal 'contract' (para. 9). The social contract consists in the couple's reproduction of 'successive generations' (ibid). Landolt goes on to suggest that the Attorney General's Office (responsible for appealing against the gay rights judgment) is unable to perform its legal duty because of bias. According to REAL Women, the federal government's favouritism towards 'radical feminist, lesbian and homosexual groups' disqualifies it from properly performing its role to argue on behalf of the traditional family (para. 12) – hence, the need for intervenors such as REAL Women.

It could be argued, however, that the affidavit is rather deceptive. While the meaning of 'interdenominational' may be somewhat ambiguous (referring popularly to either a range of Christian denominations or different religious faiths), the word is no doubt intended to suggest that the group has no 'one' religious orientation, or that religion itself is not necessarily the organization's *raison d'être*. However, while there are some Catholic members, there is no indication that Buddhists, Hindus, Jews, Muslims, and so on either belong or are welcome. As I noted in chapter 5, REAL Women's president quite clearly stated that, while the organization was fundamentally Christian, this was not an element of RW's politics leaders chose to share with the public (Anderson interview).

It is as well rather dubious for RW to suggest that it 'supports policies for women that provide equal opportunity in all areas, including education, employment, and retirement' (para. 3). REAL Women adamantly opposes universal child care, equal pay legislation, sex education, human rights provision, and an assortment of other 'equal opportunity' initiatives (see chapter 5). While they might argue that the policies they *do* advocate would 'help' many women, particularly those who work solely in the home, they remain opposed to what are commonly understood as 'equal opportunity policies' for women.

What is both interesting and yet, perhaps, predictable about RW's claims is that the organization's legal strategy so earnestly attempts to render RW's politics compatible with liberal equality discourse. REAL Women has accepted that, with respect to its public involvement in litigation, the dominant liberal ethos must be adopted. Thus, the REAL

Women legal submission, while remaining 'true' to the organization's perspective on 'the family', seeks to conceal both its New Right and Christian politics.

Yet, it does not do this completely. The 'radical feminist' conspiracy theme makes its appearance in Landolt's discussion of government bias. I would argue that Landolt's views here are an honest, and to some extent accurate, assessment of why the REAL Women coalition has something different to offer the court. She is right that the Department of Justice seems to have put little effort into its case; they called no witnesses at the tribunal, and their factum makes its arguments in a perfunctory fashion. Whether or not Justice bureaucrats are conspiring with gay rights activists is beside the point; for whatever reason, it remains the case that the government's defence was, arguably, half-hearted and ill planned.

The Affidavit of James A. Sclater, Assistant to the President for Public Policy and Research, Focus on the Family Association (in the Federal Court of Appeal)

Jim Sclater (subsequent to this promoted to national director of public policy) combines the 'child welfare' rhetoric of William Speck with the government-bias thesis of Gwen Landolt. Sclater first claims that the 'primary function' of Focus on the Family is to provide assistance to 'families' (para. 4). Focus, he states, 'believes strongly' that 'the welfare of children requires a mother and a father ... in order that they may attain a strong sense of self, and a healthy ability to relate to others, and in order that they may, in turn, fulfil a normal male or female role' (para. 5). The recognition of 'same-sex relationships' as families poses a 'serious threat to the structure of society and the health and viability of future generations' (para. 6).

Only once does Sclater identify Focus as a 'Christian organization' (para. 4). As with the Salvation Army and REAL Women affidavits, Focus on the Family's submission renders almost invisible the conservative Christian theology animating every facet of the organization's work. Sclater discusses the servicing role Focus plays for 'families,' but does not note that only Christian families are welcomed. Furthermore, Sclater's affidavit contains no mention of the 'appalling' sexual practices 'homosexuals get up to' (Sclater interview). In contrast to Focus's internal documents, which highlight the 'diseased' and 'predatory' 'homosexual lifestyle', or allege the covert infiltration of the 'homosexual agenda' into institutional life (see chapter 5), Jim Sclater's *legal* construction of homosexuality is most notable for its *lack* of definition.

Factum of the Intervenors, The Salvation Army, Focus on the Family Association Canada, REAL Women, The Pentecostal Assemblies of Canada, and the Evangelical Fellowship of Canada (in the Federal Court of Appeal)

The coalition's factum, their joint submission, is perhaps most remarkable for its paucity of argument and contribution to debate. The primary purpose of the factum appears to be to cite and quote from precedent. A variety of previous 'gay rights' cases, all decided negatively, are listed in support of the basic premise that 'family' means a heterosexual marriage (pp. 3–5). The public, argues the coalition, has an interest in the preservation and continuing state privileging of the traditional family. This interest is based on the family's role in procreation, and in providing societal stability (p. 3).

The document takes issue with the 'sociological definition' of 'family' adopted by the tribunal (pp. 5–8). While the coalition acknowledges in this document that the popular meaning of 'family' may have changed, it argues that the *legal* meaning has not. Using a variety of legal rhetorical techniques, such as the 'slippery slope' analogy, the factum urges the court to adopt the 'plain' meaning of the word, which, it suggests, can be discovered by reading dictionaries (p. 12). The intervenors further argue that Parliament did not intend, when enacting the Canadian Human Rights Act, to protect homosexual relations, and it is not for the court to usurp the role of Parliament.[18] There is little else to the factum but this.

Has the conservative Christian coalition made a unique contribution towards the judicial appraisal of this case? I would argue that the factum offers no hint of the actual expertise and knowledge the coalition members possess. Legal precedent has replaced God's word as Truth, the dictionary supplanting the authority of the Scriptures. What the coalition had to offer was their Christianity, their world-view as to the imminent and serious threat posed by the conspiracy to further the 'homosexual agenda.' Instead, the legal process appears to have subverted these beliefs, rendering them invisible. The homosexuals who 'eat and rub themselves with faeces,' 'defecate on their partners,' and 'drink urine' (Hayton n.d.) are nowhere to be found. References to the homosexual 'sub-culture of prostitution' flourishing in the 'inner cities'[19] are notably absent.

Instead, the factum offers an exercise in legal logic that provides only a faint echo of the coalition's politics. In fact, there is little to distinguish the NCR's factum from that of the attorney general.[20] The same arguments are made, the same cases cited. The AG's factum does not, however, discuss the function of family and marriage in society, nor does it offer as much in the way of legal rhetoric (for example, the government does not make a 'slippery slope' argument). In these respects, the intervenors have presented additional *legal* knowledge, and, perhaps, Landolt's and Sclater's argument, with respect to a lack of governmental commitment to defending 'the family,' is justified.

Nevertheless, a review of the coalition's legal submissions in *Mossop* shows the extent to which the right-wing, evangelical Christian politics of these organizations has been muted. This phenomenon can be evaluated in different ways. On the one hand, it could be argued that the NCR's agenda has been marginalized (or co-opted), its leaders' evangelism usurped by its lawyers' legalism. On the other hand, I could suggest my own version of a 'conspiracy thesis,' arguing that the NCR has deliberately chosen to hide its politics beneath a cloak of respectability. In this way, judges and others are potentially deceived, remaining unaware of the real 'New Christian Right Agenda.' Or, is a more accurate view somewhere in between – a mixture of legal colonization and pragmatic politics?

Feminist legal submissions do not necessarily reveal the radical politics of, for example, the many lesbian feminists who work for feminist legal action groups and participate in the drafting of documents. Is this a deliberate strategy of deception or an example of pragmatic political struggle (or both)? What is interesting about this process are the specific ways in which legal discourse compels the adoption of a particular pragmatic politics (liberal legalism) and that it appears to affect social movements on either side of the political spectrum. Further, as I discuss in chapter 7, even when alternative perspectives *are* submitted to courts, they tend then to be simply ignored.

It is worth considering NCR leaders' own explanations for the process of legalization that occurred for the coalition members in *Mossop*. According to Judy Anderson, Jim Sclater, and Don Hutchinson, there could never be any question of submitting an overtly Christian document to the courts (interviews). They and their organizations view society as profoundly *anti*-Christian, and hence their political communication must be informed by other knowledge sources in order to be publicly credible. Judy Anderson, for example, stated in an interview that 'Christianity is allowed to be lambasted at every opportunity ...

things can be said about us you can't even say about gays any more ... Christianity is low man on the totem pole, anybody can give a kick and get away with it. We're at the back of the bus now ... everywhere Christianity is derided and treated with disrespect.'

As I left Judy Anderson's house, following this interview, she pointed to a Christian prayer hanging in the front hallway. She told me that every time someone came to interview her she considered whether or not to take this prayer down and hide it, knowing that this symbol of religion could lead journalists and researchers to 'totally dismiss' her. She likened her feelings to those of closeted lesbians and gay men, who 'were' (in her view) once reduced to similar 'sterilization procedures' (my interpretation) in their homes. Now, she feels the tables have turned. According to Anderson, neither group should be in such a position (although she was perhaps unable to understand how REAL Women's potential success could substantially reduce the possibility of lesbians and gay men being out).

Don Hutchinson, the Salvation Army's legal adviser, has a similar, although somewhat more complex analysis:

... in today's society there's a sense that Christianity was or is the faith of the majority, that the majority has imposed its will on others, and that we are in an era where minority rights should be recognized as much as possible ... there's a perception that Christianity is responsible for the abuse of rights, rather than any kind of recognition that the Christian faith works hand in hand with the [sic] societal development to recognize the need and the granting of certain rights for people.

There's a societal backlash if you stand up and say I'm speaking from a Christian perspective ... there's a tendency in the church to be fearful ... or to wisely temper their Christian perspective with the appropriate supporting documentation from other sources. (interview)

Hutchinson's last comment captures what conservative Christians feel to be the pragmatic reality they face when attempting to communicate publicly, whether within law or any other discursive field. For Focus on the Family, a key activity is gathering together certain 'scientific truths' and disputing others (see Hayton n.d.). Unlike fundamentalists, these Christians do not hesitate to engage the secular world on its own terms.

Jim Sclater, national policy director for Focus on the Family, asks,

Why waste our words? The truth is that we are not in a Christian society and we don't believe that it is even necessarily appropriate to appeal to our Christian theology. Our only argument that has validity in our society is whether it bene-fits our society and the individuals in it. We argue on the facts, we argue out of our conviction, we're there because we believe that the Christian Scripture gives us an agenda and because that's who we are. But we'll argue the facts, as we think they're relevant in law.

We also believe that all truth is God's Truth. The truth about my body as a sex-ual being is Truth. Christians shouldn't view the body or the mind as separate from what we can find out about it through other means. When we talk about the family, we understand it psychologically as well as theologically. We know, from the history of psychology and human history, that males that aren't raised by a mom and dad don't always turn out the same way as those who are. Model-ling happens. Maleness is picked up. Of course the men's movement right now in North America and around the world is based on the idea that men need a father, and if they don't have one they need a surrogate father. If they don't have a surrogate father at least they need male bonding, because men are finding out that the nature of their manhood is that it needs affirmation from other males, particularly from preceding generations.

Those are 'facts' that can be discovered by studying the social sciences, we don't need to bring our theology into court to prove that. If we did, most people would turn off immediately anyway. (interview)

In this way, the discourses of psychology, sociology, and the modern 'men's movement' can be woven together to form a coherent, non-reli-gious public statement. Internally, the effort can even be justified theo-logically – 'all truth is God's Truth' – meaning, presumably, that God creates all *legitimate* forms of knowledge, not just those contained in the Bible. Knowledge perceived to conflict with biblical pronouncements however, such as 'evidence' that children are not harmed by being raised in fatherless homes, would presumably be viewed as false knowledge, rather than God's Truth.

The ways in which conservative Christians tailor argument to audi-ence is reiterated by Judy Anderson.

I can write from a religious point of view, my own faith, or I can take the same thing and say it not using the code words for religion ... if I'm going to talk to the Catholic Women's League, sure, I'll talk about faith there because we all under-stand it, but if I'm talking to the Royal Canadian Yacht Club, I can say the same thing, but without using my own particular faith language. (interview)

There is nothing particularly startling or unusual about this. Academics and activists, feminists, lesbians, socialists – we all give different speeches to different audiences. What is interesting about Judy Anderson and REAL Women is the extent to which their conservative, evangelical Christianity has deliberately been completely submerged and unacknowledged, even though their 'faith' clearly underlies much of their political agenda. Even the Salvation Army, an organization very publicly identified as Christian (although perhaps, mistakenly, no longer as evangelical), feels unable to present its biblical position to the court (Hutchinson interview).

Thus far, I hope to have shown how the sexual politics of the New Christian Right, as evidenced within the movement texts of three organizations active in Canada today, was considerably altered, and indeed cut out of the legal submissions in one particular intervention. I have suggested a partial reason for this – namely, the views of leaders as to what can be publicly communicated. Quite clearly, an initial period of self-censorship took place, as it does for many movements on the left (see chapters 3 and 4).

It would be misleading to suggest that something called 'law' was necessarily responsible for this. Social-movement actors are no doubt aware of the conventions, practices, and rhetoric of legal discourse; as a result, many may feel that litigation is a particularly fraught exercise. At the same time, however, those who believe themselves to hold marginalized perspectives on social life often feel that *any* engagement in 'the public realm' necessitates the translation of their radical politics into a more acceptable (liberal) form (see also Hertzke 1988). What is interesting about the case of the New Christian Right is that, in engaging with law, they have lost nearly all the key elements in their sexual politics. Right-wing activists have had to concede that the ideology of 'formal equality between the sexes' dominates and that support for gay rights is a relatively widespread phenomenon. Despite their 'real' belief that homosexuality is dangerous precisely because it is 'sick,' 'sinful,' and 'seductive,' coalition members have chosen not to present such a perspective. And, except for brief references to 'modelling,' NCR analyses of the relation between gender and sexuality also remain unspoken.

How seriously should we take the New Christian Right in Canada? This is the question I move on to now. For those who refuse to accept the authority of Scripture and the Second Coming of Jesus, New Christian Right politics could be perceived as a politics of hate, death, imperialism, and destruction. The theology motivating the NCR and its 'army of

saints' is frightening (even more so if you are one of those condemned to
the hell-fires of Armageddon); the relatively measured tones of the individuals I interviewed should not obscure this 'reality.'

Analysing NCR 'Success'

Academics are divided over whether the NCR can be said to be a vibrant
or a dying force in North American political struggle. In Canada, for
example, some feminist writers have attributed a great deal of success to
REAL Women. Dubinsky (1985) cautions that the Canadian New Right
has 'not yet reached its zenith,' and there is a need to pay REAL Women
'close attention.' Erwin (1988a, 1988b) alerts us to their increasing influence; Gill (1989) argues they have achieved a reorientation of media discourse on feminism; and Ross (1988) credits RW with forcing the
defunding and increased policing of lesbian projects by the Secretary of
State Women's Programme. Others, however, such as Razack (1991), find
REAL Women barely worth mentioning.

In the United States, various studies undertaken in the 1980s show
that NCR practical successes were limited, consisting of electoral victo-
ries that were few and often momentary, and a legislative agenda that
made little progress (Lipset and Raab 1981; Johnson and Tamney 1982;
Zweir 1984). Steve Bruce goes so far as to suggest that the NCR, far from
being a 'disciplined, charging army,' is, rather, a 'motley crew.'[21] This
view, however, is not shared by Sara Diamond (1989), who sees in the
NCR's world-wide network a formidable enemy to progressive social
change. Others suggest the American NCR is regrouping, redirecting its
energies locally, and most certainly not 'withering away' (Moen 1989;
Helvacioglu 1991). Further, the NCR was initially mobilized by economic new rightists, and has continued to play an important role in
facilitating new right politics generally. So long as there is a Right, it will
likely have a Christian component.

In suggesting that the NCR remains an important social actor, one
could also argue that the activities of an organization like Focus on the
Family imply, perhaps, a growing, imperialistic, American 'mission' in
Canada. NCR foreign intervention and agitation, so thoroughly
researched by Sara Diamond (1989), is unfortunately ignored by many
writers. American Christian corporations are active all over the world,[22]
often engaged in propping up brutal dictatorships. While these activities
are more common to American-based organizations, it is imperative for
Canadians as well to view the NCR's agenda in its entirety. Lesbians and

gay men are not the only targets; attempts to combat NCR influence in the realm of sexuality must take account of the connections between domestic and foreign activities.

Thus the NCR's agenda needs to be examined as a whole – their strategies in one area are often linked to their views in others. For example, as I briefly discussed in the previous chapter, the representation of the 'inner city' as a den of homosexual iniquity is intimately connected to the construction of it as a centre of non-White (predominantly Black) criminal (including illicit sexual) activity. Furthermore, the opposition of NCR constituencies to 'gay rights' is rooted not only in their Christian beliefs, but also in the White backlash to perceived antiracist initiatives. This is consequential because it can help explain the appeal of the NCR agenda to people who may not completely share all the tenets of conservative Christianity.[23]

It is also important to note that most social movements are active on several fronts at once. It does not follow from the NCR being weak in one, for example, 'winning' legal cases, that it is therefore weak in all. In the United States, the NCR and its legislative representatives (e.g., Jessie Helms) have recorded a number of successes in the field of arts censorship, achieving the public defunding of individual artists and progressive arts organizations (see also Stychin 1993a). Many American feminist, lesbian, and gay artists would find Bruce's analysis (1990), that the NCR is 'dead,' inaccurate and offensive (as would pro-choice activists).

With respect to law, the arguments made in this chapter suggest that the legal process, be it legislative or judicial, is a key site of social-movement struggle. While individual battles can be seen to be 'won' or 'lost' (such as Bill 7, or the *Mossop* case itself), the relation between legal discourse and social-movement politics is something more complex than a simple 'results tally' would indicate. For example, the NCR coalition's 'win' in *Mossop* at the Supreme Court of Canada is not necessarily an indication of NCR 'power.' It was, in fact, a *hostile* judicial climate that fuelled the American NCR eruption in the 1970s. The *Roe* v *Wade* abortion decision was instrumental in fostering NCR mobilization in that country; the more recent judicial erosion of the *Roe* privacy principle has, paradoxically, put anti-abortion forces on the defensive and facilitated pro-choice mobilization.

Nevertheless, the success of NCR organizations in achieving legal intervenor status should not be underestimated. Whether they win or lose, these organizations have been granted an official, public platform from which to preach. While their legal submissions may be unoriginal and legalistic, and only a handful of people will ever read them, the organizations' official legal status confirms the NCR as a legitimate party in more popular debates around sexuality and family. In the pages of the mainstream print media, there may be other considerations related to effective communication, but NCR activists will not be so constrained by the imperatives of *legal* discourse.

The Canadian New Christian Right is, in a sense, a novice at legal struggle. It is only beginning to flex its muscles, to extend its reach into this arena. The experience of organizations such as Focus on the Family, REAL Women, and the Salvation Army in a case like *Mossop* was a learning one for them. Through their involvement, they gained valuable contacts, achieved a degree of mainstream respectability, and, perhaps most significantly, further supplemented their own 'Truths' as well as arming themselves with legal knowledge, strategies, and argumentation. In addition, they succeeded in making the *Mossop* case a three-way site of struggle between the lesbian and gay rights movement, the government, and the New Christian Right. This last point means that both the lesbian and gay movement and various state actors must respond in some way to them. An evaluation of NCR success must, therefore, also consider the ways in which that movement affects the discourse and strategies of others. For example, the NCR's relentless attack upon the Charter may mean that left-wingers, who might otherwise be similarly critical of Charter-culture, instead defend its limited achievements. This phenomenon, whereby progressive academics and activists feel compelled to defend minimal policies and programs rather than seek substantive changes to them, is one of the most significant ways in which the Right shifts the battleground.

Having said this much, however, it is important not to overemphasize the NCR threat. For example, some writers suggest that the American NCR managed to infiltrate the Republican Party. While their candidates were somewhat unsuccessful in securing Republican nominations, the party was forced to respond to the NCR agenda, taking on board a number of evangelical Christian positions (Diamond 1989). Others, however, suggest that Republican support for the NCR agenda was largely rhetorical and, further, that the very process of 'infiltration' was a co-opting one, altering the NCR agenda as much as the Republican Party's.[24]

Neither can the NCR be said to be an instrument of corporate America. Much is sometimes made of the funds corporations contribute to the American NCR (see Diamond 1989). However, other research shows that

the major American corporations have rarely contributed to NCR cof-
fers, preferring instead the old-fashioned Republican Party, often against
NCR factions (Bruce 1990b, 54–5). Furthermore, I would suggest that,
these days, for every corporation giving funds to right-wing organizations one might find another adopting a 'sexual orientation' human
rights policy or selling its products at Lesbian and Gay Pride festivals.[25]

Furthermore, the conservative Christian movement is itself disparate
and divided. Those active in NCR politics agree to put aside theological
differences in order to unite around 'shared values' (Wuthnow 1983).
However, in the process, those shared values are compromised, organizations become unwieldy, and leaders increasingly removed from the
concerns of grass-roots constituents.[26] In the United States, several
studies indicate that those who share a number of 'pro-family' values
often neither support NCR organizations nor endorse the NCR agenda
(Simpson 1983, 1984; Shupe and Stacey 1984). I have previously shown
how Bibby's Canadian data indicate a discrepancy between NCR organizations and the belief-systems of those they claim to represent (see
chapter 5).

In this way, the setting up of structures such as the Legal Defence
Fund may have effects contrary to those intended. For example, the
increasing desire of the Canadian NCR to 'work together' and develop
political coalitions may succeed in achieving a similar atmosphere of
conflict and consensus break-down, as has been experienced in the
United States. Indeed, Don Hutchinson, the Salvation Army's legal
adviser, expressed the view that an evangelical Christian movement
could never really succeed in Canada, given the extent of internal division (interview; see also Cuneo 1989).

It is important, however, to problematize our notion of 'success.'[27]
Fields (1991) has argued that right-wing movements do not need to
mobilize large constituencies or gain 'control of the state' in order to
achieve a significant impact upon public debate. Her analysis suggests
that the 'power' of the New Christian Right lies in its ability to explain
the social world, to confidently identify problems and solutions, and to
communicate these ideas as an alternative vision (see also Heinz 1983).
Fields argues that the NCR is one oppositional social movement among
many, but one with significant powers of social interpretation (see also
Susan Harding 1991).

Although Fields does not discuss law specifically, I would suggest that
legal cases can provide the right, as well as the left, with opportunities to
contest dominant frameworks of meaning. However, the 'success' of this

struggle may be related to how well the case affords access points into other fields (such as media or politics) rather than what is written down for judges in legal submissions. With respect to *Mossop*, it would seem that, with regard to these considerations, the case was perhaps more successful for the gay litigant than for the NCR organizations. For example, Brian Mossop argues that his litigation achieved his prime objective – getting on the radio to talk about sexuality (interview) – while Judy Anderson maintains that the 'radical feminist' media has conspired to deny her an opportunity to speak on the matter at all (interview).

In analysing the 'success' of the three organizations studied here, there is little indication that REAL Women, for example, is gaining political ground. While the organization has made friends in the Conservative party, activists' language has, at times, been 'too extreme,' too hateful, for the organization to make much impact upon the 'liberal centre' (see also chapter 4). Judy Anderson quite rightly noted that RW spokeswomen often sound foolish and 'hysterical' when quoted in the media.[28]

The election of Anderson to the presidency signalled, perhaps, an attempt by REAL Women to soften its tone and change its image. Anderson is a full-time teacher, married to a divorced man, primary income provider for her family, with children in day care (interview). While she firmly believes in the 'radical feminist' conspiracy, she is somewhat sensitive to the position of lesbians and gay men, 'has gay friends,' believes gay teachers should have job protection, and expresses no wish to 'gay bash.' Thus, as I argued in chapter 4, were REAL Women to substitute its language of homosexual disease and depravity for the more muted and popular tones of, for example, rights rhetoric, they might have more communicative success.

Focus on the Family Association is an organization likely to play an important, but behind-the-scenes, role in NCR Canadian activity. Focus is, perhaps, too American, and, again, too 'over the top,' for it to be a public NCR leader in its own right. On the other hand, during battles over telecommunications licensing and the portrayal of lesbians and gay men in public broadcasting, Focus did play an important role.[29] The success of Focus on the Family may depend in part on its ability to appear 'pro-family,' while disguising its fundamental religious theology. The creation of the Legal Defence Fund may assist in this.

And, what of the Salvation Army? I have previously suggested that the Army found itself in a paradoxical position vis-à-vis the *Mossop* case. On the one hand, while they oppose homosexuality on biblical grounds and believe in the ultimate necessity of saving souls for Jesus, Salvationists, to a large extent, do not support the NCR agenda of organizations like Focus and REAL Women. Yet, they appeared in this intervention as primary funders and legal directors. Don Hutchinson was clearly uncomfortable with this role; he insisted that the coalition did not signal the Army's intention to join forces with Focus and REAL Women in the long term.

One of the things we have made quite clear is that this association or coalition is strictly for the purposes of intervention in this case, it is not a long-term arrangement ... The Salvation Army assesses its involvement with these matters on a case by case basis. We do not tend to throw our hat into the ring with coalitions that operate on a long-term basis. Principally because it's very important to us that we have some degree of control over what words are put into our mouth, and prefer to speak for ourselves. (interview)

The Salvation Army would appear to be a weak link in this particular NCR chain. The leadership is clearly uncomfortable both with their own involvement with some of the other organizations and with how this will be publicly perceived by those who support and appreciate the Army's work in other areas. Again, their continued role in similar struggles may depend on the extent to which their participation is invisible – a 'solution' that would seem to render the participation itself questionable.

In Canada, for the moment, it would seem worthwhile to consider NCR politics, neither awarding it more attention than it deserves, nor dismissing it as the absurd ravings of 'religious fanatics.' Rather, opposing activists should perhaps be informed about this movement, its history and practices, examining the, perhaps unnecessary, 'self-policing' responses they make to it. It might also be useful to consider adopting a strategy of the U.S. anti-NCR organization, People for the American Way (PAW).[30] That group has waged several successful campaigns exploiting the 'liberal consensus' in the United States. PAW has actively sought to publicize the *internal* documents, speeches, and so on of NCR organizations and leaders, thereby revealing the underlying 'politics of Armageddon' behind NCR public expressions.

A strategy such as this (used in part, for example, by the Coalition For Gay Rights in Ontario during Bill 7) is appropriate only for certain political climates; the presence of a 'liberal consensus' which would find NCR religion extreme, dangerous, and alienating must be apparent. However, in North America, we do seem to live in such a climate today;

indeed, this is recognized by the NCR itself, and PAW's campaigns have tended to be well received. Thus, progressive movements might consider such an approach, particularly in cases like *Mossop*, where the content of NCR legal submissions in lesbian/gay equality cases is as far removed from NCR sexual politics as NCR sexual politics is from the sexual politics of the 'general population.'

We must also remember, however, that 'the general consensus' can always change. There are enough historical examples of societies that quickly dispensed with concepts of equality and justice to prescribe and enforce hierarchies of race, religion, and so on. Knowing the beliefs and goals of conservative Christians may make some of us more appreciative of liberalism – this is not an unimportant point. At the same time, one ought not to lose sight of the ways in which the 'liberal centre' is susceptible to pressure from the right, and from the left.

Concluding Remarks

It is, perhaps, worth stating what has so far been implicit: the NCR and its opponents (feminists, lesbians, gay men, socialists, etc.) share similar yet irreconcilable views of their social worlds. Each believes the other (or some 'other') controls society's major institutions. They share a fear and distrust of the other, and each vilifies the other in internal communication. We each perceive our adversaries as constituting a networked, formidable obstacle to social transformation. To varying degrees, we have also linked 'the state' to our opponents' agenda. For example, left-wing academics have long suggested that judges have a conservative agenda and decide cases based on the values and politics of the privileged classes from which they are drawn. Interestingly, this is a view echoed by REAL Women. They argue that 'the ultimate decision of the courts has a great deal to do with the judge's own personal perspective of life and society ... the Supreme Court of Canada ... is in fact imposing a liberal interpretation of the Charter on our country.'[31] Thus, only the 'liberal centre' insists on maintaining notions about law's neutrality, or judicial impartiality.

How can these two very different 'right' and 'left' interpretations be reconciled? There seems little doubt that Judy Anderson, Don Hutchinson, and Jim Sclater express a 'reality' in saying that conservative Christian theology is at present not given mainstream social credibility as a source of knowledge and action. Similarly, feminist perspectives which challenge notions of gender and seek to question compulsory heterosexuality are also marginalized. REAL Women's 'radical feminist' might be labelled by others a 'liberal feminist,' and, perhaps, part of a 'liberal feminist conspiracy.' Nevertheless, feminist groups probably *do* receive more public funding than do conservative Christian groups; Brian Mossop *does* perceive himself to have had access to and success with the media, and Judy Anderson claims neither (interviews); the movement for lesbian and gay legal equality *has* made enormous strides within the last ten years. And, yet, as I have already indicated, the NCR has had its impact, although, perhaps, in Canada, not as great – yet.

The arguments I have put forward also suggest a complex and contradictory understanding of the role of 'the state,' and the concept of 'power.' For example, Brian Mossop, employed by the federal Treasury Department, could, in one sense, be seen to be making a claim against and a demand from 'the state.' Yet, the situation is somewhat more complicated than this. The *Mossop* case has seen one statutorily created, government-appointed body (the human rights tribunal) order a government ministry (Mossop's employer) to officially recognize a gay male couple as 'family'; another government-appointed agency (the Federal Court of Appeal) overturned this decision; yet another, the Supreme Court, also found against Mossop but did so in terms more sympathetic to his claim (see chapter 7). And, upon this terrain, opposing social movements struggle for interpretive authority.

Within contemporary struggles around sexuality, lesbian and gay movements and the New Christian Right each perceives 'the other' to 'have power.' Yet, the *Mossop* case, and I include the litigation's effects well beyond the confines of strict 'legal processes,' reveals the ways in which power has shifted between liberal professionals (the tribunal adjudicator and the Court Challenges administrators), conservative and liberal judges, Conservative politicians, and the irreconcilable movements of diverse social actors.[32]

I am not here subscribing to liberal pluralist theory; nevertheless, the relation between social movements, legal processes, and 'state' agents is a complicated one. For example, I have suggested that the dominance of liberal equality discourse in Canada, and the gradual 'success' of lesbian and gay movements for inclusion within its terms, has made it correspondingly difficult for right-wing movements to publicly express *virulent* homophobia. Rather than vilifying 'homosexuals,' New Christian Right activists have focused their public rhetoric around child-welfare and general 'family' principles. Interestingly, this has led to a 'new' social phenomenon – the need to defend and justify heterosexual marriage, a task inconceivable in an earlier period of homosexual pathologization. It is thus arguable that cases such as *Mossop*, regardless of outcome or possible negative effects, may succeed in putting heterosexuality on the defensive, or, at least, into question, and that liberal equality's seeming ability to accommodate 'lesbian and gay' subjects has facilitated this process.

Finally, while the New Christian Right may not be able to mobilize a massive constituency, or play a crucial role in the 'making' of political power, it is nevertheless important to avoid underemphasizing the power Christian religion continues to exercise within the lives of many people. In the fight for lesbian and gay liberation particularly, the conservative Christian tradition poses a formidable obstacle.

7

Judges and Experts

In previous chapters, I addressed several issues concerning the relationship between social movements and law reform. I deliberately avoided prioritizing what goes on 'in court' and, instead, explored how diverse texts, actors, strategies, and politics affect this engagement. Indeed, I have suggested that the outcome of particular cases, and the content of judicial utterances, are often not the most important elements in law-reform struggles. However, I now wish to consider the role and politics of judges and experts within litigation – a site where many legal analyses often begin (and end). I am concerned with pursuing two related questions. What is the role of 'experts' within litigation? Why do judges reach the decisions they do?

The ability of non-legal 'experts' to influence legal outcomes is an important issue for those concerned with achieving social change through litigation. In legal theory, the question of whether law is even open to such 'colonization' is a contested one. Yet, 'other' knowledges have had an impact on the development of lesbian and gay rights case law.

In considering the role of 'experts' in these cases, I argue that the judicial response to their intervention is ambiguous at best. While some judges are willing to embrace a sociological analysis of the issue before them, others maintain that only legal doctrine is capable of resolving the problem. At a deeper level, however, I suggest that these approaches are types of discursive strategies – that judges reach the decisions they do not because they have experienced courtroom conversions but because of the *sexual politics* they bring to the adjudication process.

The Role of 'Experts'

Those seeking both to advance and thwart social change through law reform have historically made use of 'expert' knowledges (Kargon 1986). Often, as I noted in previous chapters, this has involved the appropriation of professional discourses by social movements seeking to convince and persuade others. Within litigation, however, the 'expert witness,' a person who is deemed sufficiently knowledgeable by the court to give 'opinions' (and not simply recount 'what they saw') is the only authority permitted to expound on professional matters.

Many writers have analysed the difficulties encountered by professional 'experts,' most focusing upon the tensions to do with 'role negotiation' (e.g., scholar versus advocate).[1] For feminists and others, a more important concern has been the ability to communicate effectively the complexity of their politics within legal forums. For example, Alice Kessler-Harris, a feminist historian, has written of her experience as an 'expert witness' in the *Sears* case,[2] compelled, given the adversarial proceeding, to adopt a rigid analysis to which she did not fully subscribe.

One intuits the difference between working in a library and participating in a courtroom drama, but until one has experienced it, the disjunction between the two remains abstract. Accustomed to developing the subtle distinctions of an argument, to negotiating about fine points of interpretation, the historian quickly discovers that thesis skills must be abandoned in testifying. Maintaining a position is as important as the position taken. Consistency is not merely a virtue but evidence of one's expertise ... I got my first taste of the clear distinction made by the legal profession between learning the truth and constructing a case; between understanding and persuading. And there, I also learned for the first time, that precisely what I as a historian cared most about would surely destroy my testimony if I pursued it. My job, I was told, was to answer all questions, but to provide no more information than was demanded ... Any attempt I made to introduce controversy, disagreement and analysis merely revealed that history was an uncertain tool and invalidated both its findings and my conclusions ... I found myself constructing a rebuttal in which subtlety and nuance were omitted, and in which evidence was marshalled to make a point while complexities and exceptions vanished from sight. (1987, 61–2)

Kessler-Harris expressed 'surprise' at how the lawyer for Sears often did not challenge the substance of her testimony but, rather, the language in which it was phrased – a tactic that resulted in her comments being presented as absurd or extreme. The structure of 'yes' or 'no' answers also complicated her ability to respond: 'I was nevertheless astonished at how easy it was, within the yes or no format demanded by the court, to agree with statements simply because I could not deny them, not because they represented my understanding of the issues involved' (ibid, 64).

Margrit Eichler also confesses to having rather ambivalent feelings about her part in Canadian lesbian and gay rights cases: '[It is] very difficult for someone who defines herself as a scholar, in the sense of being involved in trying to generate knowledge, not just taking what's there and teaching it, to be put into a situation where you're under oath and where the attempt is to make scholarly research serve a purpose for which it was not created ... that's the basic problem' (interview). Eichler's evaluation of the different cases in which she was involved is mixed. The *Andrews* litigation,[3] for example, was not a 'pleasant' experience for her; she recalls that Andrews's lawyers insisted upon maintaining complete control over questioning and legal strategy. Eichler felt like 'a slot machine, different buttons are being pushed, if someone pushes the wrong button there's very little you can do about it' (interview). As I have discussed elsewhere,[4] Eichler was 'pushed' into making several statements that did not reflect the complexities of her analytical approach to 'family.'

On the other hand, Brian Mossop's counsel (lawyers with the Canadian Human Rights Commission) 'took the time' to listen, and responded positively to Eichler's suggestions for reorienting their legal argument (Eichler interview). Eichler believes her contribution is far more valuable if she is allowed to formulate the questions lawyers will ask her in direct examination. The assumptions underlying courtroom questions, and legal actors' unwillingness to admit them, are, for Eichler, the key obstacle to a successful 'expert' intervention. In her view, the ideal 'expert' contribution is, perhaps, a written paper or report, rather than oral testimony made to appear absurd or ridiculous during questioning from lawyers on *both* sides.[5]

In many cases, then, the 'expert' witness is thus prevented from displaying the full breadth of knowledge she or he possesses. Certain perspectives are excluded (by lawyers, legal conventions, and so on) from the legal process, often prior to judges even hearing the case. What, however, happens to the 'expert' evidence that is presented to the court?

Judges and Experts

Lawyers present 'expert' evidence to judicial forums for several reasons. In part, the production of an 'expert witness' has become a historical convention – each side must have at least one or risk being considered incompetent. Indeed, the federal government's failure to present an 'expert' in *Mossop* was partially responsible for the NCR deciding that the Attorney General's Office lacked the necessary commitment to defend the case (see chapter 6). Primarily, however, 'expert' evidence is offered to convince, persuade, and educate decision makers (Chesler, Sanders, and Kalmuss 1988). In this way, legal forums often become complex battlegrounds between opposing experts and their respective 'knowledges.' Judges respond to these interventions in different ways.

Knodel (1991)

In this case, a gay man sought to have his health benefits extended to his partner and the legal battle was over whether the 'opposite sex' definition of 'spouse' in the governing legislation infringed section 15 of the Charter. The judge concluded that it did, and ordered that same-sex couples be included within the legislation's definition of 'spouse.'

During the hearing of the case, Knodel's lawyer presented to the court the report of an 'expert' psychiatrist. Michael Myers, 'clinical professor of psychiatry at the University of British Columbia,' concluded that homosexuality was innate and attributable to an 'abnormality in brain differentiation of the developing fetus.' 'Homosexuals,' Myers argued, had 'no control' over their sexual proclivities. The psychiatrist also defined homosexuality for the court and stated its statistical incidence in 'Western culture.' He further presented a 'psychological portrait' of the homosexual (not dissimilar to the one painted of 'Black children' in the *Brown* civil rights litigation nearly forty years earlier; see chapter 2), based on the concept of 'stigma.'

By the time of puberty, most of these individuals, who have felt 'different' as children, begin to experience strong feelings of attraction to members of their own sex. They have no control over these feelings – they are not a deliberate choice. For most of them, this is very frightening and lonely, because they have come to believe that what they are experiencing is not considered normal by most of society. This then leads to isolation, unhappiness, self-loathing, and a sense of inferiority. I have listened to the life stories of hundreds of homosexual men and women and I can attest to the pervasive influence of discriminatory ideas, beliefs, and laws on the sense of these individuals. This indifferent or hostile climate not only damages one's worthiness but causes many people to lead double or fragmented lives. They dare not be open for fear of further ridicule and rejection. Many attempt to pass as heterosexual people and do their best to conform. When they meet someone else, fall in love, and become a couple, they are usually much happier and find it easier to cope with life. (pp. 364–5)

According to Myers, Knodel and his partner were just this type of happy couple. Adopting the analysis of Margrit Eichler (the sociologist figuring prominently in the *Mossop* litigation), the psychiatrist listed several factors 'proving' that the two men were a couple 'no different from' heterosexual ones, and that together they constituted a 'family.'

In setting out the evidence, Rowles, the B.C. Supreme Court justice hearing the case, reproduced several passages from Myers's report at length. Her decision, however, was not based at all on the psychiatrist's definition of homosexuality, or even on his evidence of the harm caused by 'stigma.' Instead, in her resolution of the dispute Rowles referred only to Myers' analysis of the two men as a 'family,' an understanding he acknowledged was borrowed from sociology. Clearly, the psychiatric evidence played some role within Rowles's text, if only as a sign of her sympathy with 'poor unfortunates.' There is, however, little indication that Rowles was persuaded, educated, or informed by the 'expert' intervention.

Andrews (1988)

Despite having a rather conservative litigation strategy, the lawyers acting on behalf of Karen Andrews' claim for 'family' health benefits presented several 'alternative' knowledge sources to the court. No psychiatric evidence was offered; instead, 'expert' contributions were solicited from three sociologists, two of whom had written extensively on lesbian and gay issues.

These latter two, Barry Adam and Mariana Valverde, discussed, in their affidavits, historical persecution and the formation of sexual identities, respectively.[6] Each scholar attempted, within the limits set by Andrews's attorneys, to offer the court elements of a 'social constructionist' approach to sexuality (see chapter 2); however, the primary paradigm they each employed was the 'minority' one (see chapter 3). Valverde's affidavit noted arguments for the immutability of homosexuality; however, she chose neither to reject nor to endorse such perspectives (nor did she offer a 'choice' analysis). While both these 'expert' interventions sought to inject some alternative perspectives from feminist and lesbian and gay studies, their overriding effect was to suggest that lesbians and gay men were a fixed minority deserving of legal equality.

Margrit Eichler, who submitted an affidavit and testified in court, argued on behalf of a 'functional definition' of family (later adopted by the tribunal in *Mossop*), and stated that Karen Andrews's relationship met the criteria for this. Offering the perspective adopted by Myers in *Knodel*, Eichler argued that Karen Andrews and her partner displayed qualities 'similar to' those exhibited by heterosexual 'spouses.'

In deciding Andrews's action, McCrae chose to ignore *all* the 'expert' interventions. From the judgment, one would not even know that he had been presented with this evidence. The *Andrews* decision refers only to the authority of dictionaries; sociology is deemed so irrelevant as to be unworthy of mention. Thus, despite the manner in which Adam and Valverde 'liberalized' their analyses,[7] and despite Eichler's attempts to offer a 'modern' family analysis to the court, these 'experts' would appear to have played little or no role in the judge's resolution of the complaint.

Mossop *(1989, 1990)*

In *Mossop* (1989), one of the first steps taken by the tribunal adjudicator in her decision was to establish the authority of the 'expert witness,' Margrit Eichler, upon whose testimony the tribunal judgment rests. While 'expert's' qualifications are often briefly reviewed in reasons for judgment, here Eichler's academic and professional history was given in great detail. The reader is informed not only that Eichler holds a doctorate in sociology and is a 'full' professor at the Ontario Institute for Studies in Education, but also that she holds two cross-appointments, has received 'numerous research and development grants,' and 'has published extensively' (4.4).[8] We also learn she has written the only existing textbook on 'families' in Canada, and that she provides consulting services to a host of public and private bodies (4.4).

The tribunal adjudicator, Mary-Elizabeth Atcheson, then incorporated Eichler's perspective on family within her opinion. She began by establishing a lack of 'standard definition' and 'consensus' with respect to the 'evolving' concept of family (4.7, 4.5). She went on to search for sources of meaning, finding the parliamentary record of little assistance as the minister responsible at the time simply commented on what the concept 'should mean, or might mean, as opposed to what it did mean' (4.56). Atcheson's response to the attorney general's argument that 'the' meaning was 'generally understood' was that counsel adduced no evidence to support this contention and, further, that general understandings may be discriminatory and therefore not a valid source of meaning (4.59). The adjudicator also noted that law did not always reflect the reality of people's lives; simply because a relationship had not been heretofore recognized in law did not mean it should not be now (4.61). Atcheson further attempted to minimize the relevance of current legal provision specifically based on 'opposite sex' relations (4.61).

The adjudicator concluded that the term 'family status' was 'not clear and unambiguous.' Dictionary definitions, she added, may be reasonably consistent, but they are broad, and often include non-marital and non-biological relationships (4.63). The tribunal, Atcheson argued, did not need to select 'the' 'all-inclusive meaning,' but only 'a' 'reasonable' meaning, one that *'best accords with the Act'* (4.67; emphasis in original).

Her final act of interpretation in this process was to find that the term 'reasonable' was itself fluid, and hence 'impossible of measurement' (4.70). She then put aside any formal 'test of reasonableness.'

As a practical matter, the Tribunal agrees with the Complainant that terms should not be confined to their historical roots, but must be tested in today's world, against an understanding of how people are living and how language reflects reality. Dr. Eichler's evidence, as well as that of the Complainant, was helpful in making these assessments. Value judgments should play no part in this process because they may operate to favour a view of the world as it might be preferred over the world as it is. (4.70)

Atcheson's dilemma could be interpreted as that of the progressive liberal, faced with a case where the 'law as it was' did not 'go the way' that she wanted (see Kennedy 1987). She must, therefore, develop a strategy that allows her to ignore the range of prior cases and legislative provisions that clearly did *not* help Brian Mossop.[9] In the process, she articulated a broad liberal ideology that allowed her to side-step what had heretofore stood as 'precedent' on the subject of homosexuality. There was little basis 'in law' for her decision – she must actively create new law *and rely on other sources of knowledge* to support her finding of discrimination.

Atcheson saw the tribunal's task as one of performing 'value-free' adjudication, not imposing any conception of 'the good life' upon litigants (4.70). The tribunal's society is a pluralist one, where the role of adjudicators is to protect the minority from 'majoritarian' tyranny. No one group should have the power to impose its morality on others: all people are equal and are owed equal rights and benefits.[10]

However, within this paradigm the 'same-sex couple' is seen as *equal to* or *the same as* the heterosexual couple. Heterosexuality remains unchallenged as the unproblematic norm. The tribunal adopted a 'same as' approach to counter the usual 'different from' analysis exhibited in earlier cases on sexual orientation. Atcheson recognized that these 'sameness' principles are what had animated Canadian liberal human rights law in the 1980s. However, these principles had not yet been extended to the legal treatment of homosexuality. It was this failure of law, both judge-made and statutory (with some exceptions), that compelled the tribunal to rely on the insights of sociology. Throughout Atcheson's decision, she underscored the *compatibility* of law and sociology. 'The evidence of Dr. Eichler was that the term does not have one definition for all purposes. Sociology and law appear to be similar in this regard' (4.65).

In contrast, the Federal Court of Appeal, in judicially reviewing the tribunal decision, made every effort to distance law from sociology. 'Status,' Marceau stated, was a 'legal concept' (p. 674). The 'functional definition given by the sociological approach' was 'ad hoc' and not 'acceptable' (ibid). Marceau misrepresented the sociology of which he was critical, arguing that the 'functional approach' had simply taken 'some attributes usually ascribed to families' as being 'the essence of the concept itself being signified.' Eichler, on the other hand, had specifically maintained that family could not be reduced to an 'essence.'

At times, the court's approach is quite derisive. Although the tribunal had decided that Mossop and his lover constituted 'sociologically speaking a sort of family,' the court held that *no* approach 'other than the legal one' could lead to a proper understanding of what is meant by the phrase 'family status' (ibid). 'Family,' Marceau continued, did not have a meaning 'so uncertain, unclear and equivocal' that it could not be defined (p. 673). The word signified a 'basic concept' that had 'always been' (673). Non-biological formations had been rendered 'normal' through marriage and other legal mechanisms, but these did not affect the 'core meaning' of the word (ibid). Marceau described other meanings as 'peripheral,' 'residual ... analogical uses' (ibid).

Family, according to Marceau, was not a 'fluid term' (p. 674). As noted above, the 'sociological approach' had missed the 'essence of the concept' (ibid). There was, for the court, a 'generally understood meaning to the word family' (p. 675). This last point was legitimated through the judicial strategy of 'common-sense knowledge.' Phrases such as 'generally seen', 'no one would want,' or 'generally understood' (pp. 673–5) were employed to persuade the reader of the 'normalcy' of the judge's views.[11] This contrasted sharply with the tribunal's explicit critique of such understandings as being potentially discriminatory. The court then concluded its discussion of the meaning of 'family status' by arguing that the 'real issue underlying the complaint' was 'sexual orientation' (p. 675). Sexual orientation was not a protected ground in the CHRA at the time of Mossop's complaint, and it was not for the court to make it so. The 'real issue' was thus disposed of.

Marceau went on, however, to consider the applicability of the Charter – despite Charter arguments not having been made before the court. He argued that, although sexual orientation might be an analogous ground under section 15, the Charter could not be used as a 'legislative amendment machine' to be read into human rights legislation (676). According to Marceau, only Parliament could legislate the inclusion of sexual orientation in the Canadian Human Rights Act (pp. 675–8). Stone, in his concurring judgment in the case, stressed that he would have considered Charter arguments seriously if they had been raised.

For the tribunal, then, the 'real issue' or subject of the complaint began and ended with the meaning of 'family.' The question to be decided was whether or not Mossop and his partner constituted a 'family.' If so, they were clearly being discriminated against on 'family status' grounds as their 'kind of family' (as Marceau later put it) was being denied a benefit given to others. Once having determined they were a family 'sociologically speaking,' there was little else to adjudicate (other than to diffuse the attorney general's arguments). The tribunal was clearly not concerned with 'homosexuality' per se, but only with its manifestation in a category called 'same-sex couple.' In fact, the entire tribunal judgment functions to render *sexuality* itself invisible.

On the other hand, the judges of the Federal Court of Appeal refused to allow this. Their subject was indeed 'the homosexual,' who, according to their interpretation, was the 'real issue' missed by the tribunal. Marceau insisted that 'sexual orientation' lay at the root of the complaint; his strategy of conservative judicial restraint allowed him to maintain the status quo of exclusion.

For the most part, Marceau and his colleagues refrained from making obviously 'partisan' arguments, such as those expressed by McCrae in *Andrews*. As I noted above, McCrae based his finding that a 'homosexual partner' could not be a 'spouse' on the 'fact' that homosexuals were unable to marry and procreate (*Andrews*, p. 16, 193). He argued that the government's definition of 'spouse' was related to the important objective of 'establishing and maintaining traditional families' (ibid, p. 16, 194). In *Mossop*, Marceau is never quite this explicit, although these views are certainly implied within his search for the meaning of 'family' (see also Layland 1993). When the *Mossop* case reached the Supreme Court of Canada, however, the judges shied away from this sort of discourse.

Mossop *(1993)*

The majority decision of the Supreme Court of Canada (SCC) in *Mossop* adds little to the reasoning of Marceau at the Federal Court of Appeal. The distinction, if any, is in form, rather than substance. While Marceau embedded his conservative legal approach within an implicitly conservative sexual politics, the Chief Justice, writing for the majority, chose to couch his within a somewhat more liberal discourse.

Following Marceau, Chief Justice Lamer insisted that 'sexual orientation' was the 'real' issue underlying the complaint, and that Parliament had clearly not intended the 'family status' ground to provide sexual orientation protection. The Court, Lamer argued, could only, in this case, provide a 'statutory interpretation'; this litigation was not the place to determine whether lesbians and gay couples *should* receive equal employment benefits, nor was it open for the court to subject the Canadian Human Rights Act to Charter scrutiny (as this had not been argued before them). The majority did, however, hint that a different result might have been reached with a Charter analysis.

The SCC judgment was short and, in principle, the judges took an 'original intent' approach to their interpretive task. Parliament did not intend, when enacting the relevant provisions, to protect lesbians and gay men from discrimination. It was not for the Court (in the absence of a Charter challenge) to construe legislative terms in ways contrary to manifest parliamentary intention.

The sociological evidence reviewed by the two courts below was ignored. In fact, there was almost no discussion of what 'family' *meant*; the issue that concerned the parties and intervenors was virtually invisible in the majority judgment. Perhaps the most revealing aspect of Lamer's opinion is his insistence that 'sexual orientation' was the 'real' issue at stake. 'While, with respect, I am not in agreement with all of Marceau JA's judgment, I believe that he correctly identified the relationship which exists between sexual orientation and the discrimination at issue in this case ... [quoting Marceau] "in the final analysis, sexual orientation is really the ground of discrimination involved ..."'

The Court, by closing off 'family'-related grounds, is ensuring that lesbians and gay men claim under the 'sexual orientation' ground and no other; the discrimination faced by lesbians and gay men is, according to the Supreme Court, solely the result of this orientation, and, by implication, not attributable to wider relations of gender and family.[12] Lesbians and gay men, in order to receive section 15 protection, will be forced to claim that protection by invoking the analogous ground of 'sexual orientation' and hence their history of 'disadvantage.' This may effectively enshrine such claims within a 'minority paradigm' (see chapter 3) and render more difficult an action which actually sought to challenge, for example, the social legitimacy of marriage.

The dissenting judgment in *Mossop* (1993), written by L'Heureux-Dubé and concurred in, for the most part, by Cory and McLaughlin, is, I think, of greater interest and, perhaps, long-term significance. In effect, L'Heureux-Dubé adopts the tribunal's reasoning with more depth, contextual analysis, and referencing. Her judgment also illustrates better the questions I pose in this chapter – to do with the role of experts and the relationship between legal and other forms of knowledge.

In contrast to the majority, the dissent explicitly adopts a 'living tree' approach to their decision making in this area. 'Courts have recognized that statutory interpretation is not such a strict science, and that there are situations where it may be less appropriate to speak of "the correct answer" and more appropriate to speak about ranges of acceptable answers.' In clear disagreement with Marceau at the Federal Court of Appeal, L'Heureux-Dubé advocates for greater appreciation of the specific skills and knowledge possessed by human rights adjudicators. While her argument relates to a jurisdictional issue I am not pursuing here,[13] L'Heureux-Dubé's analysis of this question indicates an approach less formalistic and more open to the entry of non-legal discourses.

This is most evident in her discussion of the meanings of 'family.' L'Heureux-Dubé, in contrast to Marceau and the older line of cases relying on dictionary definitions, questions the so-called plain meaning of 'family' which, she argues, is merely an 'unexamined consensus.' She then proceeds to draw upon a wide range of feminist, lesbian, and other literatures to argue that law must shift to take account of 'the lived experience of family' and that 'non-traditional family forms may equally advance true family values.'

While many of her sources are 'legal' ones, others are not. For example, L'Heureux-Dubé quotes both Audre Lorde and Adrienne Rich – two lesbian feminist theorists whose work articulates a radical sexual politics.[14] Her reliance upon the factum submitted by EGALE et al. (the coalition of progressive *Mossop* intervenors) is also apparent (see chapters 2 and 4). She uses it to challenge the appropriateness of 'functional' family definitions and to argue for an 'intersectionality' approach to analysing the relationship between different grounds of discrimination. The factum, in turn, relied upon the work of several feminist writers to make these and other points (see Duclos 1993; Gavigan 1993). That L'Heureux-Dubé could take two other Supreme Court justices with her in validating this knowledge is also significant.[15]

Mossop's final Supreme Court disposition, then, perhaps gives little comfort to social conservatives. With the possible exception of brief comments made by La Forest (with Iacobucci concurring),[16] none of the judges supported in principle a 'heterosexuals only' definition of family. And the 'procreation' discourse of conservative judges (see, for example, *North* and *Layland*) was nowhere in evidence. Indeed, the majority explicitly left the Charter gate open, and the dissenting judges seem to have signalled their intentions when faced with such a challenge in the future.

In the Afterword, I consider how the *Mossop* litigation has shifted dominant understandings of 'family.' For now, I wish to continue on the themes of this chapter by considering the relationship between 'experts,' judges, and judicial decision making.

Judges, Experts, and the Politics of Judging

Chesler, Sanders, and Kalmuss (1988, 204–5) have suggested that lawyers present 'expert' opinion in order to 'convert' judges through a process of education. Their research, based on a study of American school-desegregation litigation, is somewhat inconclusive. Some judges did report having been 'converted,' while others used social science evidence to legitimate the imposition of activist remedies (ibid, 208–16).

While 'expert' evidence may have educational and reforming effects in some cases, this model of change rests upon the assumption that judges really are the 'neutral arbiters' of liberal discourse, and that, with 'correct' information, they will reach 'right' decisions.[17] Several writers have argued, and I would agree, that in the majority of cases judges bring to court the politics and vested interests that will lead them to certain decisions and not others.[18] Expert witnesses will provide evidence legitimizing these decisions, but are unlikely to cause much judicial 'conversion.' In *Mossop*, for example, the tribunal adjudicator was a feminist lawyer – one of the founders of the feminist legal action group LEAF (see also Atcheson et al. 1984). While feminist credentials by no means guarantee a pro–gay rights stance, the two do, often, go together.[19] Marceau, on the other hand, was a Federal Court justice with a history of conservative decision making. Two years prior to *Mossop*, he had dissented in an opinion giving rights to unmarried heterosexual couples (*Re Schaap* 1988). In *Mossop* at the Supreme Court, the two women members of the Court were in dissent.

In lesbian and gay rights cases, what judges 'know' about homosexuality is less a consequence of 'expert' courtroom interventions, and more the result of the sexual politics they bring to the decision-making process – a politics informed by their social location and experience, as well as any or all of several other sources, including religion, psychiatry, biology, feminism, and sociology. Indeed, one possible interpretation of current lesbian and gay rights litigation is to view these cases as struggles between the new liberal professionals (who may also be élite participants in social movements), often holding positions within the legal process somewhat low in the hierarchy (such as human rights adjudicators), and the higher courts, still largely dominated by White, middle-class, conservative men. The current tensions in Canadian lesbian and gay rights jurisprudence often reflect the entry of judges who do not conform to some aspects of the traditional judicial stereotype. Should 'out' lesbians and gay men come to be selected for judicial appointment, perhaps they will bring to case-law development another 'new,' local knowledge.

All this is not to say that judges are 'free' to come to any decision they want. The restrictions of precedent, appellate review, legal technicalities, and a host of other factors play an important role. The legitimacy of law depends, to a large extent, on the practice of *stare decisis*, the adherence to past decisions as legal 'truths.' Even when judges are extremely keen to overturn precedent with which they do not politically agree, there are strong cautionary compulsions. In the summer of 1992, the U.S. Supreme Court refused to completely overturn the *Roe* abortion rights decision, despite most of the justices having been selected for appointment on the basis that they would do so.

The *Brown* case (noted in chapter 2) is another such example, where the judge, despite his obvious sympathy with the gay litigants, felt unable, in light of binding precedent, to offer them a remedy. Although the plaintiffs were denied relief, Coultas's sympathy with them, and his implicit condemnation of the moralistic conservatism of the Social Credit government, was apparent.

The history of western civilisation records that, from biblical times to our own, homosexuals have been subjected to discrimination because of their sexual orientation. As with other forms of discrimination, it is unjust for it fails to take into account individual merit, character or accomplishment. The form and extent of it is uglier, the cry more shrill since the onset of AIDS. I accept that those who suffer HIV or AIDS, often very ill, are discriminated against and persecuted in various subtle ways, and some not so subtle at all. (*Brown*, p. 309)

The comments of the B.C. Minister of Health were characterized as 'unnecessary, inflammatory, and reflecting ignorance of the disease that one would not expect' (*Brown*, 311).

Coultas's concluding comments perhaps exemplified the best that liberal law had to offer: 'I have found that the funding policy does not contravene the law. Nevertheless, I recognize that AIDS is one of the great tragedies of our age. It behoves those in private life and in government whose actions affect the well-being of those suffering the disease to act decently, fairly, compassionately' (ibid, 322). Coultas gives the impression here of someone who feels their hands are tied by the wording and existing interpretations of the Charter. His decision is thus more obviously an example of how judges are constrained than is the tribunal ruling in *Mossop* where Atcheson felt free to make new law.

The politics of judges, and the constraints within which these politics can be expressed, is the key to understanding why they reach the decisions they do. However, it is also important to draw attention to the ways in which judges and other legal actors disqualify alternative accounts and interpretations (Smart 1989), and also the hierarchy of 'expert' knowledges acknowledged by 'law.' By stating that sociology is 'not law,' the Federal Court of Appeal in *Mossop* both excluded sociology from being a valid source of knowledge *and* further created and solidified what was law itself. I noted in chapter 5 that New Christian Right activists partly constitute their own identity through the vilification of 'others.' Similarly, law and its judges maintain their integrity partly through 'knowing' *what* is *not* law and *who* are *not* legal 'experts.'

Nevertheless, Margrit Eichler's prominence within Canadian lesbian and gay rights cases reveals the extent to which sociological analyses have supplanted psychiatric understandings in the formation of legal knowledge about homosexuality. While conservative judges continue to emphasize the 'reproductive function' of 'traditional families,' even they are now unwilling to engage in public discussions of homosexuality's 'causes' and 'effects.' Instead, conservative judges simply rely upon well-established precedent denying rights to lesbians and gay men, while liberal judges, on the other hand, deploy sociological analyses in their attempts to make the law respond to 'new realities.' Legal discourse, once 'knowing' homosexuality only through the lenses of religion and conservative medicine, has slowly been influenced by 'new' ways of understanding social relations. L'Heureux-Dubé's dissent in *Mossop* is a clear indication of this.

Concluding Remarks

In analysing the role of 'other' knowledges within legal discourse, it may be useful to consider the relative advantages of different epistemological paradigms. For example, sociology's increasing influence within legal constructions of homosexuality is, on the whole, I would argue, something to be cautiously welcomed. As a discipline, sociology is ostensibly concerned with social relations, group interactions, and structural dynamics, and hence less focused on individual pathologies. As several cases thus far demonstrate, adjudicators have deployed sociological analyses to show the historical discrimination and prejudice lesbians and gay men have faced. In this way, the harm, and even the 'illness,' is seen to lie within society, and not 'the homosexual.' Within such an approach, lesbians and gay men are viewed as a legitimate collectivity struggling for justice within a social-conflict paradigm, and not as 'poor unfortunates.' The lesbian or gay 'subject' of sociology is thus, potentially, an empowered, contextualized one.

Furthermore, sociology's potential to explain sexuality (and law) in terms which recognize its contingent and constructed character is witnessed by the fact that many oppositional writers have found a home in the discipline. In several of the cases I have described above, the 'experts' appearing in favour of lesbian and gay rights were feminist and gay scholars, many of whom had been active themselves within social-movement struggles. These appearances are, on first glance, a positive development. If we want public institutions to take oppositional analyses seriously, then we must surely welcome the increased prestige, status, and credibility that attach to the work of such scholars as a result of their entry into legal arenas. This is particularly true where 'new' scholarship is informed by marginalized voices, ones emerging from the local experience and analyses of subordinated groups.

At the same time, there are also troubling effects to these kinds of developments. In chapter 1, for example, I discussed my own ambivalence around the role of 'lesbian legal theorist,' and in other chapters I have questioned whether lesbian and gay rights movements need or want 'spokespeople' and considered issues to do with co-optation, institutionalization, and deradicalization. Furthermore, in this chapter I have argued that 'expert' evidence seldom convinces legal forums of anything, and thus that we perhaps need to think more critically about the *purpose* of these interventions.

It is also important to note that 'sociology' is not a monolithic, uniform approach to understanding social relations. On the contrary, there are many different kinds of sociology; as Barry Adam has himself noted (1986), much *mainstream* sociology (e.g., standard introductory textbooks) remains largely conservative in its approach to homosexuality. In *Vogel*, a 1992 trial court decision in Manitoba, the provincial government presented to the court its own 'sociological expert' who argued, in contrast to Margrit Eichler (appearing again), that lesbian and gay households were *not* 'families.' According to Dr Lyle Larson,

... it has been established by social science scholars that the universal family may be defined as 'a kinship group normatively defined to carry out the nurturant socialization of dependent children ... the basic thing about a family is that it involved children. It involves children. It always involves children ... The basic characteristic of [marriage is] that it involves a male and a female and that involves the potential for the eligibility for procreation. (testimony cited in *Vogel* 1992)

In adopting this definition, the judge in *Vogel* implicitly accepted that lesbians and gay men did not and could not have children, and, presumably, that 'infertile' heterosexuals could never form families either. The judge and his expert went even farther, declaring that 'a majority of social scientists and a majority of society do not as yet approve of homosexual relationships in the context of marriage or as a vehicle for raising children.'

Vogel shows that 'sociology,' like psychology, biology, and other 'expert knowledges,' has its conservative side, and its entry into legal constructions of gay rights will not always be uniformly positive.[20] Furthermore, I have also indicated, in cases such as *Mossop* and *Andrews*, that oppositional analyses of sexuality may be watered down in order to be judicially palatable. Nevertheless, sociology can potentially turn law's gaze away from 'individual pathologies,' sympathetic or hostile, and towards the 'ills of society.' It is the efforts of lesbian and gay rights activists, litigants, lawyers, and supporters, however, that have enabled these epistemological and other struggles to take place.

8

Afterword: *Mossop* and Beyond

For radical gays or lesbian feminists, one test of the 'merits' of lesbian and gay rights reform might be whether such activities lead to the overthrow, or at least the destabilisation, of heterosexuality's claim to 'normalcy.' When I began asking the questions that led to my writing this book, providing some kind of response to this 'test' was part of my motivation. In most of these pages, however, I have suggested that we cannot predict with any certainty the effects our actions will have. For example, long-term consequences often contradict short-term gains; engagements between opposing social movements may produce unexpected results; particular, perhaps temporary, configurations of power enable or constrain possibilities; and the ways in which social identities and practices are shaped by inclusion within certain kinds of legal regimes can never be anticipated fully.

Nevertheless, in this afterword, I wish to reflect upon what has come before, and suggest some possible ways of thinking about the challenge posed to heterosexuality by struggles for lesbian and gay rights. I do this by examining the potential effects of lesbian and gay rights reform upon a concept at the heart of many law-reform campaigns and epitomized by the *Mossop* litigation: *family*. In previous chapters, I have discussed the relationship between law reform and social-movement mobilization; I have also considered when and how a radical sexual politics can be publicly communicated during legal struggle. Here, while I pick up some of these points, I am more concerned with shifts in the meanings of concepts themselves, and the effects those shifts have upon broader ideologies and practices. By this I mean, did the dominant understandings of 'family' change through the struggles of lesbians and gay men to be included within its terms? Did these struggles entrench or undermine dominant paradigms? Or, are these questions posed too starkly; is it even possible to make such an assessment?

In several chapters, I argued that legal cases, such as Brian Mossop's, had indeed succeeded in destabilizing conventional definitions of 'family'. Lesbians and gay men, by insisting that our relationships were as valid as heterosexual units and as entitled to be described by the politically meaningful word 'family,' had contributed to a social climate in which it was possible to talk about non-traditional family configurations. As a result, conservatives were on the defensive, forced to rationalize what had previously been taken as inevitable, and 'natural.'

Brian Mossop and Ken Popert's claim for 'family status' helped to open up for discussion the meanings and purposes of one of society's most fundamental concepts. Their legal challenge was explicitly directed at shifting the dominant understandings of 'family,' thus rendering the heterosexual unit less able to claim superiority. Other similar claims, to 'spousal' pension or health benefits for example, raise the kinds of concrete issues sometimes marginalized by more abstract human rights struggles. Demands perceived to implicate the distribution of 'real' benefits and resources are often far more controversial than adding 'sexual orientation' to a pre-existing list within legislation widely recognized as ineffective anyway.

At the same time, however, there are those who would argue, as I have done previously (Herman 1990), that the 'family' model is itself conservative, and exclusionary. By adopting the qualities perceived to be held by the idealized heterosexual family, lesbians and gay men simply reinforce and affirm this idealization. If, as many feminists argue (see, for example, Barrett and McIntosh 1982), this dominant familial ideology is a key ingredient in the subordination of women, then such a strategy by lesbians and gay men is fundamentally antithetical to 'women's' interests. In this sense, then, the meaning of 'family' has not really shifted; rather, it has simply, as I argued with respect to the concept 'minority,' been extended to include certain 'approved of' relationships within lesbian and gay communities. In the process, the dominance of 'coupledom,' and the qualities such couples exhibit that are akin to traditional marriage, are affirmed (see also Smart 1984). Marriage, and its foundation – heterosexuality – are not very bothered.

One argument against this interpretation can, however, be drawn from the work of Judith Butler (1990). She has suggested that all sexual identities are 'performances.' For example, gay drag, she argues, is a parody. But this copy has no 'original'; in fact, '"the original" is revealed to be a copy, and an inevitably failed one, an ideal that no one *can* embody' (ibid, 139). The process of *performance* 'troubles' the 'naturalness' of sexual / gender categories by revealing them to be what they are – constructed, and inherently unstable.

Perhaps, then, the legal recognition of lesbian and gay families does not so much approve a mimicking of the idealized 'norm' as 'trouble' the norm itself. Certainly, the vociferous opposition of conservatives to lesbian and gay familial claims might suggest this. One of the key 'secular' arguments made by conservative Christians against the legal recognition of lesbian and gay families is that children will not be given appropriate gender role models. Children, if they have two mothers or two fathers, rather than one of each, will grow up confused about their gender role in life.[1] The implication of this argument is that the official affirmation of lesbian and gay families may thus contribute to the deconstruction of gender itself. For activists and theorists who actually desire such a result, lesbian and gay family claims may be just the thing to help achieve it.

Furthermore, although I have previously suggested that human rights challenges tend to entrench the public / private divide by locating the source of problems in the state or 'public' realms and leaving the site of 'family' unaddressed (chapter 4), it is also possible to view lesbian and gay family challenges as transcending this dichotomy. Brian Mossop's claim, for example, centred on work-related discrimination; however, in disputing the employer's benefits policy, Mossop and Popert also effectively highlighted 'the family' as an area of contestation. I think that there is much to be said for these more generous interpretations (see also Weston 1991), however, at the same time, the problematic effects of lesbian and gay family rights remain.[2]

Despite the destabilization of the traditional family, it remains the case that uncoupled lesbians and gay men, or those whose relationships do not fulfil the 'functions' of sociological definitions (see chapters 2 and 7), are excluded from the group seeking inclusion. As many feminist theorists have advocated, entitlement to social benefits should not be based on the degree of intimacy attained with a 'significant other.' Rather, the privileging of marriage can be challenged by policies which, for example, allow individuals to designate a person, any person, as a co-recipient or beneficiary (see Gavigan 1993). This would avoid the need to 'prove' relationships were 'familial'; it would also remove from judges the power to issue authoritative definitions in such cases.

I would suggest again, however, that this is, perhaps, a 'next stage' rather than an alternative strategy. The official acknowledgement that lesbians and gay men form important, positive, useful personal relationships may need to precede rights or entitlements being offered on a different basis. Furthermore, in such areas as immigration law, for example, it is difficult to envision alternative standards coming into play in the near future. Nevertheless, the rights claims of lesbians and gay men, by undermining the dominance of traditional family forms, assists in creating a climate where this might be possible.

Concluding Remarks

One question somewhat beyond the scope of this book is the relationship between the lesbian and gay rights movement and other social movements on the left struggling for social change. I believe that the undermining of heterosexuality, and eventually the deconstruction of gender itself,[3] is a necessary part of any larger project of social transformation. I have argued, however, that lesbian and gay rights reforms may not achieve this, or may do so partially and with ambiguous side-effects. At the same time, not all such reforms inevitably challenge other sets of social relations, such as those based on economic class or race. On the contrary, these hierarchies are reproduced within lesbian and gay communities.

I would suggest that there is no necessary link between rights for lesbians and gay men and the transformation of social relations not premised upon sexuality. Rather, I would agree with Laclau and Mouffe (1985) that diverse social movements must build 'chains of articulation' – create mechanisms and processes whereby the 'other' is identified *with*, and the interests of individual groups are seen to be shared by all. For lesbians and gay men, this means moving beyond 'interest group' politics. Lesbian and gay struggle, in legal arenas and elsewhere, ought to be broad, encompassing, and inclusive. Individuals are made up of complex identities, some often contradictory. When we argue for rights as a fixed 'minority,' claiming that we were 'born this way,' we simultaneously imply that our demands 'stop here.'

In interviewing lesbians and gay men for this book, I was struck by how most seemed not to have thought about how they would ideally want sexuality to be organized. Although 'the future' can be neither planned nor predicted, it may be useful to encourage debate around values and visions (see also Weeks 1991, 183). For example, do we want the freedom to live out our 'selves' within existing frameworks of social relations? Or, are we fighting for substantial shifts in these relations themselves?

The 'lesbian and gay rights problematic,' I would argue, must involve questions about underlying political analyses and about the power relations that shape the terms of equality. More often than not, rights-claims are neither inherently radical rearticulations nor dangerous and diversionary; occasionally, they may be both. To say that rights are difficult, complicated tools for social change does not mean that the struggle for their acquisition is doomed or that 'real issues' are being obscured. At the same time, an unreflexive seeking of rights and yet more rights may not bring about the changes to social relations many of us would like to see.

Notes

Chapter 1

1 Broad studies of lesbian and gay movements are found in Adam 1987; Altman 1982; Cruikshank 1992; D'Emilio 1983; Faderman 1991; Kinsman 1987; Weeks 1977, 1981, 1985.
2 When using the phrase 'lesbian and gay rights movement,' I refer to a loose coalition of rights-campaigning groups and individuals. The lesbian and gay rights movement is, itself, part of a broader 'lesbian and gay movement.' My concern is with the former. Much of the sociology of social-movements literature is concerned with defining and delimiting the substance and activities of social movements themselves – such an inquiry is not the focus of this book. See, generally, Handler 1978; Zald and McCarthy 1987; Touraine 1985; Melucci 1989; Offe 1985. See Epstein 1990 and Plotke 1990 for a critique of 'new movement' theory.
3 Jefferson 1985; Harvard Law Review 1989; Mohr 1988; Tatchell 1992.
4 Lynch 1982; Kinsman 1987; Eaton 1991.
5 I use the word 'ideology' to mean a framework of meaning within which social relations are understood.
6 This book owes a great deal to past and present research into Canadian lesbian and gay legal issues. See, for example, Arnup 1984, 1989; Bruner 1985; Coffey 1986; Eaton 1991; Faulkner 1991; Gavigan 1993; Girard 1986, 1987; Green 1987; Gross 1986; Jefferson 1985; Leopold and King 1985; McIntosh 1988; Rayside 1988; Richstone and Russell 1981; Ryder 1990; Stychin 1993b.
7 The sources I rely on here include Butler 1990; Lorde 1984; Mackinnon 1983, 1987; Rich 1981; and Weeks 1985, 1991. This is by no means a comprehensive list. A full discussion of what a radical 'left' sexual politics 'looks like' is not the topic of this book. While the analyses I bring to the issues stand on their

own, the reader should note that my approach is premised on the relative 'correctness' of the statement to which this note applies. It is not necessary, however, to agree with me in order to find the analyses helpful. Note that, in chapter 5, I give an account of a radical *right-wing* sexual politics.

8 See Bumiller 1988, drawing on Foucault 1976 and Gordon 1980.

9 I am indebted to many writers for their analyses of legal ideology, institutions, and discourse. See Bakan 1990, 1991; Boyd 1989, 1991; Fudge 1987, 1989; Gavigan 1986, 1987; Glasbeek and Mandel 1984; Hunt 1985; Kline 1992; Mandel 1989; Smart 1984, 1989; Sumner 1979.

10 For an analysis of one such 'takeover' in Britain, see Cooper 1994b.

11 For a fuller discussion of this topic see Herman 1993b.

12 This is true for any academic writer. On research reflexivity, see Atkinson 1990 and Woolgar 1988.

13 Sandra Harding 1986, 1991; Harstock 1983; Smith 1987.

14 See Herman 1993b, chapter 1 and appendices, for a fuller discussion.

Chapter 2

1 Ross 1990.

2 The early work of Mary McIntosh ([1968] 1981) paved the ground for many subsequent theoretical developments. Michel Foucault (1976) is, perhaps, most often associated with articulating this 'social constructionist' perspective. Other sources in which this approach is developed include D'Emilio 1983; Faderman 1991; Kinsman 1987; Mort 1987; Weeks 1977, 1981; and the collection edited by Ken Plummer (1981). See also, however, the debates in Stein 1990.

3 For a brief review of this history see Tarnopolsky 1979.

4 For discussion of the Damien case and its political role within lesbian and gay communities, see Jackson and Persky 1982; Hofsess 1987; Kinsman 1987.

5 For a discussion of the legal issues see Richstone and Russell 1981.

6 The applicability of the 'sex' ground to a gay newspaper seems to have been accepted and was not in dispute.

7 In the late 1980s, Chris Vogel relaunched a similar case only to have both the human rights adjudicator and a lower court judge refuse to consider it (*Vogel* 1992); see also chapter 7.

8 'Statement of the principles, structure, program and strategy of the Coalition for Gay Rights in Ontario (CGRO),' ratified at the founding conference in Toronto, 18 and 19 January 1975, and revised at the Steering Committee of the Coalition in Ottawa, 31 July and 1 August 1976, Gay Archives of Canada.

9 Ibid.
10 Ibid.
11 Ibid.
12 CGRO, Brief to Ontario Legislature, March 1978, Gay Archives.
13 Ibid, 3.
14 Ibid, 4–5. The brief went on to describe a history of religious and other persecution of homosexuals, concluding with examples of present-day discrimination in Canada. The CGRO concluded by listing various groups, municipalities, and other organizations that had publicly supported the campaign for human rights.
15 In 1979, Michael Lynch wrote in *The Body Politic* that, despite the failure of the various bills, the campaigns themselves had achieved great successes. Indeed, he argued that winning human rights amendments should no longer even be on the movement's agenda; see Jackson and Persky 1982, 244. I return to these ideas in subsequent chapters where I problematize notions of 'success' and 'failure.'
16 As I noted in chapter 1, this book is about only one branch of the lesbian and gay movement. During the period I am discussing here, other lesbians and gay men were active in struggles that had little to do with reforming human rights laws. See, for example, Creet 1990; Davies 1988; Jackson and Persky 1982; Kinsman 1987; Weir and Steiger 1981; Stone 1991; the documents of the Revolutionary Marxist Group, Gay Archives of Canada; and the publications *The Body Politic*, *Broadside*, and *Fireweed*, for example.
17 At the same time, and in order to pacify Conservative back-benchers, a proposal was made to amend the act to include a definition of 'marital status' intended to exclude lesbians and gay men from claiming under this ground.
18 Further discussions of this case are found in chapters 4, 6, and 7. Here I am simply setting it out for what follows.
19 Recall that this act did not contain a 'sexual orientation' ground.
20 For example, *North* 1974; *Vogel* 1983.
21 For example, Lorde 1984.
22 See chapter 7 and Herman 1991 for further discussion of these decisions.
23 See, for example, the furore over the possible implications of the *Leshner* decision in P. Small and M. Maychak, 'Gay ruling on benefits seen costing "millions,"' *Toronto Star*, 2 September 1992. The Charter can also play an important role in redefining concepts employed in other regulatory regimes; see discussions in chapters 4 and 6.
24 See *Brown* 1990; *Knodel* 1991; *Haig* 1992; *Egan* 1991, 1993.
25 *Haig* 1992.

26 This was not without protest from several provincial governments.
27 In chapter 4, I explore the 'politics of rights.' Some of this discussion concerns issues involving the supremacy of Parliament, democracy, and judicial power. The 'politics of entrenched constitutions' is, however, not a primary focus of this book. In Canada, there is a large legal literature concerned with this question. For critical approaches see Bakan 1990, 1991; Glasbeek and Mandel 1984; Knopff and Morton 1992; Mandel 1989.
28 See, for example, the discussion of the *Klippert* case in Kinsman 1987; see also Freedman 1989. Psychiatric constructions of 'dangerousness' have shaped the content of legislation and case law generally; see Menzies 1986.
29 See discussion of liberal psychology in Kitzinger 1987.
30 See Gross 1986; Leopold and King 1985. For a critical approach to liberal 'expertise' see Cooper and Herman 1991.
31 A key enunciator of this form of psychology is Dr Richard Green (1988, 1992); in the United States he has appeared as an expert witness in several gay rights cases. See also Eve Sedgwick's critique (1991); Kitzinger 1987; and chapter 7.
32 The latter argues, for example that Black parents 'choose' to live in Black neighbourhoods for entirely 'rational' reasons (e.g., they want to be near other Black families), and not because institutional racism prevented the exercise of real choice.

Chapter 3

1 The previous autumn, Gigantes had introduced an unsuccessful private member's Bill to achieve the same purpose.
2 My focus is upon the CGRO. For a discussion of the RTPC (not re Bill 7) see, for example, McCaskell 1988.
3 Coalition for Gay Rights in Ontario, CGRO Brief Support Group, Minutes, 23 April 1986, Gay Archives of Canada.
4 See comments of Attorney General Ian Scott, *Canadian Press*, 6 May 1986.
5 David Rayside (1988), an academic active in the CGRO at the time seems to suggest that the CGRO deliberately chose to conduct a quiet, non-confrontational campaign, and did not actively seek to mobilize lesbian and gay communities around the amendment. Chris Bearchell, another Bill 7 CGRO activist, disagrees, and argues that large numbers of lesbians and gay men were mobilized by the CGRO across the province (interview). I discuss this further below.
6 See chapters 5 and 6 for full consideration of this movement.
7 In 1985, a federal all-party committee had recommended the inclusion of sexual orientation in the Canadian Human Rights Act, and had agreed that sec-

tion 15 of the Charter protected lesbians and gay men by way of analogy. See *Equality for All*, Report of the Federal Equality Committee, 1985.

8 REAL Women, formed in 1984, is dedicated to overturning what they perceive to be the successful 'anti-woman' initiatives of the Canadian women's movement. The National Citizens' Coalition is a neoconservative lobby group, backed by wealthy individuals and corporations. REAL Women is discussed further in chapters 5 and 6.

9 For example, the REAL Women 'sexual orientation' pamphlet, discussed further in chapter 5, was widely distributed. See also Coalition for Family Values, Open Letter to Fellow Ontarians from Rev. Hilsden, 4 October 1986, Gay Archives of Canada.

10 See, for example, Brief of the Evangelical Fellowship of Canada on Homosexual Legislation: An Evangelical Response,' July 1986, Gay Archives of Canada. See chapter 6 for a consideration of the process whereby conservative Christian beliefs are translated into legal language.

11 See, for example, S. Oziewicz, 'Ontario Liberals divided over homosexual rights legislation,' *The Globe and Mail*, 18 October 1986.

12 Endorsements were also sought and obtained from a variety of organizations, including the Ontario Federation of Labour, the Canadian Auto Worker's Union, the Ontario Secondary School Teachers' Federation, the National Action Committee on the Status of Women, the Women's Legal Education and Action Fund, and the United Church of Canada.

13 The personal support of Liberal Whip Joan Smith is evident from CGRO documents. She was in regular contact with the CGRO and, together with Scott and Peterson, was instrumental in ensuring the amendment's passage. See CGRO, Steering Committee Meeting, 20–1 September 1986, Appendix 16, *Spokesperson's Report re Bill 7*, Gay Archives of Canada.

14 See, for example, J. McLeod, 'Bill banning anti-gay bias "powder keg,"' *The Toronto Sun*, (10 October 1986; P. Comeau, 'Gay rights bill tests Grit will,' *The Toronto Sun*, 5 November 1986; C. Cornacchia, 'Planned bill to protect gays is in trouble, churchman says,' *The Globe and Mail*, 3 November 1986).

15 'Rights and Sexuality,' *The Globe and Mail*, 19 November 1986. See also, 'Of homosexuals and discrimination,' *The Toronto Star*, 15 November1986.

16 See, for example, S. Oziewicz, 'Tory MPPs assail bill banning homosexual bias,' *The Globe and Mail*, 27 November 1986.

17 Equality Rights Statute Law Amendment Act, 1986, S.O. 1986, c.64. Some provisions relating to disability were not declared at that time.

18 For a review of this history see chapter 2.

19 See Handler 1978; Jenkins and Eckert 1986; Simon 1982; Staggenborg 1988. Piven and Cloward (1977) argue formal structures are depoliticizing,

although other research suggests this is not an 'iron' rule. See also Morris 1984.

20 It is worth noting, again, that other CGRO activists may assess the campaign rather differently.

21 See, for example, *Hunter* 1984; *Big M Drug Mart* 1985; *Morin* 1985; *Singh* 1985; *Edwards Books* 1986; *Oakes* 1986.

22 Mandel and Glasbeek (1984) argue that the Charter has fostered a depoliticization of social struggle through the reification of abstract rights. See also Mandel 1989; Glasbeek 1989a; Fudge and Glasbeek 1992. I discuss these ideas further in chapter 4.

23 In keeping with these developments, the Supreme Court of Canada endorsed, during this period, a 'living tree' approach to interpreting human rights code legislation, which, the judges pronounced, was a 'special case' of law standing above other regulatory regimes. See, for example, *O'Malley* 1985; *Bhinder* 1985; subsequent decisions reiterated this approach, including *Action Travail* 1987 and *Robichaud* 1987.

24 This ground featured in the *Mossop* litigation where federal human rights legislation contained no 'sexual orientation' provision.

25 Witness George Bush's struggle around the 1990 Civil Rights Act in the United States.

26 *Discrimination Against Lesbians and Gay Men: The Ontario Human Rights Omission, A brief to the Ontario Legislature, Coalition for Gay Rights in Ontario, October 1986*, 5.

27 Ibid, 8.

28 This last factor is often noted by marxist Charter critics who argue that the Charter functions as an instrument of class rule.

29 CGRO brief, 5.

30 See also Johnstone, Ontario Hansard, 26 November 1986, 3670.

31 See, respectively, Ontario Hansard: 1 December 1986, 3790; 2 December 1986, 3838 and 3856; 1 December 1986, 3805; 2 December 1986, 3842 and 3853.

32 Susan Fish, one of four sympathetic Tory MPPs to vote in favour, did so explicitly: Ontario Hansard, 1 December 1986, 3806–7. Liberal MPP Caplan, for example, referred a number of times to lesbians and gay men as a 'class of persons': Ontario Hansard, 1 December 1986, 3790. Another Liberal, describing himself as a 'psychiatrist and amateur social political philosopher' spoke of his dilemma over attempting to resolve the question of 'homosexual causation': Henderson, Ontario Hansard, 26 November 1986, 3676.

33 See, for example, McKessock, Ontario Hansard, 25 November 1986, 3629; Bernier, ibid, 3634; Haggerty, ibid, 3639; Runciman, ibid, 3673; Hennessy, ibid,

3678; Villeneuve, ibid, 26 November 1986, 3682; Gregory, ibid, 27 November 1986, 3738; Marland, ibid, 3743; Sheppard, ibid, 3748; Pope, ibid, 1 December 3786; McCague, ibid, 3782; Wiseman, ibid, 3797; Leluk, ibid, 2 December 1986, 3835.

34 See in particular: Gregory, Marland, McCague, Leluk, ibid.

35 See particularly *The Toronto Star* columns of Rosemary Spiers: 'Beware! Propaganda at work,' 29 November 1986; 'Grossman shows he's no captive leader,' 3 December 1986; 'Thou shalt not defame others,' 6 December 1986. Also, Editorial: 'Conscience prevails,' 3 December 1986, and previous editorial endorsing amendment: 'Of homosexuals and discrimination,' 15 November 1986.

36 See 'Rights and Sexuality' *The Globe and Mail*, 19 November 1986. Also, opinion column by O. French, 'Society's values weighed,' *The Globe and Mail*, 3 December 1986.

37 E.g., 'Unreasonable act,' *The Toronto Sun*, 3 December 1986.

38 Particularly in the *The Toronto Sun*, see for example: J. McLeod, 'Bill banning anti-gay bias "powder keg,"' 10 October 1986; L. Goldstein, 'Group raises new adoption fears,' 3 December 1986.

39 See previous discussion; also M. Maychak, 'Emotions ran high as lobbyists swamped Queen's Park,' *The Toronto Star*, 3 December 1986.

40 See above. The hegemony of liberal ideology is further demonstrated in action taken by the Ontario Conference of Catholic Bishops following the amendment's passage. A member of the Coalition for Family Values, the Conference later insisted that it did not approve the CFV's press releases, had not supported the organization financially, and were in favour of 'basic human rights.' See M. McAteer, 'Catholic bishops deny launching campaign against homosexuals,' *The Toronto Star*, 4 December 1986; R. Spiers, 'Thou shalt not defame others,' *The Toronto Star*, 6 December 1986.

41 I am not suggesting that none of these people were lesbian or gay, but that they were not speaking 'as' lesbians or gay men.

42 Some activists were quoted in the press the day after the amendment's passage, see M. Maychak, 'MPPs vote to give homosexuals protection from discrimination,' *The Toronto Star*, 3 December 1986; G. Drummie, 'Victory for "dignity" applauded,' *The Toronto Sun*, 3 December 1986.

43 See also Carole Vance's (1989) discussion of the relationship between lesbian and gay movements and notions of immutability. The relevance or appropriateness of the concept 'minority' to lesbian and gay identity is a historical debate within the movement – see, for example, Weeks 1985, 95–201, and Kinsman, 1987, 90–3, for different views. Here, I am focusing upon how human rights law compels its adoption, despite this debate. See chapter 8 for further discussion.

44 I continue this point in the conclusion to this chapter.

45 See *Discrimination Against Lesbians and Gay Men: The Ontario Human Rights Omission, A Brief to the Ontario Legislature*, Coalition For Gay Rights in Ontario, October 1986.

46 Ibid, 16.

47 This was a point stressed by Ontario Attorney General Ian Scott in the aftermath of the amendment's passage.

48 However, one could also argue that the legitimacy of lesbian and gay equality in the 'public sphere' has long-term effects on 'private' relations; for example, by contributing to the production of a 'new' consciousness on the part of parents. See my comments in the Afterword.

49 The more recent advent of AIDS and Queer Nation activisms has shifted this somewhat.

50 E.g., D. Harrington, 'Rights watchdog fails racial groups director admits,' *The Toronto Star*, 14 September 1985. See also Frideres and Reeves 1989; Iyer 1993.

51 Re sex discrimination, see Coté and Lemonde 1988; Mossman and Jai 1979; Réaume 1979; Backhouse 1981.

52 See Habermas's (1987a, 290–3) critique of Foucault.

53 See Ontario Human Rights Commission, *Annual Reports*.

54 CGRO Brief, 8.

55 See, respectively, Ontario Hansard: 25 November 1986, 3619; 26 November 1986, 3669; 1 December 1986, 3788, 3804; 2 December 1986, 3838, 3849, 3856. See, also, Cicchino, Deming, and Nicholson (1991) for a discussion of a similar process in an American campaign.

56 L. Hurst, 'Courts the place to fight for rights homosexuals told,' *The Toronto Star*, 13 December 1986.

57 For a discussion of the role of 'symbolic politics', see Elder and Cobb 1983; Edelman 1988.

58 Quoted in M. Maychak, 'MPPs vote to give homosexuals protection from discrimination,' *The Toronto Star*, 3 December 1986.

59 Quoted in L. Hurst, 'Homosexuals see rights bill as key to new benefits,' *The Toronto Star*, 6 December 1986.

60 See his comments quoted in L. Goldstein, 'Group raises new adoption fears,' *The Toronto Sun*, 3 December 1986; L. Hurst, 'Courts the place to fight for rights homosexuals told' *The Toronto Star*, 13 December 1986.

61 The history of systemic and institutionalized racism in Canada has been well documented in hundreds of sources which I cannot do justice to here. A very broad sweep, in relation to the development of human rights law, is given by Anand 1985.

62 See, for example, the Bill 7 coverage in *Rites* 3/8 (1987), including comments by CGRO activists Bearchell and LaChance.

63 For one such attempt, see the factum of EGALE et al. in *Mossop* (at the Supreme Court of Canada). Further discussion in chapters 6 and 7.

Chapter 4

1 See chapter 2 for a description of this case.

2 Freeman 1982; Fudge 1987, 1989; Fudge and Glasbeek 1992; Gabel 1984; Glasbeek 1989a, 1989b; Kingdom 1991; Mandel 1989; Smart 1989; Tushnet 1984.

3 Hunt 1990; Matsuda 1987; Minow 1990; Schneider 1986; P. Williams 1987; R. Williams 1987.

4 For a critical review of much of this literature, see Bartholomew and Hunt 1990.

5 For example, a *Toronto Sun* columnist asserted the rights of families and social agencies, likening the amendment to laws curtailing individual rights in a wide range of areas (including anti-smoking by-laws). The amendment is viewed as one more assault on individual freedom by a pandering, overly interventionist state. See J. McLeod, 'Gay way is 'ok' ... so there!,' *The Toronto Sun*, 14 October 1986. Another editorial lamented the amendment's impact upon employers' and landlords' rights: see 'Sober look needed before Bill passed,' *Niagara Falls Review*, 9 October 1986.

6 Some 'critics' are speaking about only constitutional rights when discussing abstraction. However, this is not always made clear.

7 See comments by the following during debate: Haggerty, Ontario Hansard, 25 November 1986, 3639; Villeneuve, Ibid, 26 November 1986, 3682; Gregory, ibid, 27 November 1986, 3738; McCague, ibid, 1 December 1986, 3792; Leluk, ibid, 3835.

8 See Bernier, Ontario Hansard, 25 November 1986, 3634; Johnson, ibid, 26 November 1986, 3642; Hennessy, ibid, 3678; Partington, ibid, 3684; Barlow, ibid, 3688; Marland, ibid, 27 November 1986, 3743; Sheppard, ibid, 3748.

9 See, for example, Brief of the Evangelical Fellowship of Canada on Homosexual Legislation: An Evangelical Response, July 1986, Gay Archives. Interestingly, it could be argued that this process helped to legitimize the pre-existing Code protections, despite the likelihood of right-wing objections to human rights regimes generally (see chapters 5 and 6). For a fuller exposition of this conservative position, see T. Marco, 'Oppressed Minority, or Counterfeits,' *Focus on the Family Citizen* 6/4 (20 April 1992).

10 Abortion is Alan Hunt's (1990) example; however, it may be an inappropriate one from which to draw broad conclusions. Elizabeth Kingdom (1991) notes

the specificity of this example, although much of her book nevertheless seems to generalize from it.

11 See discussion of the *GATE* case in chapter 2.

12 See comments in conclusion to chapter 2.

13 See CGRO brief and issues of *The Body Politic* and *Rites*.

14 I have, however, previously discussed the dangers of presenting just such a view to the press and public, see chapter 3. It seems to me that these two points are different.

15 Interview. Brodsky further discusses access to justice issues in Brodsky and Day 1989.

16 Similar processes appear to have taken place elsewhere, see, for example, the *Pandora Magazine* litigation as described by Anne Derrick at the National Association of Women and the Law conference, Vancouver, 20 February 1993.

17 Becki Ross (1990) has written about her feelings, sitting in the Ontario legislature, day after day, like I did. She, too, had no illusions about the ability of the Code amendment to effect major social change; however, her experience of 'house sitting' had a significant impact upon her view of the bill.

18 See Scheingold 1974. Hunt argues that his conception of rights is not the neutral one advanced by Scheingold.

19 See comments of Susan Fish and Yuri Shymko, *Canadian Press*, 1 December 1986.

20 Minow 1990, 297. Elsewhere in her book, Minow clearly implies that many powerful 'decision makers' are well-intentioned people doing their best to resolve 'the dilemma of difference' (ibid, 44–7). All that is needed to overcome inequality is for judges to *understand* the experience of 'others' – hence, Minow's relatively uncritical perspective on rights, which, in her view, facilitate such understandings.

21 This struggle also can be seen to have exacerbated a division between urban and rural communities, strengthening each against each other.

22 It could also be argued that the Charter, and perceptions of its 'misuse by special interest groups,' has resulted in the delegitimising of human rights codes as these are increasingly identified with the 'new selfish rights seekers.'

23 See also my discussion of 'standpoint epistemology' in chapter 1.

24 For example, MPPs received far more phone calls, letters, and petitions from CFV supporters than from those in favour of the amendment.

25 For example, analyses found in the work of Lorde (1984); Mackinnon (1983); Rich (1981); Weeks (1985, 1991); and in movement publications such as *The Body Politic*, *Rites*, *Broadside*.

26 See Gwen Brodsky's comments earlier in this chapter.

27 See *In Re Kowalski*, 1991. Remember, also, the comments of Evelyn Gigantes during the Bill 7 debate: 'There is no task that I have undertaken that has made me feel more radical than this one': Ontario Hansard, 25 November 1986, 3629.

28 See Bakan 1991; Glasbeek and Mandel 1984; Glasbeek 1989a; Fudge and Glasbeek 1992; Mandel 1989.

29 As I explain in chapter 6, however, the New Christian Right would vehemently disagree with this statement. They argue the courts are controlled by socialist feminist gay rights advocates. For further discussion of the relationship between class analyses and sexuality see Herman 1993a.

30 Open letter from CFV to Fellow Ontarians, 4 October 1986, Gay Archives of Canada.

31 Taylor and Condit (1988) have shown how religious conservatives used equality discourse to their advantage in battles over the teaching of evolution in schools. See also Kaplan's study (1989) of Jehovah Witness struggles for civil rights.

32 See also my discussion of 'family' in chapter 8.

Chapter 5

1 From Dobson and Bauer 1991, 223.

2 E.g., Dubinsky 1985; Luker 1984; Ginsburg 1984; De Hart 1991; Petchesky 1984, 245. But see Erwin 1988b and Klatch 1987.

3 McKessock, Ontario Hansard, 25 November 1986, 3629. See also Haggerty, ibid, 3640; Johnson, 26 November 1986, 3668; Runciman, ibid, 3673; Davis, ibid, 3682; Barlow, ibid, 3689; Pope, 1 December 1986, 3787; McCague, ibid, 3795; Wiseman, ibid, 3798; Leluk, 2 December 1986, 3836; Taylor, ibid, 3841. Note that all of these politicians explicitly relied upon 'Christian morals' and/or discussed the dangers of 'secularization.'

   There is reason to believe that *atheism* is an important factor leading people to *support* lesbian and gay equality (Bibby 1987, 155).

4 Other than Lorna Erwin (1988a, 1988b), whose research I draw upon greatly, one of the few other sources on the Canadian NCR is Haiven's (1984) journalistic account. Barrett (1987) and Robin (1992) have written on the 'extreme' right in Canada, a movement also very much shaped by a sense of religious destiny, but one I do not consider here.

5 A 1985 study revealed that, while Canadian's overall disapproval of premarital sex stands at 22 per cent, conservative Christians disapprove at a rate of 61 per cent. Similarly, the figures for homosexuality disapproval are, compara-

tively, 70 per cent and 89 per cent. Additionally, 73 per cent of conservatives are 'uneasy' at the thought of meeting a lesbian or gay man, compared with 62 per cent of the national population. In all areas, those individuals profess-ing agnostic or atheist positions were by far the *least* disapproving, see Bibby 1987.

6 However, they are considerably less *concerned* about poverty, unemployment, etc., listing drugs and pornography near the top of their 'social concerns agenda': Bibby 1987.

7 Within the sociology of religion literature, a distinction is sometimes made between 'evangelicals' and 'fundamentalists': see Ammerman 1991. This dis-tinction is not important for my purposes, and I use the word 'evangelical' to mean proselytizing or missionary.

8 One of the distinguishing characteristics of this movement, what partly makes it, perhaps, 'new,' has been the forging of a Christian alliance between Protestants and Catholics. Given the historical anti-Catholicism of conserva-tive Protestantism, however, this has not been without conflict, see Wilcox and Gomez 1989–90.

9 See also Chandler 1984; Lienesch 1982. Chandler discusses how certain Truths are selected for observance, and others ignored.

10 Chandler 1984; Diamond 1989. There is some disagreement over whether Christians will reign for 1,000 years before or after the Second Coming. The majority of North American conservative Christians are pre-millennialists, meaning they believe that Christ will return first. This eschatology (belief about how the world will end) is known as dispensationalism.

11 12,000 for each of the 12 tribes of Israel: see Revelations 7:4–8.

12 This version is put forth by Hal Lindsey in his book *Late Great Planet Earth* which has sold more than 18 million copies; see Bruce 1990, 87.

13 I cannot here trace the history of the NCR's emergence, nor explain its organi-zation and structure. Two comprehensive accounts, which offer different assessments, are found in Bruce 1990 and Diamond 1989. The edited collec-tion of Liebman and Wuthnow (1983) is also useful, as is Allen Hunter's pre-scient analysis (1981). Jerome Himmelstein's (1990) book is more analytical than some others, and also considers the 'new right' as a whole.

14 See Bruce 1990; Chandler 1984; Diamond 1989; Hunter 1981; Jorstad 1987; Lienesch 1982. Needless to say, NCR activists might choose to describe their political platform using different terminology.

15 The relationship between some of these positions and foundational conser-vative theology is not always clear, indicating both the NCR's absorption of a general New Right agenda, and the distancing of NCR leaders from their constituency. For example, evangelical Christianity has, in the United States,

a large Black following, particularly in the South. Many of the political positions adopted by NCR organizations and their leaders would by no means reflect the beliefs of this religious constituency. An inquiry into the relation between the New Right and the New Christian Right is beyond the scope of this book. While there would be much agreement between the two, areas of conflict include the role of religion in public life and ideas about civil liberties.

16 In chapter 2, I outline the background to this case and in chapter 7 analyse its judgments. Two other organizations intervened with these three: the Evangelical Fellowship of Canada, an umbrella organization to which most of the others belong, and the Pentecostal Assemblies of Canada, an association of Pentecostal churches with a long history in Canada. For reasons of time and space, I have not been able to devote attention to these two.

17 The three other coalition members, however, are harder to place. The Pentecostal Assemblies, the Evangelical Fellowship, and the Salvation Army have long histories, stretching back decades – even to the last century in the case of the Army. Their participation in the *Mossop* litigation can be seen to reflect the new agenda of old evangelical Christianity. Focus on the Family and REAL Women, on the other hand, are organizations with clear links to the New Right generally.

18 The Salvation Army Positional Statements, Canada and Bermuda Territory, 1990.

19 For historical information on the Army see Coutts 1974; Handy 1976; Marks 1992; Valverde 1991. See also Submission of the Salvation Army to the Royal Commission on New Reproductive Technologies, January 1991.

20 Focus on the Family, with Dr James Dobson, Special Introductory Issue, 1990.

21 FFA (U.S.), in addition to maintaining its telecommunications empire, operates the Washington-based Family Research Council, a right-wing think-tank.

22 Books published include *Guiding Your Family in a Misguided World* and *How to Know God's Will*.

23 For example, in 1991 Focus urged the Canadian government to delay ratification of the United Nations Convention on the Rights of the Child as 'parental rights' were not recognized within it: see Letter from J. Sclater to Friends, FFA, 14 June 1991.

24 See, generally, Focus on the Family in Canada: Purpose and Services, Vancouver, 1991.

25 REAL Women is against publicly funded feminism, pornography, liberal divorce laws, equal pay for women, publicly provided universal childcare, and tax policies which are perceived to encourage family breakdown. They are for the family, heterosexuality, marriage, motherhood and homemaking.

See, for example, *Position Papers*, Pamphlet, REAL Women, n.d.; *Who We Are: Brief to the Members of Parliament*, 19 November 1985, REAL Women, Pub. No. 6; *Pornography in Canada*, Pamphlet, REAL Women, n.d.; *Easy Divorce?*, Pamphlet, REAL Women, n.d.; *Equal Pay for UnEqual Work*, Pamphlet, REAL Women, n.d.; *Child Care: Whose Responsibility*, Pamphlet, REAL Women, n.d.; and various issues of REAL Women's newsletter *Reality Up-Date*.

26 *Laws Protecting Homosexuals or so-called "Sexual Orientation" Legislation: How it will affect Canadians*, Pamphlet, REAL Women, 1985.

27 According to Erwin's data (1988b), *all* REAL Women members are Christian. Although the organization claims to have Jewish and Muslim members, all RW respondents to Erwin's survey identified themselves as Christian, and she has found no other evidence to substantiate RW's claim to religious diversity (Erwin, personal communication to author).

28 Anderson, interview. The significance of conservative Christianity in the lives of American anti-feminist women is also noted by Jerome Himmelstein (1986) in his research into anti-ERA campaigns. He concludes that common religious beliefs and networks are what, more than anything else, women share. See also Klatch 1987 and Erwin (1988a, 1988b).

29 There is a fifth theme – that of rights versus responsibilities. I have discussed the politics of rights extensively in chapter 4.

30 Concern for 'the family' is not the sole province of conservative Christians. Other Christians, and many liberals generally, prioritize the family, and define it in various ways. What distinguishes the Christian conservatives are the perceived *threats* to the family, as well as a particularly exclusive definition of the unit; for discussion of conservative and liberal approaches to 'the family' see Cooper and Herman 1991.

31 Letter from J.A. Sclater to Student, FFA, 20 March 1991.

32 The Salvation Army Positional Statements, Canada and Bermuda Territory, 1990, p.18.

33 Ibid, p. 12.

34 *Focus on the Family*, Special Introductory Issue, 1990. See also Dobson 1991.

35 The theologically based NCR prescription for family and gender roles is discussed in Diamond 1989, 104–10; Erwin 1988; Hadden 1983; Hunter 1981, 129–30; Jorstad 1987, 79–80; Klatch 1987; Mathews and De Hart 1990, 163–4 and ch. 8). For a critical discussion of New Right conservative theory on gender see David and Levitas 1988.

36 M. Hodgson, '10 Ways Wives Can Say "I Love You,"' *Focus on the Family*, June 1991, 11.

37 Erwin 1988b. I stress again that these are *not* necessarily the views of conservative Christians generally, just those of the organizational memberships.

38 See also *Reality Up-Date*, November 1984, 5, and the contributions of Laura McArthur and Gwen Landolt, two Canadian anti-feminists, to Rowland 1984. Once again, however, the Salvation Army is somewhat of an 'odd "man" out' in this debate as it tends not to engage directly in prescribing strict gender roles; indeed, the Army has been seen as a religious pioneer in breaking down work-related gender discrimination. See also Marks 1992.

39 *Citizen* 5/9 (16 September 1991).

40 Studies of conservative Christian communities show how women negotiate power, rarely feeling completely 'powerless.' The women emphasize how, while gender roles are necessarily different and rigidly circumscribed, within the religious community neither is necessarily valued more highly than the other. See, for example, Ammerman 1987; Rose 1989; McNamara 1985.

41 *Laws Protecting Homosexuals or So-Called "Sexual Orientation" Legislation: How it will affect Canadians*, Pamphlet, REAL Women, n.d. The spectre of 'homosexual rights' was invoked in similar language by anti-feminist campaigners during the American ERA battles, see Mathews and De Hart 1990, 166–7.

42 The portrayal of the 'corrupt inner city' also has deep racist implications in NCR ideology; see below.

43 I discuss these links further below.

44 See Conservative comments during Bill 7 struggle, chapter 3. See also speech by Lord Halsbury during British parliamentary debate on sexuality, where lesbians are explicitly distinguished from the predatory, diseased 'homosexual': quoted in Cooper and Herman 1991.

45 In the following chapter, I consider more closely the relationship between Christian, and other forms of knowledge.

46 Ibid. Again, the authority for this statement is a publication of the Institute for the Scientific Investigation of Sexuality, see Haylon, n.d., fn.12.

47 See Foucault 1976; Weeks 1981; Mort 1987; Walkowitz 1980; Valverde 1991.

48 Altman 1986; Patton 1985, 1990; Crimp 1988; Sontag 1988; Williamson 1989.

49 Gilman 1985, 1988; Sontag 1988. Interestingly, the recent texts of Focus on the Family, REAL Women, and other similar organizations are *not* AIDS-obsessed. While HIV remains an important symbol of the consequences of homosexual activity, other illnesses, infections, and disease syndromes play an equally important discursive role.

50 See re historical Christian anti-communism: Speer 1984 and Wilcox 1987–8. See re articulation of communism with homosexuality, Edelman 1992; D'Emilio 1989; Faderman 1991, and re homosexuality and antisemitism, Mosse 1985 and Gilman 1985, 1988.

51 In Canada, a central Christian 'devil' has been Henry Morgentaler, the Jewish doctor who pioneered abortion practice and services. He has played the his-

torical role of 'Jewish baby killer,' and his experience as a Holocaust survivor has also played a complex role within anti-choice rhetoric.

52 During the Bill 7 struggle, a Catholic anti-communist organization produced a newsletter identifying homosexuals with communism and the destruction of a 'Christian Canada.' See 'Where Is Canada Heading,' Canadian Society for the Defense of Tradition, Family, and Property (January–February 1987).

53 For discussions see Bruce 1990; Diamond 1989, 84–5; Heinz 1983, 134–5; Jorstad 1987, 28–34. On the role of conspiracy theories generally, see Davis 1971.

54 Dobson and Bauer 1990; see also Dugan 1991. The NCR 'conspiracy' theme has interesting links to the recent (secular) backlash against 'political correctness.'

55 Dobson and Bauer 1990, 115–16. One edition of Focus's political magazine was entirely devoted to media bias during an anti-abortion 'rescue' operation, see *Citizen* 5/11 (18 November 1991).

56 See generally Mosse 1985; Parker et al. 1992; Seidel and Gunther 1988.

57 See, generally, 'How Homosexuals Push Their Agenda,' *Citizen* 5/6 (17 June 1991).

57 This infiltration has occurred ostensibly in a covert manner. Teachers have been the victims of 'desensitisation techniques,'' including being 'exposed to graphic depictions of perverted sexual acts' (Newsletter from Geoffrey Still, president, Focus on the Family, to Friend, April 1991). Thus, the homosexual agenda has even infected teacher training. A newsletter quotes one teacher complaining of 'psychological manipulation' during training classes (ibid). See also Heinz 1983; Rose 1989.

59 Newsletter, Ibid

60 See, for example, B. Mitchell, 'Radicals Intimidate Christians on Campus,' *Citizen* 5/10 (21 October 1991).

Conspiracy and mind control are not, however, themes stressed in FFA's public expressions. For example, a letter from Jim Sclater, FFA policy director, to a student requesting information, contains no allusions to civil war or conspiratorial infiltration (March 1991). On the contrary, this letter, while describing the threat posed by the success of cases like *Mossop*, offers to lesbians and gay men a few words of sympathy and understanding.

61 See, also, *Who We Are*, REAL Women, n.d., and C. Hoy, 'Campbell panders to feminist forces,' *Law Times*, 11 November 1991.

62 Bertha Wilson (now retired) was a Supreme Court justice popularly identified as having 'feminist sympathies.'

63 Anderson, interview. I consider REAL Women's view of law and the legal system more fully in the next chapter.

64 The National Action Committee on the Status of Women is the Canadian national umbrella organization of feminist groups (like the American NOW).

65 See 'Commentary: What Happened to the Family,' *The War Cry,* 27 May 1989, 2.

66 During my interview with him, Don Hutchinson drew a diagram of three circles, representing this encroachment.

67 For a discussion of right-wing articulations of race, gender, and sexuality during anti-ERA campaigns, see Mathews and De Hart 1990, 173–4, 224. Allen Hunter (1981) also discusses the racist content in New Right thinking.

68 Foucault 1976. As Valverde (1991) has argued, in her study of social purity movements in Canada, Christian conservatives do not advocate the wholesale repression of sexual expression; on the contrary, they seek to contain it within 'healthy' channels (see also Petchesky 1984, 263–4). Dobson himself is something of a sexual guru to Focus on the Family subscribers, he has authored a number of books purporting to advise married couples on improving their sex lives.

69 See Cooper and Herman 1991 for its manifestation in British politics.

70 It could be argued that the Salvation Army takes a different position, regarding the 'origins of a homosexual orientation as a mystery'; however, according to them, some people are clearly 'disposed' to homosexual behaviour and others are not (The Salvation Army Positional Statements, Canada and Bermuda Territory, 1990, 13). This may partly account for why the 'fifth column' theme plays such a limited rhetorical role for Salvationists. Arguably, as the Army becomes more involved in NCR coalitions, these views may change. See also the Salvation Army newsletter *War Cry,* 27 May 1989, 2. Note also, that the Army's head office in Britain publishes a more severe statement on homosexuality, describing it as an 'innate tendency' in need of suppression, see 'Homosexuality,' The Salvation Army – A Positional Statement, International Heritage Centre, London, n.d. When interviewed, however, Don Hutchinson appeared to contradict this opinion. In response to a question asking whether he agreed with the sexuality views of Jim Sclater, Hutchinson, while expressing some reservations, stated that 'no one is born gay'.

71 I discuss in chapter 4 the problems around defining what is meant by 'rights.'

72 Quoted from T. Marco, 'Oppressed Minority, or Counterfeits' *Citizen* 6/4 (20 April 1992). See also 'Sexual Disorientation: Faulty Research in the Homosexual Debate,' Family Policy 5/2 (1992) (Publication of the Family Research Council).

73 I am not concerned here with analysing possible 'illogicalities' in this formulation.

Chapter 6

1 Letter from James Sclater, director of public policy, FFA, to 'Friends,' 14 June 1991.
2 In American constitutional interpretation, a conservative judicial approach is usually noted by adherence to the doctrine of 'original intent' rather than the 'living tree' approach of liberal justices. The latter approach interprets the U.S. Constitution in light of modern developments and social change, while the former insists upon 'reading the minds' of its eighteenth- and nineteenth-century writers. For an interesting discussion see Bork 1990.
3 For example, during the 1988 federal elections, NCR groups ranked candidates on their abortion stands, and publicly sought, and to a small extent succeeded, in having their chosen candidates elected.
4 Ottawa Conference on the Family, 1991, Agenda.
5 I am simply presenting the views of the NCR here, not debating the issue. While it is no doubt true that feminist groups receive far more in litigation funds than REAL Women, section 15 of the Charter ostensibly exists to assist 'disadvantaged' groups seeking equality. Federal administrators decided that REAL Women did not meet this qualification, and, no doubt, given the intentions of the section, they were right. The Court Challenges Programme was not set up to assist battles between social movements with different societal visions; if it had been, then 'equality' might require the funding of REAL Women. Rather, the programme was meant to assist 'disadvantaged groups' seeking to challenge potentially discriminatory legislation. It is, therefore, assumed that the government will mount an effective defence of the legislation; however, the NCR has identified, in cases like *Mossop*, the government's failure to do this. If this is so, then the assumptions upon which section 15, and the Court Challenges Programme, are based are undermined. This, however, is a different issue from REAL Women's not receiving 'equal' rights to programme funds.
6 See, for example, G. Koch, 'Rise of the Court Party,' *Western Report*, 18 November 1991, 10–11; I. Benson, 'Claims about LEAF popularity must be viewed with caution,' *Law Times*, 11–17 March 1991; C. Hoy, 'Campbell panders to feminist forces,' *Law Times*, 11–17 November 1991. Copies of these articles were given to me by Judy Anderson.
7 See 'Rise of Court Party,' ibid, and Knopff and Morton 1992; also A. Strachan, 'The hidden opposition,' *The Globe and Mail*, 11 January 1992. The authors

have written against 'equal opportunity' policies long before the Charter's effects were known, see, for example, Knopff 1985.

8 E.g., see note above. It is worth noting, again, that the 'left's' perception of the Charter and the courts is similarly critical, although for different reasons, see also chapter 4.

9 I have discussed these views more fully in chapter 4.

10 Ibid. Hutchinson's comments echo a point I have made at various stages in this book and echoed by the work of Gusfield (1981). Social movements struggle on a number of fronts, some of which may even be incompatible with each other. Focus on the Family remains a primarily pastoral agency, and the Salvation Army remains predominantly a community social service. REAL Women, on the other hand, is almost entirely a political lobby.

11 The following account is based upon interviews with Jim Sclater, Don Hutchinson, and Ian Binnie, the lawyer for the coalition (with the firm McCarthy Tétreault).

12 Interestingly, Ian Binnie, McCarthy's lawyer on the case, similarly knew very little about Focus on the Family. He noted, however, that the participation of the Salvation Army gave the entire coalition credibility with the courts, which they might not otherwise have had (interview).

13 This is the coalition of progressive groups intervening on Mossop's behalf. See chapter 2 for brief discussion of the social-movement organizations involved in this coalition.

14 The process is a similar one to achieving 'standing.'

15 The Salvation Army Positional Statements, Canada and Bermuda Territory, 1990, 18.

16 Ibid, 15.

17 Ibid, 12–13, 18.

18 Ibid, 8–9. Ultimately, this was the view accepted by the majority of the Supreme Court of Canada in *Mossop* 1993.

19 *Laws Protecting Homosexuals or So-called 'Sexual Orientation' Legislation: How it will affect Canadians*, Pamphlet, REAL Women of Canada, 1986.

20 See Factum of the Attorney General of Canada, Federal Court of Appeal, *Mossop v A.G.*

21 Bruce 1990, 175. See also Hadden 1983; and, re abortion, Petchesky 1984, 259–61.

22 Most recently, in the former communist countries. See re Albania, for example, E. MacDonald, 'US Baptists Corner a Muslim Market,' *Independent on Sunday*, 18 October 1992.

23 Again, this is linked to the 'political correctness' backlash.

24 Bruce 1990, 149–54. Furthermore, this process should not be analysed solely as 'history'; the early 1992 battles for the Republican nomination between Bush, Buchanan, and Duke reminded us both that the right is divided and that conservative Christianity remains a potent political force. At the same time, the later stages of the 1992 presidential campaign suggested that the Republicans courting of the Christian right had backfired. Re Canada, see M. Cernetig, 'Preston Manning and his faith,' *The Globe and Mail*, 2 December 1991.

25 See, for example, 'Advertisers, Gays March with Pride,' *Marketing* 96 (24 June 1991), 8; T.A. Stewart, 'Gay in Corporate America,' *Fortune*, 16 December 1991, 42.

26 Lienesch 1982; Wilentz 1990. Chandler (1984) discusses how the NCR's attempts to ally with earlier-reviled Catholics and Mormons caused problems for the movement; see also Wilcox and Gomez 1989–90 re alliances with Catholics.

27 Joel Handler's (1978) book on social movements and the legal system tends to use a narrower and perhaps more traditional framework for evaluating 'success.'

28 Anderson interview. As I discussed in chapter 4, the mere fact of entry into media texts says little about how activists' views will be represented.

29 See also, D. Todd, 'Evangelical Christians argue gay bashing a God-given right,' *Vancouver Sun*, 30 November 1991. The title of this article would seem to confirm NCR constructions of media bias.

30 Discussed, for example, in Bruce 1990, 178–9 and many other NCR analyses.

31 'Charter of Rights – Effects on Women and the Family,' Pamphlet, REAL Women of Canada, n.d.

32 See also Beckford's (1990) understanding of the different forms of power potentially wielded by NCR movements, and Cooper's (1994a, forthcoming) theorization of power vis-à-vis feminist struggles.

Chapter 7

1 See, for example, Gothard 1986; Levine 1983; M. Rose 1986; Rosen 1977.

2 The details of this American case are not important for my purposes. Briefly, the claim against the company was initiated by the human rights regulatory body on behalf of the class 'women.' The claim alleged that Sears had engaged in hiring and other practices which effectively prohibited women from taking up more lucrative sales positions. One legal issue revolved around whether women 'chose' not to take up such positions (e.g., they preferred to work part-time, did not feel comfortable in high-powered sales jobs,

etc.) or were structurally prevented from doing so as a result of Sears's discriminatory practices. The company won the case. For comment, see Kessler-Harris 1987; Scott 1988a, 1988b; Milkman 1986. Several court documents are reproduced in Hall 1986.

3 See chapter 2 and later in this chapter.

4 Herman 1991. In this article, I was not particularly sympathetic to Eichler's intervention, and tended to underestimate the limitations within which her testimony was given.

5 Ibid. In *Knodel*, the psychiatric report was given in such a manner (see chapter 2 and below).

6 Affidavits of Barry Adam and Mariana Valverde, *Andrews v Ont. (Min. of Health)*.

7 Their own academic writings are far more complex and radical; see, for example, Valverde 1985 and Adam 1987.

8 Paragraph numbers in brackets refer to the report as noted in 'Cases Cited' in References.

9 See chapter 2 for a discussion of these cases.

10 See use of words and phrases like 'harmony' (4.47) and 'equal opportunity' (4.49). The tribunal also expresses the liberal view that values 'should play no part' in the adjudication process (4.70). See chapter 3 for a discussion of legal liberalism.

11 See Goodrich 1986 for a discussion of how judges deploy linguistic techniques.

12 In a related development, the Ontario Court of Appeal ruled in 1991, in a case about common-law heterosexual partners, that 'unmarried persons living together' do not constitute a 'disadvantaged group' as envisioned by section 15 (*Leroux* 1991). *Mossop* (1993) may confirm this (as does *Egan* 1993).

13 *Mossop* at the SCC contains lengthy analyses of the appropriate role of the courts in reviewing the decisions of human rights tribunals.

14 See Lorde (1984); Rich (1981).

15 In contrast, see Muldoon's derisory approach to similar arguments in *Nielsen* 1992. Thanks to Bruce Ryder for bringing this to my attention.

16 Re family: the 'ordinary use of language' does not admit a 'same-sex arrangement.'

17 As I discussed in chapter 4, this is the model underlying some American conceptions of rights reform (e.g., Minow 1990).

18 On 'reading' ideologies in law see Sumner 1979. See also Olsen 1980 for a study of the Canadian judiciary as a 'state élite.'

19 Arguably, female, especially feminist, judges are more likely to reach decisions favouring 'untraditional' families. Aside from Atcheson, Rowles in

Knodel, and L'Heureux-Dubé in *Mossop*, see Arbour's decision in *Leroux* 1990 and Dawson's in *Leshner* 1992.
20 See also the sociological evidence presented in *Layland* 1993.

Chapter 8

1 A version of this argument is also used against 'single' heterosexual parents.
2 And, as Butler herself notes, 'parody by itself is not subversive' (1990, 139).
3 By this I mean dissolving 'male' and 'female' categories currently perceived as 'fixed.'

References

Bibliographical References

Adam, Barry D. 1986. 'The Construction of a Sociological "Homosexual" in Canadian Textbooks.' *Canadian Review of Sociology and Anthropology* 23, 399ff.
– 1987. *The Rise of a Gay and Lesbian Movement.* Boston: Twayne
Aho, James A. 1990. *The Politics of Righteousness: Idaho Christian Patriotism.* Seattle: University of Washington Press
Altman, Dennis. 1982. *The Homosexualization of America.* Boston: Beacon
– 1986. *AIDS and the New Puritanism.* London: Pluto
Ammerman, Nancy Tatom. 1987. *Bible Believers: Fundamentalists in a Modern World.* New Brunswick, NJ: Rutgers University Press
– 1991. 'North American Protestant Fundamentalism.' In M.E. Marty, and R.S. Appleby, eds., *Fundamentalisms Observed.* Chicago: University of Chicago Press
Andrews, Karen. 1989. 'We Are Family,' *Healthsharing* (Fall), 18ff.
Arnup, Kathy. 1984. 'Lesbian Mothers and Child Custody.' *Atkinson Review of Canadian Studies* 1, 35ff.
– 1989. '"Mothers Just Like Others": Lesbians, Divorce, and Child Custody in Canada.' *Canadian Journal of Women and the Law* 3, 18ff.
Atcheson, M. Elizabeth, et al. 1984. *Women and Legal Action: Precedents, Resources and Strategies.* Ottawa: Canadian Advisory Council on the Status of Women
Atkinson, Paul. 1990. *The Ethnographic Imagination: Textual Constructions of Reality.* London: Routledge
Backhouse, Constance B. 1981. 'Bell v The Flaming Steer Steak House Tavern: Canada's First Sexual Harassment Decision.' *University of Western Ontario Law Review* 19, 141ff.

Bakan, Joel. 1990. 'Strange Expectations: A Review of Two Theories of Judicial Review.' *McGill Law Journal* 35, 439ff.

– 1991. 'Constitutional Interpretation and Social Change: You Can't Always Get What You Want (Nor What You Need).' *Canadian Bar Review* 70, 307ff.

Barrett, Michele, and McIntosh, Mary. 1982. *The Anti-Social Family.* London: Verso

Barrett, Stanley. 1987. *Is God a Racist? The Right-Wing in Canada.* Toronto: University of Toronto Press

Bartholomew, Amy, and Alan Hunt. 1990. 'What's Wrong with Rights.' *Law and Inequality* 9, 1ff.

Bayefsky, Anne F., and Mary Eberts. 1985. *Equality Rights and the Canadian Charter of Rights and Freedoms.* Toronto: Carswell

Beckford, James. 1990. 'Religion and Power.' In Thomas Robbins, and Dick Anthony, eds., *In Gods We Trust: New Patterns of Religious Pluralism in America,* 2d ed. New Brunswick, NJ: Transaction

Bell, Colin. 1978. 'Studying the Locally Powerful: Personal Reflections on a Research Career.' In Colin Bell, and S. Encell. *Inside the Whale.* Oxford: Pergamon

Bibby, Reginald W. 1987. *Fragmented Gods: The Poverty and Potential of Religion in Canada.* Toronto: Irwin Publishing

Bork, Robert H. 1990. *The Tempting of America: The Political Seduction of the Law.* London: Sinclair-Stevenson

Boyd, Susan. 1989. 'From Gender Specificity to Gender Neutrality? Ideologies in Canadian Custody Law.' In Carol Smart, and Selma Sevenhuijsen, eds., *Child Custody and the Politics of Gender.* London: Routledge

– 1991. 'Some Postmodern Challenges to Feminist Analyses of Law, Family and State: Ideology and Discourse in Child Custody Law.' *Canadian Journal of Family Law* 10, 79ff.

Brodsky, Gwen and Shelagh Day. 1989. *Canadian Charter Equality Rights for Women: One Step Forward or Two Steps Back?* Ottawa: Canadian Advisory Council on the Status of Women

Bromley, David G., and Anson Shupe, eds., 1984. *New Christian Politics.* Macon: Mercer University Press

Bruce, Steve. 1984. *Firm in the Faith.* Aldershot: Gower

– 1990. *The Rise and Fall of the New Christian Right: Conservative Protestant Politics in America 1978–1988.* Oxford: Clarendon Press

Bruner, Arnold. 1985. 'Sexual Orientation and Equality Rights.' In Anne Bayefsky, and Mary Eberts, eds., *Equality Rights and the Canadian Charter of Rights and Freedoms.* Toronto: Carswell

Bulmer, Martin. 1988. *Social Research Ethics.* London: Macmillan

Bumiller, Kristen. 1988. *The Civil Rights Society: The Social Construction of Victims.* Baltimore: Johns Hopkins University Press

Burt, Sandra. 1990. 'Canadian Women's Groups in the 1980s: Organizational Development and Policy Influence.' *Canadian Public Policy* 16, 17ff.

Butler, Judith. 1990. *Gender Trouble: Feminism and the Subversion of Identity.* New York: Routledge

– 1991. 'Imitation and Gender Insubordination.' In Diana Fuss, ed., *Inside/Out: Lesbian Theories, Gay Theories.* New York: Routledge

Cain, Patricia. 1989. 'Feminist Jurisprudence: Grounding the Theories.' *Berkeley Women's Law Journal* 4, 991ff.

Canada. Statistics Canada. 1993. *Religions in Canada.* Ottawa

Chandler, Ralph Clark. 1984. 'The Wicked Shall Not Bear Rule: The Fundamentalist Heritage of the New Christian Right.' In David Bromley, and Anson Shupe, eds., *New Christian Politics.* Macon: Mercer University Press

Chesler, Mark, Joseph Sanders, and Debra S. Kalmuss. 1988. *Social Science in Court: Mobilizing Experts in the School Desegregation Cases.* Madison: University of Wisconsin Press

Cicchino, Peter, Bruce Deming, and Kate Nicholson. 1991. 'Sex, Lies and Civil Rights: A Critical History of the Massachusetts Gay Civil Rights Bill.' *Harvard Civil Rights–Civil Liberties Law Review* 26, 549ff.

Coffey, Mary Anne. 1986. 'Of Father Born: A Lesbian Feminist Critique of the Ontario Law Reform Commission Recommendations on Artificial Insemination.' *Canadian Journal of Women and the Law* 1, 424ff.

Collins, Hugh. 1982. *Marxism and Law.* Oxford: Oxford University Press

Cooper, Davina. 1989. 'Positive Images in Haringey: A Struggle for Identity.' In Carol Jones, and Pat Mahoney, eds., *Learning Our Lines: Sexuality and Social Control in Education.* London: Women's Press

– 1994a. *Power in Struggle: Feminism, Sexuality, and the State.* Milton Keynes: Open University Press. Forthcoming

– 1994b. *Sexing the City: Community Politics and the Limits of State Activism.* London: Rivers Oram. Forthcoming

Cooper, Davina, and Didi Herman. 1991. 'Getting the Family "Right": Legislating Heterosexuality in Britain, 1986–1991.' *Canadian Journal of Family Law* 10, 41ff.

Coté, André, and Lucie Lemonde. 1988. *Discrimination et Commission des Droits de la Personne.* Montreal: Les Editions Saint-Martin

Cotterrell, Roger. 1986. 'Law and Sociology: Notes on the Constitution and Confrontations of Disciplines.' *Journal of Law and Society* 13, 9ff.

Coutts, Frederick. 1974. *No Discharge in This War.* London: Hodder and Stoughton

Creet, M. Julia. 1990. 'A Test of Unity: Lesbian Visibility in the British Columbia Federation of Women.' In Sharon Dale Stone, ed., *Lesbians in Canada.* Toronto: Between the Lines

Crenshaw, Kimberley. 1989. 'Demarginalizing the Intersection of Race and Sex: A Black Feminist Critique of Antidiscrimination Doctrine, Feminist Theory and Antiracist Politics.' *University of Chicago Legal Forum* 89, 139ff.

Crenshaw Williams, Kimberley. 1988. 'Race, Reform and Retrenchment: Transformation and Legitimation in Antidiscrimination Law.' *Harvard Law Review* 101, 1331ff.

Crimp, Douglas, ed. 1988. *AIDS: Cultural Analysis Cultural Activism*. Cambridge, MA: MIT Press

Cruikshank, Margaret. 1992. *The Gay and Lesbian Liberation Movement*. New York: Routledge

Cuneo, Michael. 1989. *Catholics against the Church: Anti-Abortion Protest in Toronto, 1969–1985*. Toronto: University of Toronto Press

David, Miriam and Ruth Levitas. 1988. 'Antifeminism and the British and American New Rights.' In Gill Seidel, ed., *The Nature of the Right*. Amsterdam: John Benjamin's

Davies, Megan. 1988. '"Culture Is Politics Is Unity": LOOT and the Growth of Lesbian Feminist Consciousness.' *Rites* 4 (March), 12ff.

Davis, David Brion. 1971. *The Fear of Conspiracy: Images of Un-American Subversion from the Revolution to the Present*. Ithaca, NY: Cornell University Press

De Hart, Jane Sherron. 1991. 'Gender on the Right: Meanings Behind the Existential Scream.' *Gender and History* 3, 246ff.

D'Emilio, John. 1983. *Sexual Politics, Sexual Communities: The Making of a Homosexual Minority in the United States, 1940–1970*. Chicago: University of Chicago Press

– 1989. 'The Homosexual Menace: The Politics of Sexuality in Cold War America.' In Kathy Peiss, and Christina Simmons, eds., *Passion and Power: Sexuality in History*. Philadelphia: Temple University Press

Diamond, Sara. 1989. *Spiritual Warfare: The Politics of the Christian Right*. Boston: South End

Dobson, James C. 1991. *Straight Talk: What Men Need to Know, What Women Should Understand*. Dallas: Word

Dobson, James, and Gary L. Bauer. 1990. *Children at Risk: The Battle for the Hearts and Minds of Our Kids*. Dallas: Word

Donzelot, J. 1980. *The Policing of Families*. London: Hutchinson

Dubinsky, Karen. 1985. *Lament for a 'Patriarchy Lost'? Anti-Feminism, Anti-Abortion, and R.E.A.L. Women in Canada*. Ottawa: CRIAW/ICREF

Duclos, Nitya. 1993. 'Disappearing Women: Racial Minority Women in Human Rights Cases.' *Canadian Journal of Women and the Law* 6, 25ff.

Dugan Jr, Robert P. 1991. *Winning the New Civil War*. Portland: Multnomah

Durham, Martin. 1991. *Sex and Politics: The Family and Morality in the Thatcher Years*. Houndmills: Macmillan

Dworkin, Ronald. 1984. 'Liberalism.' In Michael J. Sandel, ed., *Liberalism and Its Critics*. Oxford: Basil Blackwell

Eaton, Mary. 1991. 'Theorizing Sexual Orientation.'" LLM Thesis, Queen's University

Edelman, Lee. 1992. 'Tearooms and Sympathy, or, the Epistemology of the Water Closet.' In Andrew Parker, Mary Russo, Doris Sommer, and Patricia Yaeger, eds., *Nationalisms and Sexualities*. New York: Routledge

Edelman, Murray. 1988. *Constructing the Political Spectacle*. Chicago: University of Chicago Press

Elder, Charles D., and Roger W. Cobb. 1983. *The Political Uses of Symbols*. New York: Longman

Epstein, Barbara. 1990. 'Rethinking Social Movement Theory.' *Socialist Review* 20, 35ff.

Epstein, Lee. 1985. *Conservatives in Court*. Knoxville: University of Tennessee Press

Epstein, Steven. 1991. 'Democratic Science? AIDS Activism and the Contested Construction of Knowledge.' *Socialist Review* 21, 35ff.

Erwin, Lorna. 1988a. 'REAL Women, Anti-Feminism, and the Welfare State.' *Resources for Feminist Research* 17, 147ff.

– 1988b. 'What Feminists Should Know About the Pro-Family Movement in Canada: A Report on a Recent Survey of Rank-and-File Members.' In Petra Tancred Sherif, ed., *Feminist Perspectives: Prospect and Retrospect*. Montreal and Kingston: McGill-Queen's University Press

Faderman, Lillian. 1991. *Odd Girls and Twilight Lovers: A History of Lesbian Life in Twentieth-Century America*. New York: Penguin

Faulkner, Ellen. 1991. 'Lesbian Abuse: The Social and Legal Realities.' *Queen's Law Journal* 16, 261ff.

Fields, Echo E. 1991. 'Understanding Activist Fundamentalism: Capitalist Crisis and the "Colonization of the Lifeworld.' *Sociological Analysis* 52, 175ff.

Findlay, Sue. 1987. 'Facing the State: The Politics of the Women's Movement Reconsidered.' In Heather Jon Maroney and Meg Luxton, eds., *Feminism and Political Economy: Women's Work, Women's Struggles*. Toronto: Methuen

Findlay, Sue, Frank Cunningham, and Ed Silva. 1988. 'Introduction.' In Frank Cunningham, Sue Findlay, Marlene Kadar, Alan Lennon, and Ed Silva, eds., *Social Movements/Social Change: The Politics and Practice of Organizing*. Toronto: Between the Lines

Fitzpatrick, Peter. 1987. 'Racism and the Innocence of Law.' *Journal of Law and Society* 14, 119ff.

Flax, Jane. 1987. 'Postmodernism and Gender Relations in Feminist Theory.' *Signs* 12, 621ff.

Foucault, Michel. 1976. *The History of Sexuality: An Introduction*. London: Penguin Books

Freedman, Estelle. 1989. '"Uncontrolled Desires": The Reponse to the Sexual Psychopath, 1920–1960.' In Kathy Peiss, and Christina Simmons, eds., *Passion and Power: Sexuality in History*. Philadelphia: Temple University Press

Freeman, Alan. 1982. 'Antidiscrimination Law.' In David Kairys, ed., *The Politics of Law: A Progressive Critique*. New York: Pantheon Books

Frideres, James S., and William J. Reeves. 1989. 'Research Note: The Ability to Implement Human Rights Legislation in Canada.' *Canadian Review of Sociology and Anthropology* 26, 311ff.

Fudge, Judy. 1987. 'The Public/Private Distinction: The Possibilities of and the Limits to the Use of Charter Litigation to Further Feminist Struggles.' *Osgoode Hall Law Journal* 25, 485ff.

– 1989. 'The Effect of Entrenching a Bill of Rights Upon Political Discourse: Feminist Demands and Sexual Violence in Canada.' *International Journal of the Sociology of Law* 17, 445ff.

Fudge, Judy, and Harry Glasbeek. 1992. 'The Politics of Rights: A Politics with Little Class.' *Social and Legal Studies* 1, 45ff.

Gabel, Peter. 1980. 'Reification in Legal Reasoning.' In S. Spitzer, ed., *Research in Law and Sociology*. Greenwich, CT: JAI

– 1984. 'The Phenomenology of Rights-Consciousness and the Pact of the Withdrawn Selves.' *Texas Law Review* 62, 1563ff.

Gabel, Peter, and Jay Feinman. 1982. 'Contract Law as Ideology.' In David Kairys, ed., *The Politics of Law: A Progressive Critique*. New York: Pantheon Books

Gavigan, Shelley. 1986. 'Women, Law and Patriarchal Relations: Perspectives Within the Sociology of Law.' In Neil Boyd, ed., *The Social Dimensions of Law*. Scarborough: Prentice-Hall Canada

– 1987. 'Women and Abortion in Canada: What's Law Got to Do with It?' In Heather Jon Maroney and Meg Luxton, eds., *Feminism and Political Economy: Women's Work, Women's Struggles*. Toronto: Methuen

– 1992. 'Paradise Lost, Paradox Revisited: The Implications of Familial Ideology for Feminist, Lesbian and Gay Engagement with Law.' *Osgoode Hall Law Journal* 31

Gill, Donna. 1989. 'REAL Women and the Press: An Ideological Alliance of Convenience.' *Canadian Journal of Communication* 14, 1ff.

Gilman, Sander L. 1985. *Difference and Pathology: Sterotypes of Sexuality, Race and Madness*. Ithaca, NY: Cornell University Press

– 1988. *Disease and Representation: Images of Illness from Madness to AIDS*. Ithaca, NY: Cornell University Press

Ginsburg, Faye. 1989. 'The Body Politic: The Defense of Sexual Restriction by Anti-Abortion Activists.' In Carole S. Vance, ed., *Pleasure and Danger: Exploring Female Sexuality* London: Pandora [orig. pub. 1984]

Girard, Philip. 1986. 'Sexual Orientation as a Human Rights Issue in Canada 1969-1985.' *Dalhousie Law Journal* 10, 267ff.

- 1987. 'From Subversion to Liberation: Homosexuals and the Immigration Act, 1952–1977.' *Canadian Journal of Law and Society* 2, 1ff.

Glasbeek, H.J. 1989a. 'A No-Frills Look at the Charter of Rights and Freedoms or How Politicians and Lawyers Hide Reality.' *The Windsor Yearbook of Access to Justice* 9, 293ff.

- 1989b. 'Some Strategies for an Unlikely Task: The Progressive Use of Law.' *Ottawa Law Review* 21, 387ff.

Glasbeek, Harry, and Michael Mandel. 1984. 'The Legalization of Politics in Advanced Capitalism: The Canadian Charter of Rights and Freedoms.' *Socialist Studies/Etudes socialistes* 2, 84ff.

Goodrich, Peter. 1986. *Reading the Law*. Oxford: Basil Blackwell

Gordon, Colin, ed. 1980. *Power / Knowledge: Selected Interviews and Other Writings, 1972–1977, By Michel Foucault*. New York: Pantheon

Gothard, Leonard. 1986. 'The Sociological Expert Witness in a Case of Collective Interracial Violence.' *Clinical Sociology Review* 4, 107ff.

Green, Richard. 1987. '"Give Me Your Tired, Your Poor, Your Huddled Masses" (of Heterosexuals): An Analysis of American and Canadian Immigration Policy.' *Anglo-American Law Review* 16, 139ff.

- 1988. 'The Immutability of (Homo)Sexual Orientation: Behavioural Science Implications for a Constitutional (Legal) Analysis.' *Journal of Psychiatry and Law* 16, 537ff.

- 1992. *Sexual Science and the Law*. Cambridge, MA: Harvard University Press

Gross, Wendy L. 1986. 'Judging the Best Interests of the Child: Child Custody and the Homosexual Parent.' *Canadian Journal of Women and the Law* 1, 505ff.

Gusfield, J. 1981. 'Social Movements and Social Change: Perspectives in Linearity and Fluidity.' *Research in Social Movements, Conflicts and Social Change* 4, 317ff.

Habermas, Jurgen. 1987. *The Philosophical Discourses of Modernity*. Cambridge, MA: MIT Press

- 1987b. *The Theory of Communicative Action*, vol. 2. Boston: Beacon Press

Hadden, Jeffery K. 1983. 'Televangelism and the Mobilization of a New Christian Right Family Policy.' In William V. D'Antonio and Joan Aldous, eds., *Families and Religion: Conflict and Change in Modern Society*. Beverly Hills: Sage

Haiven, Judith. 1984. *Faith, Hope, No Charity*. Vancouver, BC: New Star Books

Hall, Jacquelyn Dowd. 1986. 'Women's History Goes to Trial: *EEOC* v. *Sears, Roebuck and Company*.' *Signs* 11, 751ff.

Halley, Janet E. 1991. 'Misreading Sodomy: A Critique of the Classification of "Homosexuals" in Federal Equal Protection Law.' In Julia Epstein and Kristina Straub, eds., *Body Guards: The Cultural Politics of Gender Ambiguity.* New York: Routledge

Handler, Joel. 1978. *Social Movements and the Legal System: A Theory of Law Reform and Social Change.* New York: Academic Press

Handy, Robert T. 1976. *A History of the Churches in the United States and Canada.* Oxford: Clarendon Press

Harding, Sandra. 1986. *The Science Question in Feminism.* Milton Keynes: Open University Press

– 1991. *Whose Science? Whose Knowledge?: Thinking from Women's Lives.* Milton Keynes: Open University Press

Harding, Susan. 1991. 'Representing Fundamentalism: The Problem of the Repugnant Cultural Other.' *Social Research* 58, 373ff.

Harstock, Nancy. 1983. 'The Feminist Standpoint: Developing the Ground for a Specifically Feminist Historical Materialism.' in Sandra Harding and Merrill B. Hintikka, eds., *Discovering Reality: Feminist Perspectives on Epistemology, Metaphysics, Methodology, and Philosophy of Science.* Dordrecht: D. Reidel

Harvard Law Review. 1989. *Sexual Orientation and the Law.* Cambridge, MA: Harvard University Press

Hayton, Brad. n.d. *The Homosexual Agenda: Changing Your Community and Nation.* Focus on the Family

Heinz, Donald. 1983. 'The Struggle to Define America.' In Robert C. Liebman and Robert Wuthnow, eds., *The New Christian Right: Mobilization and Legitimation.* Hawthorne: Aldine

Helvacioglu, Banu. 1991. 'The God-Market Alliance in Defence of Family and Community: The Case of the New Right in the United States.' *Studies in Political Economy* 35, 103ff.

Herman, Didi. 1990. 'Are We Family?: Lesbian Rights and Women's Liberation.' *Osgoode Hall Law Journal* 28, 789ff.

– 1991. '"Sociologically Speaking": Law, Sexuality, and Social Change.' *Journal of Human Justice* 2, 57ff.

– 1993a. 'Beyond the Rights Debate' (1993) *Social and Legal Studies* 2, 25ff.

– 1993b. 'Reforming Rights: Struggles for Lesbian and Gay Legal Equality in Canada.' Ph.D. thesis, University of Warwick

Herman, Didi and Davina Cooper. 1991. 'Getting the Family "Right": Legislating Heterosexuality in Britain, 1986-1990.' *Canadian Journal of Family Law* 10, 41ff.

Hertzke, Allen. 1988. *Representing God in Washington: The Role of Religious Lobbies in the American Polity.* Knoxville: University of Tennessee Press

Himmelstein, Jerome. 1986. 'The Social Basis of Antifeminism: Religious Networks and Culture.' *Journal for the Scientific Study of Religion* 25, 1ff.
- 1990. *To the Right: The Transformation of American Conservatism*. Berkeley: University of California Press
Hirst, Paul. 1979. *On Law and Ideology.* London: Macmillan
Hoagland, Sarah Lucia, and Julia Penelope, eds. 1988. *For Lesbians Only: A Separatist Anthology.* London: Onlywomen
Hofsess, John. 1987. 'Damien's Thwarted Justice.' *Now,* 15–21 January, 9ff.
hooks, bell. 1991. *Yearning: Race, Gender, and Cultural Politics*. London: Turnaround
Hunt, Alan. 1985. 'The Ideology of Law: Advances and Problems in Recent Applications of the Concept of Ideology to the Analysis of Law.' *Law and Society Review* 19, 11ff.
- 1990. 'Rights and Social Movements.' *Journal of Law and Society* 17, 309ff.
Hunter, Allen. 1981. 'In the Wings: New Right Ideology and Organization.' *Radical America* 15, 113ff.
Iyer, Nitya. 1993. 'Categorical Denials: Equality Rights and the Shaping of Social Identity.' *Queen's Law Journal* 19, 179ff.
Jackson, Ed, and Stan Persky, eds. 1982. *Flaunting It! A Decade of Journalism from The Body Politic*. Vancouver / Toronto: New Star / Pink Triangle
Jefferson, James. 1985. 'Gay Rights and the Charter.' *University of Toronto Faculty Review* 43, 70ff.
Jenkins, Craig, and Craig M. Eckert. 1986. 'Channeling Black Insurgency: Elite Patronage and Professional Social Movement Organizations in the Development of the Black Movement.' *American Sociological Review* 51, 812ff.
Johnson, Stephen D., and Joseph B. Tamney. 1982. 'The Christian Right and the 1980 Presidential Election.' *Journal for the Scientific Study of Religion* 21, 123ff.
Jorstad, Erling. 1987. *The New Christian Right, 1981–1988*. Lewiston: Edwin Mellen
Kaplan, William. 1989. *State and Salvation: The Jehovah's Witnesses and Their Fight for Civil Rights*. Toronto: University of Toronto Press
Kargon, Robert. 1986. 'Expert Testimony in Historical Perspective.' *Law and Human Behaviour* 10, 15ff.
Kennedy, Duncan. 1987. 'Toward a Critical Phenomenology of Judging.' in Allan Hutchinson and Patrick Monahan, eds., *The Rule of Law: Ideal or Ideology.* Toronto: Carswell
Kessler-Harris, Alice. 1987. 'Equal Employment Opportunity Commission v. Sears, Roebuck and Company: A Personal Account.' *Feminist Review* 25, 46ff.
Khayatt, Madiha Didi. 1992. *Lesbian Teachers: An Invisible Presence*. Albany: State University of New York Press

– 1990. 'Legalized Invisibility: The Effect of Bill 7 on Lesbian Teachers.' *Women Studies International Forum* 13, 185ff.

Kingdom, Elizabeth. 1991. *What's Wrong with Rights?: Problems for a Feminist Politics of Law.* Edinburgh: Edinburgh University Press

Kinsman, Gary. 1987. *The Regulation of Desire: Sexuality in Canada.* Montreal: Black Rose Books

Kitzinger, Celia. 1987. *The Social Construction of Lesbianism.* London: Sage

Klatch, Rebecca E. 1987 *Women of the New Right.* Philadelphia: Temple University Press

Kline, Marlee. 1989a. 'Race, Racism and Feminist Legal Theory.' *Harvard Women's Law Journal* 12, 115ff.

– 1989b. 'Women's Oppression and Racism: A Critique of the "Feminist Standpoint."' In Jesse Vorst, et al., eds., *Race, Class, Gender: Bonds and Barriers.* Toronto: Between the Lines

– 1992. 'Child Welfare Law, "Best Interests of the Child" Ideology, and First Nations.' *Osgoode Hall Law Journal* 30, 375ff.

Knopff, Rainer. 1985. 'The Statistical Protection of Minorities: Affirmative Action Policy in Canada.' In Neil Nevitte and Allan Kornberg, eds., *Minorities and the Canadian State.* Oakville, ON: Mosaic

Knopff, Rainer, and F.L. Morton. 1992. *Charter Politics.* Scarborough, ON: Nelson Canada

La Follette, Marcel C., 1983. *Creationism, Science, and the Law: The Arkansas Case.* Cambridge, MA: MIT Press

Laclau, Ernesto, and Chantal Mouffe. 1985. *Hegemony and Socialist Strategy: Towards a Radical Democratic Politics.* London: Verso

Lechner, Frank J. 1990. 'Fundamentalism Revisited.' In Thomas Robbins and Dick Anthony, eds., *In Gods We Trust: New Patterns of Religious Pluralism in America,* 2d ed. New Brunswick, NJ: Transaction

Leonard, Leigh Megan. 1990. 'A Missing Voice in Feminist Legal Theory: The Heterosexual Presumption.' *Women's Rights Law Reporter* 12, 39ff.

Leopold, Margaret and Wendy King. 1985. 'Compulsory Heterosexuality, Lesbians, and the Law: The Case for Constitutional Protection.' *Canadian Journal of Women and the Law* 1, 163ff.

Levine, Saul. 1983. 'The Role of the Mental Health Expert Witness in Family Law Disputes.' *Canadian Journal of Psychiatry* 28, 255ff.

Liebman, Robert C., and Robert Wuthnow. 1983. *The New Christian Right: Mobilization and Legitmation.* Hawthorne: Aldine

Lienesch, Michael. 1982. 'Right-Wing Religion: Christian Conservatism as a Political Movement.' *Political Science Quarterly* 97, 403ff.

Lipset, Seymour M. and Earl Raab. 1981. 'The Election and the Evangelicals.' *Commentary* 71, 25ff.

Lorde, Audre. 1984. *Sister Outsider.* Trumansburg, NY: Crossing Press

Luker, Kristin. 1984. *Abortion and the Politics of Motherhood.* Berkeley: University of California Press

Lynch, Michael. 1982. 'The End of the "Human Rights Decade"' In Ed Jackson and Stan Persky, eds., *Flaunting It! A Decade of Gay Journalism from the Body Politic.* Vancouver / Toronto: New Star / Pink Triangle

McCaskell, Tim. 1988. 'The Bath Raids and Gay Politics.' In Frank Cunningham, Sue Findlay, Marlene Kadar, Alan Lennon, and Ed Silva, eds., *Social Movements/Social Change: The Politics and Practice of Organizing.* Toronto: Between the Lines

McIntosh, Deborah. 1988. 'Defining "Family" – A Comment on the Family Reunification Provisions in the Immigration Act.' *Journal of Law and Social Policy* 3, 104ff.

McIntosh, Mary. 1981. 'The Homosexual Role.' In K. Plummer, ed., *The Making of the Modern Homosexual.* London: Hutchinson

Mackinnon, Catharine. 1983. 'Feminism, Marxism, Method and the State: Towards a Feminist Jurisprudence.' *Signs* 8, 635ff.

– 1987. *Feminism Unmodified: Discourses on Life and Law.* Cambridge, MA: Harvard University Press

McNamara, Patrick H. 1985. 'The New Christian Right's View of the Family and Its Social Science Critics.' *Journal of Marriage and the Family* 47, 449ff.

MacNeil, Michael. 1989. 'Courts and Liberal Ideology: An Analysis of the Application of the *Charter* to Some Labour Law Issues.' *McGill Law Journal* 34, 87ff.

Mandel, Michael. 1989. *The Charter of Rights and the Legalization of Politics in Canada.* Toronto: Wall and Thompson

Marcus, Eric. 1992. *Making History: The Struggle for Gay and Lesbian Rights,1945–1990.* New York: Harper Collins

Marks, Lynne. 1992. 'The "Hallelujah Lasses": Working-Class Women in the Salvation Army in English Canada, 1882–92.' In Franca Iacovetta and Mariana Valverde, eds., *Gender Conflicts: New Essays in Women's History.* Toronto: University of Toronto Press

Mathews, Donald, and Jane Sheron De Hart. 1990. *Sex, Gender, and the Politics of the ERA.* New York: Oxford University Press

Matsuda, Mari. 1987. 'Looking to the Bottom: Critical Legal Studies and Reparations.' *Harvard Civil Rights–Civil Liberties Law Review* 22, 323ff.

Melucci, Alberto. 1989. *Nomads of the Present: Social Movements and Individual Needs in Contemporary Society.* London: Century Hutchinson

Menzies, Robert. 1986. 'Psychiatry, Dangerousness and Legal Control.' In Neil Boyd, ed., *The Social Dimensions of Law*. Scarborough, ON: Prentice-Hall

Merrett, Jim. 1991. 'America's Gay Legal Crusaders.' *The Advocate* 569 (29 January 1991), 42ff.

Milkman, Ruth. 1986. 'Women's History and the Sears Case.' *Feminist Studies* 12, 375ff.

Milner, Neil. 1986. 'The Dilemmas of Legal Mobilization: Ideologies and Strategies of Mental Patient Liberation Groups.' *Law and Policy* 8, 105ff.

– 1989. 'The Denigration of Rights and the Persistence of Rights Talk: A Cultural Portrait.' *Law and Social Inquiry* 14, 631ff.

Minow, Martha. 1990. *Making All the Difference: Inclusion, Exclusion, and American Law*. Ithaca, NY: Cornell University Press

Moen, Mathew C. 1989. *The Christian Right and Congress*. Tuscaloosa: University of Alabama Press

Mohr, Richard D. 1988. *Gays / Justice: A Study of Ethics, Society, and Law*. New York: Columbia University Press

Morris, Aldon. 1984. *The Origins of the Civil Rights Movement: Black Communities Organizing for Change*. New York: The Free Press

Mort, Frank. 1987. *Dangerous Sexualities: Medico-Moral Politics in England Since 1830*. London: Routledge and Kegan Paul

Mosse, George L. 1985. *Nationalism and Sexuality: Middleclass Morality and Sexual Norms in Modern Europe*. Madison: University of Wisconsin Press

Mossman, Mary Jane, and Julie R. Jai. 1979. 'Women and Work in the Canadian Human Rights Act.' In Ceta Ramkhalawansingh, ed., *(Un)equal Pay: Canadian and International Perspectives*. Toronto: Ontario Institute for Studies in Education

Mouffe, Chantal. 1988. 'Hegemony and New Political Subjects: Toward a New Concept of Democracy.' In Cary Nelson and Lawrence Grossberg, eds., *Marxism and the Interpretation of Culture*. Houndmills: Macmillan

– 1992. 'Preface: Democratic Politics Today.' In Chantal Mouffe, ed., *Dimensions of Radical Democracy: Pluralism, Citizenship, Community*. London: Verso

Oakley, Ann. 1981. 'Interviewing Women: A Contradiction in Terms.' In Helen Roberts, ed., *Doing Feminist Research*. London: Routledge

Offe, Claus. 1985. 'New Social Movements: Challenging the Boundaries of Institutional Politics.' *Social Research* 52, 817ff.

Olsen, Dennis. 1980. *The State Elite*. Toronto: McClelland and Stewart

Opie, Anne. 1992. 'Qualitative Research, Appropriation of the 'Other' and Empowerment.' *Feminist Review* 40, 52ff.

Palmer, Susan J. 1990. 'Virus as Metaphor: Religious Responses to AIDS.' In Thomas Robbins and Dick Anthony, eds., *In Gods We Trust: New Patterns of Religious Pluralism in America*. 2d ed. New Brunswick, NJ: Transaction

Parker, Andrew, Mary Russo, Doris Sommer, and Patricia Yaeger, eds. 1992. *Nationalisms and Sexualities*. New York: Routledge

Pateman, Carole. 1989. *The Disorder of Women*. Cambridge: Polity

Patton, Cindy. 1985. *Sex and Germs: The Politics of AIDS*. Boston: South End

– 1990. *Inventing AIDS*. New York: Routledge

Peshkin, Alan. 1986. *God's Choice: The Total World of a Fundamentalist Christian School*. Chicago: University of Chicago Press

Petchesky, Rosalind Pollack. 1984. *Abortion and Woman's Choice: The State, Sexuality, and Reproductive Freedom*. Boston: Northeastern University Press

Petersen, Cynthia. 1991. 'A Queer Response to Bashing: Legislating Against Hate.' *Queen's Law Journal* 16, 231ff.

Phelan, Shane. 1989. *Identity Politics: Lesbian Feminism and the Limits of Community*. Philadelphia: Temple University Press

Piven, Frances Fox, and R. Cloward. 1977. *Poor People's Movements*. New York: Pantheon

Plotke, David. 1990. 'What's So New about New Social Movements?' *Socialist Review* 20, 81ff.

Plummer, Kenneth, ed. 1981. *The Making of the Modern Homosexual*. London: Hutchinson

Rayside, David. 1988. 'Gay Rights and Family Values: The Passage of Bill 7 in Ontario.' *Studies in Political Economy* 26, 109ff.

Rayside, David and Scott Bowler. 1988. 'Public Opinion and Gay Rights.' *Canadian Review of Sociology and Anthropology* 25, 649ff.

Razack, Sherene. 1991. *Canadian Feminism and the Law: The Women's Legal Education and Action Fund and the Pursuit of Equality*. Toronto: Second Story

Reaume, Denise. 1979. 'Women and the Law: Equality Claims Before Courts and Tribunals.' *Queen's Law Journal* 5, 3ff.

Rich, Adrienne. 1981. *Compulsory Heterosexuality and Lesbian Existence*. London: Onlywomen

Richstone, Jeff, and J. Stuart Russell. 1981. 'Shutting the Gate: Gay Civil Rights in the Supreme Court of Canada.' *McGill Law Journal* 27, 92ff.

Roberts, Helen. 1981. *Doing Feminist Research*. London: Routledge

Robin, Martin. 1992. *Shades of Right: Nativist and Fascist Politics in Canada, 1920–1940*. Toronto: University of Toronto Press

Robson, Ruthann. 1990a. 'Lavender Bruises: Intra-Lesbian Violence, Law and Lesbian Legal Theory.' *Golden Gate Law Review* 20, 567ff.

– 1990b. 'Lesbian Jurisprudence?' *Law and Inequality* 8, 443ff.

– 1990c. 'Lifting Belly: Privacy, Sexuality and Lesbianism.' *Women's Rights Law Reporter* 12, 177ff.

- 1990d. 'Lov(h)ers: Lesbians as Intimate Partners and Lesbian Legal Theory.' *Temple Law Review* 63, 511ff.
- 1992. *Lesbian (Out)Law: Survival Under the Rule of Law.* Ithaca, NY: Firebrand

Rose, Michael. 1986. 'Commentary: The Academic as Expert Witness.' *Science, Technology, and Human Values* 26, 68ff.

Rose, Susan. 1988. *Keeping Them Out of the Hands of Satan: Evangelical Schooling in America.* New York: Routledge and Kegan Paul
- 1989. 'Gender, Education and the New Christian Right.' *Society* 26, 59ff.

Rosen, Lawrence. 1977. 'The Anthropologist as Expert Witness.' *American Anthropologist* 70, 555ff.

Ross, Becki. 1988. 'Heterosexuals Only Need Apply: The Secretary of State's Regulation of Lesbian Existence.' *Resources for Feminist Research / DRF* 17, 35ff.
- 1990. 'Sexual Dis/Orientation or Playing House: To Be or Not to Be Coded Human.' In Sharon Dale Stone, ed., *Lesbians in Canada.* Toronto: Between the Lines

Rowland, Robyn, ed. 1984. *Women Who Do and Women Who Don't Join the Women's Movement.* London: Routledge and Kegan Paul

Ryder, Bruce. 1990. 'Equality Rights and Sexual Orientation: Confronting Heterosexual Family Privilege.' *Canadian Journal of Family Law* 9, 39ff.

Sagoff, Mark. 1983. 'Liberalism and Law.' In Douglas Maclean and Claudia Mills, eds., *Liberalism Reconsidered.* Totowa, NJ: Rowman and Allanhead

Sandler, Michael, ed. 1984. *Liberalism and Its Critics.* Oxford: Basil Blackwell

Scheingold, Stuart A. 1974. *The Politics of Rights.* New Haven, CT: Yale University Press

Schneider, Elizabeth. 1986. 'The Dialectic of Rights and Politics: Perspectives from the Women's Movement.' *New York University Law Review* 61, 589ff.

Schraeder, Alicia. 1990. 'The State Funded Women's Movement: A Case of Two Political Agendas.' In Roxana Ng, Gillian Walker, and Jacob Muller, eds., *Community Organizing and the Canadian State.* Toronto: Garamond

Scott, Joan. 1988a. 'Deconstructing Equality-Versus-Difference: Or, the Uses of Poststructuralist Theory for Feminism.' *Feminist Studies* 14, 33ff.
- 1988b. *Gender and the Politics of History.* New York: Columbia University Press

Sedgwick, Eve Kosofsky. 1991. 'How to Bring Your Kids Up Gay'. *Social Text* 29, 18ff.

Seidel, Gill, and Renate Gunther. 1988. '"Nation" and "Family" in the British Media Reporting of the "Falklands Conflict."' In Gill Seidel, ed., *The Nature of the Right.* Amsterdam: John Benjamin's

Shupe, Anson, and William A. Stacey. 1984. 'Public and Clergy Sentiments Toward the Moral Majority.' In David G. Bromley and Anson Shupe, eds., *New Christian Politics.* Macon: Mercer University Press

Simon, Barbara. 1982. 'In Defense of Institutionalization: A Rape Crisis Center as a Case Study.' *Journal of Sociology and Social Welfare* 9, 485ff.

Simpson, John H. 1983. 'Moral Issues and Status Politics.' In Robert C. Liebman and Robert Wuthnow, eds., *The New Christian Right: Mobilization and Legitimation.* Hawthorne: Aldine

– 1984. 'Support for the Moral Majority and Its Sociomoral Platform.' In David G. Bromley and Anson Shupe, eds., *New Christian Politics.* Macon: Mercer University Press

Smart, Carol. 1984. *The Ties That Bind: Law, Marriage and the Reproduction of Patriarchal Relations.* London: Routledge and Kegan Paul

– 1989. *Feminism and the Power of Law.* London: Routledge

– 1990. 'Law's Power, the Sexed Body, and Feminist Discourse.' *Journal of Law and Society* 17, 194ff.

Smith, Dorothy. 1987. *The Everyday World As Problematic: A Feminist Sociology.* Stony Stratford: Open University Press

Sontag, Susan. 1988. 'AIDS and Its Metaphors.' *New York Review of Books* 35, 89ff.

Speer, James A. 1984. 'The New Christian Right and Its Parent Company: A Study in Political Contrasts.' In David G. Bromley and Anson Shupe, eds., *New Christian Politics.* Macon: Mercer University Press

Staggenborg, Suzanne. 1988. 'The Consequences of Professionalization and Formalization in the Pro-Choice Movement.' *American Sociological Review* 53, 585ff.

Stanley, Liz. 1990. '"A Referral Was Made": Behind the Scenes During the Creation of a Social Services Department "Elderly" Statistic.' In Liz Stanley, ed., *Feminist Praxis: Research, Theory and Epistemology in Feminist Sociology.* London: Routledge

Stein, Edward, ed. 1990. *Forms of Desire: Sexual Orientation and The Social Constructionist Controversy.* New York: Garland

Stone, Sharon Dale, ed. 1990. *Lesbians in Canada.* Toronto: Between the Lines

– 1991. 'Lesbians Against the Right.' In Jeri Dawn Wine and Janice Ristock, eds., *Women and Social Change: Feminist Activism in Canada.* Toronto: Lorimer

Stychin, Carl. 1993a. 'Identities, Sexualities, and the Postmodern Subject: An Analysis of Artistic Funding by the National Endowment for the Arts.' *Cardozo Arts and Entertainment Law Journal* 12, 901ff.

– 1993b. 'A Postmodern Constitutionalism: Equality Rights, Identity Politics, and the Canadian National Imagination.' Paper presented at the Canadian Law and Society Association Conference, 6–9 June

Sugarman, David, ed. 1983. *Legality, Ideology and the State.* London: Academic Press

Sumner, Colin. 1979. *Reading Ideologies.* London: Academic

Tait, Ann. 1990. 'The Mastectomy Experience.' In Liz Stanley, ed., *Feminist*

Praxis: Research, Theory and Epistemology in Feminist Sociology. London: Routledge

Tarnopolsky, W.S. 1991. 'The Control of Racial Discrimination.' In Ormond McK-
ague, ed., *Racism in Canada.* Saskatoon: Fifth House

Tatchell, Peter. 1992. 'Equal Rights for All: Strategies for Lesbian and Gay Equality in Britain.' In Ken Plummer, ed., *Modern Homosexualities: Fragments of Lesbian and Gay Experience.* London: Routledge

Taylor, Charles Alan, and Celeste Michelle Condit. 1988. 'Objectivity and Elites:
A Creation Science Trial.' *Critical Studies in Mass Communication* 5, 293ff.

Thompson, Karen, and Julie Andrzejewski. 1986. *Why Can't Sharon Kowalski
Come Home?* San Francisco: Spinsters / Aunt Lute

Touraine, Alain. 1985. 'An Introduction to the Study of Social Movements.' *Social
Research* 52, 749ff.

Tushnet, Mark. 1984. 'An Essay on Rights.' *Texas Law Review* 62, 1363ff.

Valverde, Mariana. 1985. *Sex, Power and Pleasure.* Toronto: Women's Press

– 1991. *The Age of Light, Soap, and Water: Moral Reform in English Canada, 1885–
1925.* Toronto: McClelland and Stewart

Vance, Carole. 1989. 'Social Constructionist Theory: Problems in the History of
Sexuality.' in Dennis Altman, et al., *Homosexuality, Which Homosexuality?* London: GMP

Walkowitz, Judith. 1980. *Prostitution and Victorian Society.* Cambridge: Cambridge
University Press

Weeks, Jeffrey. 1977. *Coming Out: Homosexual Politics in Britain From the 19th Century to the Present.* London: Quartet

– 1981. *Sex, Politics and Society: The Regulation of Sexuality Since 1800.* London:
Longman

– 1985. *Sexuality and Its Discontents: Meanings, Myths, and Modern Sexualities.*
London: Routledge and Kegan Paul

– 1991. *Against Nature: Essays on History, Sexuality and Identity.* London: Rivers
Oram

Weir, Lorna, and Brenda Steiger. 1981. 'Coming Together in a Hot Gym.' *Broadside*, August / September, 7ff.

Weston, Kath. 1991. *Families We Choose: Lesbians, Gays, Kinship.* New York:
Columbia University Press

Wilcox, Clyde. 1987/80. 'Popular Backing for the Old Christian Right: Explaining Support for the Christian Anti-Communism Crusade.' *Journal of Social History* 21, 117ff.

Wilcox, Clyde and Leopoldo Gomez. 1989/90. 'The Christian Right and the Pro-
Life Movement: An Analysis of the Sources of Political Support.' *Review of
Religious Research* 31, 380ff.

Wilentz, Sean. 1990. 'The Trials of Televangelism.' *Dissent*, Winter, 42ff.

Williams, Patricia. 1987. 'Alchemical Notes: Reconstructing Ideals from Deconstructed Rights.' *Harvard Civil Rights–Civil Liberties Law Review* 22, 401ff.

Williams, Robert. 1987. 'Taking Rights Aggressively: The Perils and Promise of Critical Legal Theory for Peoples of Colour.' *Law and Inequality* 5, 103ff.

Williams, Toni. 1990. 'Re-forming "Women's" Truth: A Critique of the Report of the Royal Commission on the Status of Women in Canada.' *Ottawa Law Review* 22, 725ff.

Williamson, Judith. 1989. 'Every Virus Tells a Story: The Meanings of HIV and AIDS.' In Erica Carter and Simon Watney, eds., *Taking Liberties*. London: Serpent's Tail

Wine, Jeri Dawn, and Janice L. Ristock. eds., 1991. *Women and Social Change: Feminist Activism in Canada*. Toronto: Lorimer

Wishard, Darryl Robin. 1989. 'Out of the Closet and Into the Courts: Homosexual Fathers and Child Custody.' *Dickinson Law Review* 93, 401ff.

Woolgar, Steve. 1988. *Knowledge and Reflexivity: New Frontiers in the Sociology of Knowledge*. London: Sage

Wuthnow, Robert. 1983. 'The Political Rebirth of American Evangelicals.' In Robert C. Liebman and Robert Wuthnow, eds., *The New Christian Right: Mobilization and Legitimation*. Hawthorne: Aldine

Zald, Meyer, and J.D. McCarthy, eds., 1987. *Social Movements in an Organizational Society.* New Brunswick, NJ: Transaction

Zweir, Robert. 1984. 'The New Christian Right and the 1980 Elections' In David G. Bromley and Anson Shupe, eds., *New Christian Politics*. Macon: Mercer University Press

Cases Cited

Reports are Canadian unless otherwise noted

BCLR	British Columbia Law Reports
CCC	Canadian Criminal Cases
CHRR	Canadian Human Rights Reporter
CLLC	Canadian Labour Law Cases
CR	Criminal Reports
DLR	Dominion Law Reports
FC	Federal Court Reports
FTR	Federal Trial Reports
F.2d	Federal Reports (second) (U.S.)
F. Supp.	Federal Supplements (U.S.)

LAC   Labour Arbitration Cases
NR   National Reports
NW   Northwestern Reports (U.S.)
OR   Ontario Reports
RFL   Reports on Family Law
SCR   Supreme Court Reports
S. Ct.   Supreme Court Reports (U.S.)
U.S.   United States Law Reports (U.S.)
WWR   Western Weekly Reports

Action Travail des Femmes v *C.N.R.C. et al.* (1987), 76 NR 161 (SCC)

Andrews v *Ont. (Min. of Health)* (1988), 49 DLR (4th) 584 (Ont. HC)

Bhinder v *C.NR* [1985] 2 SCR 561 (SCC)

Big M Drug Mart (1985), 18 DLR (4th) 321 (SCC)

Board of Governors of the Univ. of Sask. v *Sask. Human Rights Commission* [1976] 3
   WWR 385 (Sask. QB)

Bowers v *Hardwick*, 196 S. Ct. 2841 (1986) (U.S. SC)

Brown v *B.C. (Min. of Health)* (1990), 42 BCLR (2d) 294 (BCSC)

Brown v *Board of Education*, 347 U.S. 483 (1954) (Brown I); 349 U.S. 294 (1955)
   (Brown II) (U.S. SC)

Dolphin Delivery v *R.W.D.S.U., Local 580* (1986), [1987] 2 SCR 573 (SCC)

Edwards Books and Art v *R.* (1986), 30 CCC (3d) 385 (SCC)

Egan v *Canada* (1991), 47 FTR 305 (FCTD); aff'd. (FCA) (1993), 103 DLR (4th) 336

Gay Alliance Toward Equality v *Vancouver Sun* [1979] 2 SCR 435 (SCC)

Haig v *Canada (Min. of Justice)* (1992), 9 OR (3d) 495 (Ont. CA)

Hunter v *Southam* (1984), 11 DLR (4th) 641 (SCC)

In Re Kowalski, 478 NW 2d 790 (Minn. Ct. App. 1991)

Klippert v *The Queen*, [1967] SCR 822 (SCC)

Knodel v *B.C. (Medical Services Committee)* (1991), 58 BCLR (2d) 356 (BCSC)

Layland v *Ontario (Min. of Con. & Comm. Rel.)* (1993), 104 DLR (4th) 214 (OCJGD)

Leroux v *Co-Operators Insurance* (1990), 71 OR (2d) 641 (Ont. Ct.), rev'd. [1991] OJ
   No. 1554 (OCA)

Leshner v *Ontario* (1992), 16 CHRR D/184 (Ont. Bd. Inq.)

Morin v *National Special Handling Unit Review Commission* (1985), 49 CR 260 (SCC)

Mossop v *Dept. of Sec. State* (1989), 89 CLLC 16,041 (CHRT); rev'd. (1990), 71 DLR
   (4th) 661 (FCA); aff'd (1993), [1993] 1 SRC 554 (SCC)

Nielsen v *Canada* [1992] 2 FC 561 (FCTD)

North v *Matheson*, (1974), 20 RFL 112 (Man. Co. Ct.)

O'Malley v *Simpsons-Sears* [1985] 2 SCR 536 (SCC)

P.B. v *P.B.* (1988), [unreported] (OPCFD)

Plessy v *Ferguson*, 163 U.S. 537 (1896)

R. v *Oakes* (1986), 26 DLR (4th) 200 (SCC)

Re Carleton University and C.U.P.E., Loc. 2424 (1988), 35 LAC (3d) 96 (Ont. Arb. Bd.)

Re Schaap et al. and Canadian Armed Forces (1988), 56 DLR (4th) 105 (FCA)

Re Vancouver Sun and Gay Alliance Toward Equality (1977), 77 DLR (3d) 487 (BCCA)

Robertson v *Geisinger* (1991), 36 RFL (3d) 261 (Sask. QB)

Robichaud v *Canada* [1987] 2 SCR 84 (SCC)

Roe v *Wade* 410 U.S. 113 (1973) (U.S. SC)

Singh v *Min. Emply. Immig.* [1985] 1 SCR 177 (SCC)

Vancouver Sun v *Gay Alliance Toward Equality* (1976), [unreported] (BCSC)

Veysey v *Correctional Service of Canada* (1989), 29 FTR 74 (FTD), aff'd.

Vogel v *Manitoba* (1983), 4 CHRR D/1654 (Man. Bd. Adj.)

Vogel v *Manitoba* (1992), 90 DLR (4th) 84 (Man. QB)

Watkins v *U.S. Army,* 875 F. 2d 699 (9th Cir. 1989)

Statutes Cited

Canadian Charter of Rights and Freedoms, Part I of the Constitution Act, 1982, being Schedule B of the Constitution Act 1982 (U.K.), 1982, c. 11

Canadian Human Rights Act, RSC 1985, c. H-6

Health Insurance Act, RSO. 1980, c. 197

Human Rights Code, SO 1981, c. 53, as amended by 1986, c. 64. s. 18

Interviews

Judy Anderson, president, REAL Women of Canada, 18 December 1991

Karen Andrews, litigant, 17 December 1991

Chris Bearchell, Bill 7 campaigner, Coalition for Lesbian and Gay Rights in Ontario, 19 December 1991

Ian Binnie, legal counsel to REAL Women et al., 10 December 1991

Gwen Brodsky, legal counsel to EGALE et al., 4 December 1991

Margrit Eichler, 'expert witness,' 20 December 1991

Don Hutchinson, legal adviser, The Salvation Army, 10 December 1991

Brian Mossop, litigant, 16 December 1991

Ken Popert, litigant, 16 December 1991

James Sclater, director of public policy, Focus on the Family Association (Canada), 6 December 1991

Index